The Sacred Quest

FOURTH EDITION

The Sacred Quest

An Invitation to the Study of Religion

LAWRENCE S. CUNNINGHAM
The University of Notre Dame

JOHN KELSAY
The Florida State University

PEARSON

Prentice
Hall

UPPER SADDLE RIVER, NEW JERSEY 07458

Library of Congress Cataloging-in-Publication Data

Cunningham, Lawrence.
    The sacred quest : an invitation to the study of religion/Lawrence S. Cunningham,
John Kelsay.—[4th ed.]
        p.   cm.
    Includes bibliographical references and index.
    ISBN 0-13-192377-3
    1. Religion   I. Kelsay, John,   II. Title.

BL48.C793 2006
200—dc22

2004060158

Editorial Director: Charlyce Jones-Owen
Assistant Editor: Wendy B. Yurash
Editorial Assistant: Carla Worner
Marketing Manager: Kara Kindstrom
Production Liaison: Joanne Hakim
Manufacturing Buyer: Christina Helder
Cover Art Director: Jayne Conte
Cover Design: Bruce Kenselaar
Cover Photo/Illustration: Getty Images
Full-Service Project Management: Dennis Troutman/Stratford Publishing Services
Composition: Integra Software Services Pvt. Ltd.
Printer/Binder: The Courier Companies

Pearson Education LTD., London
Pearson Education Singapore, Pte. Ltd
Pearson Education, Canada, Ltd
Pearson Education–Japan
Pearson Education Australia PTY, Limited

Pearson Education North Asia Ltd
Pearson Educación de Mexico, S.A. de C.V.
Pearson Education Malaysia, Pte. Ltd
Pearson Education, Upper Saddle River,
    New Jersey

10 9 8 7 6 5 4 3 2 1
ISBN 0-13-192377-3

Contents

9   ## The Quest for Salvation   142

Preface

This textbook derives from a generation of experience teaching undergraduates in a course introducing the academic study of religion at the Florida State University. For well over two decades, that course has remained one of the most popular in the undergraduate curriculum. Some years ago, a team of faculty and graduate students "wrote up" and duplicated the core lectures as an aid for the students. From that somewhat modest beginning came the first edition of *The Sacred Quest*.

We are still convinced that the "core" of the course (reflected in the chapters of this book) remains valid. Nonetheless, some of our examples seemed a bit dated, we were needlessly obscure in places, and our discussion materials needed freshening. We have tried to remain faithful to our original vision while taking into serious account the many useful suggestions and criticisms of those who have used the book in their own classes.

This book is brief by design. We know that we cannot replicate the readings that an individual instructor might wish to use in class. Therefore, we trust that the individual teacher will flesh out what we have only hinted at and provide ancillary materials to enlarge the material base of the course.

Since the first edition appeared, Lawrence S. Cunningham has left Florida for the more austere pleasures of northern Indiana, while John Kelsay has moved up in the academic ranks to become chair in the Department of Religion at Florida State. The two graduate students who joined in working on the first edition, Roy Barineau and Heather McVoy, have finished their degrees and moved into full-time careers.

We wish to thank our publisher for the continued support of *The Sacred Quest* and also thank our reviewers: Allen S. Davidson, Georgia Southern University; Patricia DeFerrari, Georgetown University; Randal Cummings, California State University–Northridge; Celia Marshall, University of North Carolina, Charlotte; and Gregory L. Klein, Niagara University. They gave us valuable suggestions for improvements as we prepared this new edition.

This book is dedicated to the many students who have sat in our classes over the years. They have been our toughest critics and our best supporters.

Lawrence S. Cunningham
The University of Notre Dame

John Kelsay
The Florida State University

The Sacred Quest

Introduction

THE BREADTH AND DEPTH
OF RELIGIOUS EXPERIENCE

To study religion is a difficult yet necessary endeavor. Both the difficulty and the necessity are due to the same facts: the breadth and depth of the impact of religion on human culture.

As to breadth, we must consider that human beings show a perennial penchant for religious expression. It is common to speak of human beings as *homo sapiens*, that is, "the creature who thinks"; there is good reason also to use the phrase *homo religiosus*, "the creature who is religious." We can find examples, here and there, of persons or groups who espouse no religion. But overall, the history of human culture bears eloquent testimony to our religious capacities. Indeed, wherever we find evidence of culture, we find evidence of religion.

At the same time, we must contemplate the depth of religion's impact. Just as our cultural history bears witness to the religious tendencies of humanity, so it indicates the power of religious conviction to motivate people. Consider the beginnings of *Islam*. In Arabia, in the seventh century C.E., a young merchant named *Muhammad*, is seeking spiritual truth.[1] He has a religious experience and understands himself to be a messenger of God. By the time of his death some twenty-two years later, he is able to describe Arabia as "solidly for Islam"—that is, under the guidance of the message he has proclaimed. And within another generation, the community founded by Muhammad manages to conquer and control most of what we know as the Middle East, including parts of northern Africa.

Alternatively, consider the Protestant Reformation. In sixteenth-century Germany, an obscure monk, under vows of poverty, chastity, and obedience to church authority, is assigned to lecture on the Bible to theology students. His superiors hope the work of preparing and delivering lectures will take the young man's mind off his worries, for he is a tormented soul, constantly aware of how far short he falls of the ideals he espouses. As he prepares his lectures, this young monk—his name is Martin Luther—arrives at an interpretation of Scripture that places him at odds with important aspects of established church teaching. He challenges church authorities, and when he is ordered to submit, he refuses. Within a generation, the face of Europe is altered, for Luther's religious understanding connects with developing nationalist tendencies to create a divided Western Europe: one Protestant, the other Catholic.

In either case, we see evidence of the power of religion—of the way it reaches to the depths of the heart and mind, providing motivation and direction for human life. That such evidence continues to mount is clear; one has only to read the papers for a week.

Any intelligent account of religion must deal with the full range of its impact on human affairs. As we have said, this makes the study of religion necessary and difficult. The necessity of the study seems evident: Those who wish to understand humanity must comprehend its rich and diverse experience of religion. Equally evident is the difficulty: How can we ever hope to deal adequately with the phenomenon of religion, with its enormous scope and power?

In all probability, we cannot. What we can accomplish, however, is the development of an increased understanding of certain aspects of the religious life. The field of religious studies is devoted to the development of such understanding. To that end, it makes use of a variety of approaches. For example, it is possible to learn a great deal from the study of sacred texts: the New Testament of Christianity, the *Qur'an* (sacred in Islam), or the *Upanishads* (*Hinduism*). Many scholars of religion focus their attention on the form and substance of such texts, producing critical editions of them and commentaries on them. Scholars also concentrate on describing the origins and development of religions such as *Judaism, Buddhism,* or *Shinto.* Others focus on comparisons of particular types of religious behaviors: Sacrificial rituals, prayer, and meditation come to mind. Another approach is to deal with religion from the perspective of philosophy, in particular, to attempt to understand the nature of religious language or to evaluate arguments for or against religious faith. Finally, it is possible to study religion in the manner of intellectual or social historians who trace the development of religious ideas or institutions over time.

The diversity of approaches to the study of religion mirrors the variety of religion itself. We (the authors) do not wish to disparage any of the perspectives outlined above. Our position is that the breadth and depth of the phenomenon of religion justify all these approaches, and we make use of most of them at various points in this book. At the same time, we have our own perspective, indicated in the form and substance of this book. In essence, our approach is a loose version of the *phenomenological* method, advocated by such twentieth-century scholars as Rudolf Otto, Gerardus van der Leeuw, W. B. Kristenson, and Mircea Eliade. It is our conviction that this tack provides a perspective that unifies a number of others and that allows us to make the best use of the findings of scholars with more specialized models and techniques. Such an approach also allows us to study religion as a real phenomenon without defending or rejecting the truths claimed by this or that particular religion.

A BRIEF OUTLINE OF THE PHENOMENOLOGICAL METHOD

We begin with a quote from Mircea Eliade:

> A religious phenomenon will only be recognized as such if it is grasped at its own level, that is to say, if it is studied as something religious. To try to grasp the essence of such a phenomenon by means of physiology, sociology, economics, linguistics, art or any other study is false; it misses the one unique and irreducible element in it—the element of the sacred.[2]

At the outset, a phenomenological approach to religion as it is understood in this book resists all types of reductionism—the tendency to interpret religion as a function of one or another nonreligious aspect of human existence. A phenomenological approach will not be inclined, for example, to explain religious beliefs as the result of "wish fulfillment"—a point of view articulated by, among others, Sigmund Freud in his famous book *The Future of an Illusion*. Freud noted that there is a correlation between many religious beliefs and psychological needs—the belief in a God who is all powerful and who loves human beings, for example, relates to the need to feel secure in an overwhelming and often insecure world. He expanded this point to argue that the religious belief is a function of the psychological need. Thus, belief in God originates in and is explained by this fundamental human need.

A phenomenological approach need not deny the obvious truth that many, if not most, religious beliefs are related to psychological needs. But it will resist the attempt to say that religion is reducible to psychology, that the beliefs and practices of religious people can be fully accounted for in psychological terms.

Similarly, a phenomenological approach resists the attempt to make religion a function of economic or political interests. We can argue, for example, that differences in religious belief or practice often correspond to differences in economic or social status. Thus, in the United States we used to say that a farm laborer who began as a Baptist would, upon improving his economic status, become a Presbyterian. If the family continued to "move up" in the world, that farm laborer's children might become Episcopalians, and so on. One obvious problem with such an approach is that the scenario does not always hold. There are upper-class Baptists, for example, and there are poor Episcopalians.

From the standpoint of a phenomenological approach, however, a more basic issue is at stake. Again, a phenomenologist need not deny the obvious truth that religion and economics are related. Given the breadth and depth of religion's impact on human cultural experience, it would be surprising if this were not so. The question is how they are related, and whether we can reduce religion to a type of economics or explain the persistence of religion in terms of political needs. To adopt a phenomenological perspective is to answer in the negative.

It must be clear, however, that there are no "purely" religious phenomena. In this sense, a phenomenologist should be ready to affirm the importance of psychological, economic, and other perspectives in the study of religion. The German sociologist Max Weber captured the emphasis we are seeking when he argued that it is necessary to affirm a "relative independence" for religion as a motive for human action. During the course of his life, Weber wrote a number of studies focusing on the relationship between religion and economics. As he put it, religious practices and ideas are not fully explained by economic interests, though religious life is related to and influenced by economics. Similarly, religious factors do not fully explain economic interests, though again there is a way in which religion shapes economic interests. The point is to understand the interplay between religion and other aspects of human life. For that reason, it is necessary to resist the tendency to reduce religion to economics or to explain it as a premodern form of psychology.

At its simplest, a phenomenological approach leads to an effort to understand religious thought and behavior *from the point of view of religious persons*. A large part of our purpose, then, must be to identify and understand the *intentions* that lie behind religious behavior. As we shall argue in Chapter 1, the identifying aspect of religion has to do with a notion of the sacred that is related to certain ways of thinking, feeling, and acting. A "religious" person or group is one that demonstrates in various ways a sacred-regarding intention. We can identify four stages of a phenomenological approach, which represent an orderly approach to the study of religion without being overly rigid in their application.

Gathering Religious Data.   A phenomenological study of religion begins with certain facts drawn from observation of the behavior of religious people. The facts presented in this book are not drawn from one group or religious tradition only: Our observations come from a number of different traditions, cultures, and geographic regions. We are interested in what Christian, Jewish, Buddhist, and other believers say about the nature of religious experience. We take them at their word when they say they are religious experiences. We are likewise interested in the rituals, books, symbols, and artworks that various people use and consider part of their religion. Some of the examples will seem familiar; others will seem strange. In this respect it is important to stress the need for openness. Our emphasis will be on describing and understanding religious experience from a number of different points of view. We will not be arguing for the superiority or truth value of any particular religious tradition.

The Search for Patterns. Analysis of the data of religious experience indicates a number of common patterns. As an example, consider the widespread use of water as a symbol of cleansing and purity—as in Christian baptism or in the ritual ablutions of Muslims, Hindus, and Jews. Similarly, most religions mark off sacred places, acknowledge sacred persons, respond to questions about the nature and purposes of evil, and engage in moral teaching. Such patterns form the basis for many of the chapters in this book. They constitute the framework for a phenomenologically oriented discussion of religion.

Analysis of the Structure of Patterns. It is one thing to identify patterns that cut across several religious traditions. It is quite another to argue that such patterns indicate common meanings. Here, we make a distinction between the meanings assigned to symbols in particular religious contexts and the more universal meanings standing behind the religious use of symbols.

For example, we know that Orthodox Jews visit the ritual bath (called the *mikveh*) on the eve of the Sabbath. Similarly, we know that pious Hindus bathe daily, before morning prayers. One of the central rites of Christianity is *baptism*, which involves the suggestion of bathing or washing. Pious Muslims wash with water before they perform their obligatory prayers. Roman Catholics commonly sign themselves with holy water upon entering a church.

To observe the frequency of bathing rituals among different religious groups is to notice a pattern. It is not to identify a common intention behind the behavior. In particular religious contexts, water carries a variety of meanings. Thus, the Christian attaches an interpretation to the baptism of her child that is quite different from that which a Hindu attaches to his morning ablutions in the river Ganges. Nevertheless, we can move beyond these differences in interpretation and notice that the ritual act of bathing or washing almost universally signifies a desire to appear pure, refreshed, and cleansed in the presence of the sacred. Something deeply embedded in the religious mentality seems to insist on such cleansing. The use of water symbolizes this even when different religious traditions *intend* quite different particular meanings to such rituals.

The same issues of structure occur with respect to any number of religious behaviors. For example, what meanings, both particular and universal, stand behind the common practice of religious meals? What is the significance of marking off certain places as sacred? The phenomenological approach, as we employ it in this book, does not require that we evaluate the significance that believers in a particular tradition attach to their rituals. It does allow us to think about whether there are meanings that transcend particular religious contexts.

The Suggestion of Generalizations. It may be, then, that after one examines a variety of religious phenomena he or she will feel enabled to make some generalizations about various patterns and perhaps even about the phenomenon of religion itself. We shall be very spare in doing so, but it should be noted that certain scholars of religion are quite ready to make such generalizations and to develop overarching theories of religion. From time to time we shall consider such theories in order to suggest some of the fruits of a phenomenological approach.

ATTITUDES AND INSTITUTIONS IN THE STUDY OF RELIGION

Over a century ago, John Henry Newman said that the university is the place where "mind clashes with mind." He meant that university study is an occasion for confronting, testing, analyzing, and ultimately accepting or rejecting new ideas. Newman's general description of the university has particular application to contemporary religious studies. In particular, as the study of religion has developed in North American universities, there is a great need to recognize the difference between the type of study that tries to understand and make a contribution to some particular religious tradition and an approach that focuses on understanding a variety of religious phenomena in the context of human cultural history.

Earlier in this introduction, we listed a number of specific ways in which to study religion. Many, if not all, of these have their roots in centers of learning sponsored by particular religious communities, which focus specifically on the task of training religious leaders. Modern studies of the Bible, for example, developed in the context of schools whose mission was to train ministers, priests, and rabbis to serve as leaders of various Protestant, Catholic, and Jewish congregations. Especially for Protestants, with their historic commitment to the authority and holiness of the text of the Bible, such study could be seen as an act of devotion, as well as scholarship. We could make similar points concerning the study of theology; even disciplines such as comparative religion developed largely in the context of Protestant and Catholic departments of theology at European universities.

The link between religious studies and the goals of particular religious communities provides an important chapter in the development of contemporary religious studies. Indeed, this chapter is still being written, with much of the creative work in writing and teaching about religion continuing to occur at universities, seminaries, and divinity schools that serve and are supported by participants in particular religious traditions. In the late 1950s and early 1960s, however, the study of religion in North America began to find a home in many American public universities supported not by traditional faith communities but by public funds. Especially in the United States, wherein institutional commitments to the separation of church and state are deeply entrenched, the growth of courses and departments devoted to religious studies raises questions about purpose. What, exactly, is the place of religious studies in public institutions? How shall we talk about the purpose of courses in religion in the context of institutions that were not created by, and do not exist to serve, particular communities of faith?

It is in this connection that we recall Newman's statement concerning the university as the place where "mind clashes with mind." Although the public institutional setting does not rule out faith on the part of students or faculty, it does suggest a different or perhaps additional purpose for the study of religion than in the context of institutions supported by faith communities. In general, those studying religion in public institutions have tended to see their work as connected to the tradition of humanistic learning. Therefore, they have focused on religion in the context of trying to understand the history, literature, art, and science of *homo sapiens*. One might express the different understandings this way: The study of religion at public institutions has focused on an exercise in historical and cultural understanding, rather than on understanding and developing a particular religious or theological tradition. Such an approach even stands behind the blossoming of programs that study a particular religious tradition. Today, we frequently find funded chairs in Judaic studies or Catholic studies. The presumption is that these chairs consider a particular religion as a cultural whole.

As departments from the public setting have begun to make their contribution to the wider discipline of religious studies, the difference (and tension) between "humanistic" and "theological" approaches to religious studies has become part of an ongoing debate among students of religion. Indeed, the debate now transcends distinctions between types of institutions. Faculty and students at divinity schools, for example, discuss the value of a humanistic emphasis in connection with their overall theological aims. Similarly, faculty and students at public institutions argue over the place of theology or, better, constructive religious thought in their attempts to understand religion.

We consider the phenomenological approach, as developed in this book, to be capable of contributing to either type of context and to the interests of both humanists and theologians. It should be clear, however, that our version of phenomenology does favor the humanistic emphasis in at least one way. Specifically, we focus first on developing an *understanding* of religion; it seems obvious that those who wish to understand this phenomenon need to suspend the value judgments of their own traditions long enough to examine and comprehend expressions of religious experience quite different from, and sometimes contradictory with, their own. If we begin with the premise that we possess all religious truth and everything that cannot fit in our worldview is wrong, sympathetic understanding will be impossible. Of course, readers of *The Sacred Quest* need not become unbelievers in order to understand other people's perspectives. In fact, those who are committed to the point of view that "all religions are the same" or "all religion is nonsense" may experience as much difficulty in comprehending religious experience as those who are convinced of the truth of *Christianity*, Judaism, or Buddhism. In a sense, we are required to bracket our convictions so we can understand those of others. We must set aside the question "true or not?" long enough to inquire into the reasons *why* people believe and act as they do.

What is required is perspective. Many types of religious expression may seem strange by Western standards. A North American touring the highlands of New Guinea for a visit to one of the tribes living in the outback might well witness men decorated in bird-of-paradise feathers, nude (save for a penis sheath), covered in ashes, and dancing before a fire at the side of which are pigs bound in vines and banana leaves. His or her first reaction might well be to take some photographs in order to show "the folks back home" some of the exotic aspects of life among primitive peoples.

> But this picture can be reversed. Suppose the tribesmen of the outback visit a downtown church on Sunday morning. They observe rows of oddly dressed people (what, after all, is the purpose of a necktie?), notice that some sit while others sing, listen to one person speak at length, and see still others pass plates onto which paper and metal disks are placed. What are these tribesmen to think? Where, after all, are the pigs? The fire? The sacred feathers?

In both cases, the observer lacks a sense of perspective and context. The lesson is a simple one. It is impossible to get at the intention that lies behind religious behavior unless we have a willingness to enter sympathetically into the cultural worldview of another person, at least for a moment.

To enter sympathetically into the religious worldview of others is not simply an intellectual exercise. Many flash points of international politics are bound to profound religious differences. In contemporary India, a resurgent nationalism based on *Hinduism* reacts strongly against both *Muslims* and Christians (especially Christian missionaries). How is one to understand that fact? Can one disentangle the sociopolitical elements from the religious ones in the continuing violence in Northern Ireland? Can one simply generalize about fundamentalism in militant Islamic movements without understanding the religious passion for such belief? Can we simply dismiss such movements as "terroristic"? Is it not in our national interest to understand the equal passion of evangelical and fundamentalist Christians in this country who see their struggles as a "cultural war"?

To understand the deep religious convictions of a community or nation is to understand in a new way a great deal of what is often taken as purely social or political behavior. For example, it is impossible to think of conflicts between Serbs, Croats, and Muslims in the former Yugoslavia without understanding the role of religion, particularly among the Serbs. Closer to home, one finds that curious and indefinable yet real phenomenon called the "American character," which occasions both admiration and exasperation among other peoples. That this phenomenon has religious roots is often noted; one writer described the United States as a "country with the soul of a church." To understand the religious intentions of people is to understand a good deal about the reasons that motivate and shape other aspects of their lives.

A FINAL WORD

The most general purpose of the study of religion is the development of a heightened awareness of religion's significance in human life and culture. An ancient Greek philosopher said that wonder is the beginning of wisdom. It is in the nature of the alert person to be curious and, again to paraphrase the ancient Greeks, to desire to know. The study of religion ought to lead to a recognition of the importance of this phenomenon—so ancient and yet so contemporary—for an understanding of humanity. Such a recognition will show itself in an awareness of religion in the daily news or in the readiness to examine the religious dimensions of art, drama, or other aspects of culture.

Some years ago a group of students was touring a complex of Greek temples on the island of Sicily. One of the students asked where the worshipers stood in the temple. That question was a good one, but it assumed that a Greek temple was like a Christian church. In fact, Greek temples were designed as houses for the god or goddess to whom they were dedicated. The worshipers stood outside or walked around the central room of the temple. The altars for sacrifice were at the foot of the temple. The point is this: The arrangement of buildings can, at certain places and times, reveal a great deal about the religious experience of a culture. Beyond this, it is humanly as well as religiously significant that the architectural space of a Greek temple was organized differently than that of a Catholic church. For the Greeks, temples were for gods, and worshipers made their appeals for favors from the outside. There was no special sense of gods advocating for human beings or of a special relationship between gods and humanity. For Christians, a church is a place of fellowship between God and humanity, reflecting the notion that God has become one with humanity through the incarnation of the Son of God. The psychological and social implications of these two ways of arranging space, or really of understanding the place of human beings in the universe, are profound.

The great Muslim thinker al-Ghazali (1058–1111) wrote in his autobiography: "To thirst after a comprehension of things as they really are was my habit and custom from a very early age."[3] This "thirst" led al-Ghazali to undertake an extensive quest. He sought to master all aspects of religious thought common among Muslims: philosophy, theology, and mysticism. In the end, he claimed to achieve peace and a kind of certainty in religious matters.

For al-Ghazali, as for many others, the quest for religious certainty and the scholarly quest were the same. That is not the case for many modern students of religion. The desire to know, however—the "thirst after a comprehension of things as they really are"—remains the heart of intellectual endeavor. For the authors and, we hope, our readers, the study of religion—the "sacred quest"—makes a contribution to our understanding of our world.

NOTES

1. The designation C.E., or "common era," will be used in this book in place of A.D. or its equivalent, "Christian era." B.C.E. will be used in place of B.C.
2. Mircea Eliade, *Patterns in Comparative Religion*, trans. Rosemary Sheed (Cleveland and New York: World, 1968), p. xiii.
3. W. Montgomery Watt, *The Faith and Practice of al-Ghazali* (London: Allen & Unwin, 1953), p. 21.

SUGGESTIONS FOR FURTHER READING

ELIADE, MIRCEA, *The Sacred and the Profane*. New York: Harcourt Brace Jovanovich, 1959. This is a fundamental text for the phenomenological study of religion.

OTTO, RUDOLF, *The Idea of the Holy*. New York: Oxford University Press, 1958. A classic study of the nature of religious experience.

PALS, DANIEL L., *Seven Theories of Religion*. New York: Oxford University Press, 1996. Outlines some modern approaches to the study of religion.

SMITH, JONATHAN Z., ed., *The HarperCollins Dictionary of Religion*. San Francisco: HarperCollins, 1995. An excellent resource for the study of religion.

VAN DER LEEUW, GERARDUS, *Religion in Essence and Manifestation*. 2 vols. New York: Harper & Row, 1963. An encyclopedic survey of religion. Especially useful as a reference work.

WACH, JOACHIM, *The Comparative Study of Religion*. New York: Columbia University Press, 1958. Especially useful for its typologies of religion.

1 *Toward a Definition of Religion*

Imagine for a moment the following situation. As an employee of a company that arranges "cultural tours," you are responsible for introducing a group of tourists to aspects of American life. On Sunday morning, you take the group to observe the service of Morning Prayer at the National Cathedral in Washington, D.C. Members of the group join in the singing, listen to the sermon, and follow the prayers.

Later in the day, the group attends a political rally near the Washington Monument. Members watch attentively as a local pastor begins the meeting with prayer; they listen as various speakers address the audience; some even begin to sing along when the meeting closes with a rendition of "God Bless America." As the meeting breaks up, several of the tourists approach you. How, they ask, did these events differ from those of the morning? What marks the difference between a "religious" event and a "political" one? It seems clear that the two events bear what the philosopher Ludwig Wittgenstein calls a "family resemblance" to each other. How does one distinguish the two events?

How will you answer this question? You might refer to the *setting* of the two events. The National Cathedral is a building with religious significance. From its pews to its striking mosaics, the cathedral is a space marked with religious symbols. By comparison, the Washington Monument is steeped in political tradition, commemorating the "father of our country," the commander in chief of the Continental Army, and the first president of the United States.

This approach may not prove entirely satisfactory, however. If the members of your tourist group are not too timid, they may well press for further explanation. And you, the tour guide, may find yourself pushed to say something like this: The National Cathedral is a religious setting because of its connection with certain symbols that, in the traditions of American culture, have religious significance. The mosaics depicting scenes from the Christian gospels or the lives of the saints are associated with religious ideas. The kneelers in the pews are associated with prayer, which is a religious act. Thus, you will begin to note that the setting is "religious" not in and of itself, but because of the ideas with which it is associated. Similarly, the Washington Monument is political because of its connection with the political traditions and ideals of the United States.

Your tourists might press still further. What makes an idea "religious"? What causes you to associate a person or act with "politics"? By now you, as tour guide, may be ready to move on. But the questions of the tourists—and of many thoughtful persons—will continue.

This imaginary incident points to the following fact: The terms "religion" and "religious" are used every day to describe places, actions, ways of thinking and feeling, and the persons or groups who engage in them. The implication is that such places, actions, and thoughts are somehow different from others that are characterized as "political," "moral," "scientific," or "educational." The problem of definition—the subject of this chapter—is to come to terms with this difference. What is it that makes Morning Prayer at the National Cathedral religious and the rally near the Washington Monument political?

THE SEARCH FOR A DEFINITION OF RELIGION

The search for definitions is a search for boundaries; a desire to say that X is religious and Y is not. It is, in a sense, a prerequisite for the study of religion, or any other academic field. As such, scholars of religion are interested in the definition of religion, but an examination of their discussions yields no easy consensus on the topic.

Consider the following examples.

- "Religion is the belief in an ever living God, that is, in a Divine Mind and Will ruling the Universe and holding moral relations with mankind." (James Martineau)
- Religion is the "feeling of absolute dependence"; "the consciousness that the whole of our spontaneous activity comes from a source outside of us." (Friedrich Schleiermacher)
- Religion is "a set of rituals, rationalized by myth, which mobilizes supernatural powers for the purpose of achieving or preventing transformations of state in man or nature." (Anthony Wallace)
- "Religion is only the sentiment inspired by the group in its members, but projected outside of the consciousness that experiences them, and objectified." (Emile Durkheim)
- Religion is "a propitiation or conciliation of powers superior to man which are believed to direct and control the course of Nature and of human life." (James G. Frazer)

Even this short and somewhat random list shows that the "definition question" is controversial. We cannot expect, in this brief chapter, to settle the issue. Although we do, in the end, advance a proposal for a working definition that informs the remainder of this book, the primary purpose of this chapter is to identify and discuss several of the most important issues in defining religion. At the outset, it is helpful to keep in mind the advice of philosopher William James.

> The very fact that they [definitions of religion] are so many and so different from one another is enough to prove that the word "religion" cannot stand for any single principle or essence, but is rather a collective name. . . . Let us not fall immediately into a one-sided view of our subject, but let us rather admit freely at the outset that we may very likely find no one essence, but many characters which may alternately be equally important to religion.[1]

ELEMENTS OF RELIGION

Taking our cue from James, we begin by noting that religion is a complex phenomenon, related to a variety of aspects of existence. Any definition of religion must take this into account: Religion is not an isolated aspect of human experience but relates to thought, feeling, and action; to concerns of individual and social existence; and to the expression and recognition of values. Each of these deserves further comment.

Religion and Human Thought

In a sense, it seems unnecessary to say that religion is connected with thought. For many, religion *is* a certain type of thought, signified by the term "belief." Recall the proposal of Martineau: "Religion is the belief in an ever living God. . . ." Thus, if one wants to know about the religion of a person or group, he or she asks, "What do they believe?"

The ready identification of religion and belief relates in some sense to the influence of Protestant Christianity. To "have faith," as many Protestants put it, certainly involves more than saying that one believes or thinks certain things. But one of the ways people show their faith is by the statement "I believe"—in God, in Christ as Savior, or in the Bible as the Word of God.

Religious people differ on the place of thought in the religious life. Scholars of religion also differ, with some arguing that the influence of Protestantism distorts scholarly and popular understandings of religion. Religion, such scholars argue, is not only a matter of what people believe but also a matter of what people do or the way in which people understand themselves. Thus, Orthodox Jews emphasize living according to the *Torah* or instruction of God, and Muslims stress active submission to the will of God. Certain preliterate religions may not even have a word for religion but demonstrate a religious sensibility that is essential to their way of life.

Nevertheless, the relationship of religion to thought is undeniable. Even those who focus on practice have beliefs, develop doctrines, and emphasize the importance of certain teachings in the religious life. Although the place and focus of belief varies, the fact of a relationship between religion and thought remains constant.

Religion and Feeling

In view of the Protestant focus on religious thought, it is interesting that the nineteenth-century Protestant theologian Friedrich Schleiermacher characterized religion as a "feeling of absolute dependence."[2] In a slightly different vein, another Protestant scholar, Rudolf Otto, characterized religion as the *experience* of "the holy." According to Otto, this experience is one that inspires feelings of fear, awe, terror, and love.[3] The archetype of such experience is found in the biblical story of Job, in particular chapters 38–42, wherein after a long struggle with the question of God's role in permitting the good to suffer, God speaks to Job "out of the whirlwind" and challenges Job's ability to comprehend the workings of the divine will. Job then says:

> I know that You [God] can do all things, and that no purpose of Yours can be thwarted. Who is this that hides counsel without knowledge? Therefore I have declared that which I did not understand, Things too wonderful for me, which I did not know. . . . I have heard of You by the hearing of the ear; But now my eye sees You; Therefore I retract, And I repent in dust and ashes. (42:1–6)

The wonder and majesty of the experience of God is a humbling experience for Job. It gives rise to the feeling that the Bible calls the "fear of the Lord"—an awe tinged with fear, which nevertheless includes a sense of love. According to Otto, this feeling is characteristic of all religious experience. The *Bhagavad Gita*, Hinduism's "song of the Lord," relates this response to the vision of Almighty Krishna:

> Arjuna said: I see the gods in Thy body, O God, All of them, and the hosts of various kinds of divine beings too, Lord Brahma sitting on the lotus seat, And the seers all, and the divine serpents.
> Thy great form, of many mouths and eyes, O great-armed one, of many arms, thighs, and feet, Of many bellies, terrible with many tusks,—Seeing it the worlds tremble, and I too. (11:15, 23)

Religion and Action

We have already noted the importance of action in religion by mentioning the focus of Orthodox Judaism and Islam on obedience to God's will. According to some scholars (for example, Anthony Wallace, quoted earlier in this chapter), action, particularly ritual action, is *the* characteristic feature of religious life.

Islamic law establishes the duty of prayer. Five times daily, an observant Muslim faces toward Mecca and performs *salat*, or *worship*. Practitioners of Shinto approach the shrine of a *kami* (spirit) by washing, ringing a bell, and clapping their hands before presenting their petition to the spirit. Roman Catholics participate in the Mass; Eastern Orthodox Christians in the Divine Liturgy. In every case, the form and place of religious action varies, but the importance of action to an understanding of religion is evident.

Individual and Social Existence

Philosopher Alfred North Whitehead once wrote that religion "is what the individual does with his own solitariness" and that religion "is the art and the theory of the internal life of man. . . ."[4] There is much in religious traditions to support this thesis. Most of the great religions make a place for individual devotion and encourage persons to search for union with the ultimate reality. The teaching of the Theravada Buddhists expressly separates the monks from the laity; part of the reason for this lies in the importance of time for the monks' individual practice of meditation and search for enlightenment. No one can achieve enlightenment for another. Ultimately, one must "make it" on one's own.

It is possible to overstress the individual dimension of religion, however. Even in Theravada Buddhism, the monks form a community by which they provide support for one another in each monk's individual search. Further, in most societies influenced by Buddhism, one way for the laity to express their devotion is through support for the monks. Although the focus of Theravada Buddhism is on individual effort, there is certainly a place for the social dimension of life.

The importance of individuals becomes even less if we consider other examples. According to the French sociologist Emile Durkheim, the most "elementary" or fundamental forms of religion focus on the idea of society. The essence of religion is found in the way(s) it enables individual persons to identify with the values associated with a particular group. For example, members of the Bororo tribe in Brazil identify themselves as "red parrots." According to many interpreters, the statement "I am a red parrot," made by an individual Bororo, indicates social identity. A paraphrase of the statement might thus read: "I belong to the social unit for which the red parrot is the symbol of identification." The tribe's employment of the red parrot as a symbol of its common life may extend to special observances around it; the parrot may be a protected animal or an animal to which sacrifices are offered. In any event, the point (if we follow Durkheim) is the life of the tribe. In the end, "the idea of society is the soul of religion."[5] Insofar as groups such as the Bororo encourage personal "devotion," it is for the sake of the whole. For example, if the group recognizes that certain members are specially gifted with respect to understanding the sacred, it may authorize their training as *shamans* or "medicine men" (or women). The point remains their contribution to the life of society. Following Durkheim's suggestions, we might define religion in terms of the necessities of social life.

In reality, too great an emphasis on either individual or social elements in religion leads to an inadequate definition of religion. As the example of Theravada Buddhism indicates, it is possible for religion to stress the individual aspect of life; the example of the Bororo indicates the difficulty of Whitehead's stress on "solitariness." The phenomenon of religion is intimately connected with both of these aspects of the life of humanity.

Values and Religion

Immanuel Kant once wrote that religion is "the recognition of all duties as divine commands."[6] For Kant, religion follows from *morality*. True religion confirms the moral law and gives one power to perform one's duty. Not everyone would agree with Kant's formulation of the relationship between religion and morality. But most students of religion would agree that, in most times and places, religion has been closely connected with morality.

Religion is a way of expressing important values. When a Buddhist speaks of the Buddha as an example of compassion for all beings, or when a Christian quotes the Gospel, saying "What does it profit a man to gain the whole world, and forfeit his soul?"[7] each attempts to express a conception of "what really counts." Similarly, when believers in various settings pray or offer sacrifices to "honor God," or to ward off spirits that threaten tribal unity, they express their sense of what is important in life. In some traditions, religion is thought to provide the foundation for such values. Asked "Why do you insist on telling the truth?" believers may say, "Because God commands it." In other cases, religion may provide support for values held on other grounds. Asked "Why do you refuse to fight in war?" a pacifist may respond, "Because killing is always wrong." When asked about religion, the same pacifist may say that true religious teachings confirm the wrongness of killing and provide important examples of noble characters who preferred to suffer rather than to kill.

SUBSTANCE OR FUNCTION?

The preceding examples indicate something of the breadth of religion and the difficulty of constructing a definition of religion. An adequate definition must take into account the scope of religion's impact on human thought, feeling, and action. Individual and social needs must be considered, as must the expression and/or recognition of values.

Recognizing the breadth of religious experience only scratches the surface of the phenomenon, however. Thus, the identification of religion with various aspects of existence does not take us very far in the search for a definition of the term. We may grant that religion has an impact on human thought. We may even acknowledge religious thought as a special kind of thinking, connected with belief. But these considerations do not explain why it makes sense to use the adjective "religious" for some thoughts and not for others. Human beings have many kinds of beliefs: "moral," "scientific," "political," and "philosophical," as well as "religious." What distinguishes the various types?

We can raise the same question with respect to values. As noted, in some contexts, believers say that religion establishes certain values, as in "It is right to tell the truth because God commands it." Others say that religion provides support for values held on other (that is, nonreligious) grounds. What makes the difference?

One typical answer to this question focuses on the *function* of religion in human life. In this case, the distinguishing feature of religious thought (or feelings or actions) is identified with certain roles religion plays in the lives of persons and groups. For example, a *functionalist* definition of religion might focus on the ways religion enables people to sustain hope in the face of difficult experiences. The following comment provides a good illustration of a functionalist understanding of religion.

> Religion, then, can be described as a system of beliefs and practices by means of which a group of people struggles with . . . ultimate problems. . . . It is the refusal to capitulate to death, to give up in the face of frustration, to allow hostility to tear apart one's human associations. . . . In this sense, religion can be thought of as a kind of residual means of response and adjustment. It is an attempt to explain what cannot otherwise be explained; to achieve power, all other powers having failed us; to establish poise and serenity in the face of evil and suffering that other efforts have failed to eliminate.[8]

Definitions that emphasize such functions of religion find much evidence in the history of religions. In many cultures, for example, religion provides an answer to questions about death. Belief in an afterlife is one way to say that life really does not end when the heart stops beating or the brain ceases to operate. According to the New Testament, the struggle of Christian believers here and now "is producing for us an eternal weight of glory far beyond all comparison"—eternal life in the presence of God (II Corinthians 3:17). Similarly, the Qur'an promises that those who "keep from evil" will enter Paradise, with its "Gardens underneath which rivers flow, and pure companions, and contentment from Allah" (3:15).

There are also aspects of religious traditions that respond to problems of suffering. The Hebrew *Bible* teaches that at least some suffering serves the purpose of education.

> For whom the Lord loves He reproves, Even as a father, the son in whom He delights. (Proverbs 3:12)

And the Buddha taught that recognition and awareness of suffering is the first step on the path to *Nirvana*, the ultimate goal of life.

> What then is the Holy Truth of Ill? Birth is ill, decay is ill, sickness is ill, death is ill. To be conjoined with what one dislikes means suffering. To be disjoined from what one likes means suffering. Not to get what one wants, also that means suffering. In short, all grasping . . . involves suffering.[9]

There is much evidence to support definitions of religion that emphasize its function as a response to suffering, death, and other difficulties. Critics answer, however, with an argument that seems obvious, upon reflection. Responses to suffering and death are not necessarily religious. For some, scientific inquiry or moral philosophy or the exercise of common sense are more appropriate modes of response. In short, religion cannot simply be defined in terms of its function as "a residual means of response and adjustment." To address suffering and death in religious terms means to bring certain kinds of ideas, actions, and values to bear on these problems. Definitions of religion, therefore, must refer not only to the function of religion—the ways it helps human beings respond to difficult problems—but also must deal adequately with *substance*. It must identify what it is that makes certain responses to suffering and death religious and others not. Such a definition, to coin a phrase, must consider the *stuff* of religion.

A good example of a *substantive* definition may be found in the statement of James Martineau, quoted earlier: "Religion is the belief in an ever living God, that is, in a Divine Mind and Will ruling the Universe and holding moral relations with mankind." We might paraphrase as follows: In order for a way of thinking, feeling, and acting to qualify as religious, it must include belief in a God who can be characterized as ever living, having powers of reason and choice, having the power to rule the Universe and to hold human beings responsible for their lives. If we find ways of responding to life's problems that do not refer to such a belief, then those ways are not religious.

Martineau's is not the only or the best example of a substantive definition of religion. Many scholars would not join Martineau in identifying "belief in an ever living God" as essential to religion; they would nevertheless agree that there must be some core idea or essence that distinguishes religious approaches to life from moral or scientific ones. The distinction need not imply that religious approaches are better (or worse) than others. They are simply different: In this sense, a substantive definition of religion is proposed in order to distinguish religion from nonreligion, not from irreligion.

A substantive definition attempts to limit the range of phenomena that may be characterized as religious. All ways of thinking are not religious, nor are all responses to life's problems reflections of a religious view of the world. In this respect, substantive definitions of religion mirror the use of the terms in everyday conversation. A person can speak of Morning Prayer at the National Cathedral as religious, then of a rally at the Washington Monument as political, and think that he or she is making meaningful distinctions, despite some overlap between the two events. The difficulty lies in specifying precisely what the substance of the distinction is.

TOWARD RESOLUTION

At this point, the authors would like to advance a proposal. We can begin in this way: Considerations of function are necessary but not sufficient to the task of defining religion; an adequate definition of religion must include a substantive component. Thus, although we acknowledge the significant role of religion in human responses to such problems as suffering and death, we also follow the indications of everyday speech and make distinctions between religious and nonreligious ways of approaching such problems. "Religion" and "politics" are not synonyms, though they may be closely related. Similarly, "religion" and "morality" or "religion" and "science" should be distinguished from one another, however much they may overlap.

Our proposal for a definition of religion, then, will focus on considerations of substance, even though it will also refer to characteristic functions. The main difficulty, as indicated, lies in specifying the substance of religion. Are there any standards or rules that can help in this task?

We begin with ordinary speech. As already noted, attention to everyday conversation indicates that there are distinctions to be drawn between "religion," "politics," "science," and "morality." These distinctions are not always clear in ordinary conversation, and there will always be some disagreement over where the lines between such terms are to be drawn, but we may still find some help in the ordinary use of terms. As an exercise, consider the following. What are the clearest examples of religion you can think of? Are there some examples of human thought, feeling, and action that you can call religious without controversy? Some that are more controversial, but are still probably in the category of religion? Others that are controversial, but probably are not religious? And still others that clearly are not religious? Having distinguished the points on your own "spectrum of religion," what considerations inform you in distinguishing the various points?

The point is that we do not create definitions out of thin air. Good definitions, definitions that are helpful, are those that clarify the range of uses of terms in the everyday conversation of particular groups of people. Our proposal is thus as follows: If we consider the everyday use of terms, certain phenomena clearly are religious. Prayer is a religious act; belief in God is a religious belief. More than this, certain movements and institutions, ways of thinking and acting, over time have come to be so identified with religion that they serve as a standard for the use of the term. The Christian Church is a religious community; Christianity, Judaism, and Islam are religions—these judgments seem uncontroversial. In fact, there is no apparent difficulty in extending this: Religion is identified with the great religions. We can therefore add Hinduism and some forms of Buddhism and *Taoism* to our list. A number of traditions of smaller scale (though not necessarily of less significance) can be added: Shinto, the beliefs and practices of the Navaho, the traditions of various African tribes, Greek and Roman mystery cults—the list can become very long.

These phenomena are "clearly" religious; that is, they are uncontroversial, from the standpoint of ordinary speech. Other cases are more difficult, though many would still describe them as examples of religion. For example, many scholars debate the religious nature of certain forms of Buddhism. The difficulty is that, at least officially, such forms of Buddhism hold that belief in God or gods is a distraction and should be downplayed. "Philosophical" Hinduism also falls into this category, though its emphasis is more to the effect that belief in God or gods should be purified in order to indicate that God is not a being like others, but is Being itself. Taoism is somewhat similar insofar as it focuses on the "power" that moves through and orders all things. Lastly, *Confucianism*, with its stress on the social-political dimensions of religious practice, seems to some a controversial form of religion.

Still other cases are controversial, but probably not religion—again, following ordinary discourse. Marxism provides an important example. Marx himself thought of his philosophy as nonreligious and rejected religious belief and practice as a false response to human problems. Yet Marxism has served many as a faith that provides goals, orients behavior, and helps to resolve life's difficulties. The movements and institutions built on Marxist thought have been, in some sense, sources of devotion for believers. Observing these factors, many scholars judge Marxism to be a "functional equivalent" of religion; that is, it serves some of the same functions as religion, but does so with a set of moral and political rather than religious ideas. Nationalism and other secular ideologies present cases that are similarly controversial but probably not examples of religion.

Finally, there are cases that can apparently be labeled nonreligious, without controversy—for example, philosophies urging that human judgment be centered on a particular moral principle such as utility—the "greatest good for the greatest number."

Such an exercise helps in delineating key points in a spectrum of religion. We may still ask, however, about the considerations that lead us to draw the lines just where we do. A full answer is likely to be quite complex, relating to the history of language and of Anglo-American culture. If the examples given here are apposite, however, it is difficult to avoid the impression that the clearest, least controversial examples of religion are provided by those ways of thinking, feeling, and acting that refer to a God or gods—Judaism, Christianity, Islam, Hinduism, and the other traditions already referred to. The further one moves from such beliefs, the more controversial it becomes to use the label religion. Thus, some forms of Buddhism, philosophical Hinduism, and Confucianism are controversial, but probably still religious. They are problematic because of a lack of emphasis on God or gods, yet still religious because their affirmation of a reality that cannot be reduced to ordinary experience reflects an essential aspect of the religious worldview. The Buddhists' Nirvana, philosophical Hinduism's Brahman, Confucianism's Heaven, the reality of the *Tao*—these are not God or gods, but they affirm the irreducible nature of a reality beyond ordinary experience. Marxism, nationalism, and ultimately utilitarian moral philosophy, by contrast, are distinguished by their lack of stress on such a reality.

A Proposal

What shall we call this irreducible reality? As noted, in one sense Martineau's stress on "belief in an ever living God" is suggestive in the development of a definition of religion. If our discussion thus far is accurate, however, ordinary speech suggests we describe some things as religious that would, on Martineau's definition, be excluded. Thus, we have said that religion not only indicates the great monotheistic traditions but also serves to classify traditions that believe in many gods—for example, Shinto or the religion of the Navaho. In addition, it serves—admittedly in a more controversial way—to classify traditions that move away from or significantly revise belief in God or gods (for example, some forms of Buddhism).

Given this, some scholars propose to replace Martineau's "belief in an ever living God" and to indicate the substance of religion with phrases such as "ultimate concern" and "concern about the Ultimate." Protestant theologian Paul Tillich, for example, argued that religion "in the largest and most basic sense of the word, is ultimate concern." The attraction of Tillich's proposal is readily apparent; it is clearly more inclusive than Martineau's focus on a particular conception of God. The difficulty with the proposal, however, is that it may be *too* inclusive. Consider once more the case of Marxism. Marx considered religion an understandable though ultimately false response to the great problems of life: suffering, death, injustice. Marx's hope was to construct a philosophy that would respond to such problems, but with truth rather than illusion. Marx's intention, if nothing else, leads many to classify his thought as nonreligious. By contrast, Tillich's definition seems specifically crafted to classify Marxism and other philosophies critical of religion as religious. Because religion is ultimate concern, and ultimate concern is

> "manifest in all creative functions of the human spirit . . ." if someone rejects religion in the name of the moral function of the human spirit, he rejects religion in the name of religion. . . . If anyone rejects religion in the name of the cognitive function of the human spirit, he rejects religion in the name of religion. . . . You cannot reject religion with ultimate seriousness, because ultimate seriousness, or the state of being ultimately concerned, is itself religion.[10]

The influence of Tillich on students of religion is very deep, not least in the matter of defining religion. And, as indicated, the case of Marxism and other secular ideologies is controversial. Nevertheless, our proposal deals with them as "functional equivalents" of religion—ways of thinking that, while substantively nonreligious, often function as religions do in providing goals and responding to the great problems of life.

In the end, we follow what we hope is a middle way, more inclusive than Martineau, more exclusive than Tillich. Following historians of religion such as Mircea Eliade, Rudolf Otto, and Joachim Wach, we use the term "sacred" to capture that affirmation of an irreducible reality that seems to provide the substance of a religious worldview. At the same time, remembering the power of functionalist insights, we recognize that affirmations of the sacred are related to the human need to respond to the great problems of life in this world. Thus we propose the following definition: Religion signifies those ways of viewing the world that refer to (1) a notion of sacred reality (2) made manifest in human experience (3) in such a way as to produce long-lasting ways of thinking, feeling, and acting (4) with respect to problems of ordering and understanding existence. Each aspect of this definition can be expanded, as follows.

1. ". . . a notion of sacred reality." Earlier we indicated the importance of identifying a characteristic substance of religion. Religion serves certain functions, as noted. Our definition deals with these in (3) and (4). "A notion of sacred reality," however, is the distinguishing feature of *religious* approaches to these functions. Such a notion establishes a boundary between religion and nonreligion. A full discussion of this phrase will be the subject of the following chapter. For now, it will suffice to reiterate that "sacred" indicates a reality that is somehow distinct, "set apart," "other" than ordinary. "Sacred reality" includes the God of the Bible, the Qur'anic Allah, the Brahman of Hinduism, Buddhism's Nirvana, the *kami* of Shinto.

2. ". . . made manifest in human experience." Although the sacred is "set apart" from the ordinary, it nevertheless may be experienced, thought about, acted upon. Mircea Eliade suggests this when he writes that all religion has to do with "the element of the sacred" manifesting itself in various ways: in rituals, persons, and natural phenomena, just to cite a few

examples.[11] For Muslims, the sacred reality (Allah) is made manifest through prophecy, especially the prophecy of *Muhammad*. For Buddhists, the goal of Nirvana "comes to life" in the life and teaching of the Buddha. For the Navaho, the story of the emergence of the world and of the Navaho people makes the wisdom of the "holy people" available for those who seek harmony between all things.

3. "... in such a way as to produce long-lasting ways of thinking, feeling, and acting." The breadth of religion's impact on human culture has been noted. This part of our definition reiterates the point. In addition, we want to stress the adjective "long-lasting."[12] Religious ways develop over time. They come to constitute *traditions* that may be identified with the history of particular communities. For example, the prophecy of Muhammad is but the beginning of the tradition of Islam. Islam's message and the story of its revelation in seventh-century Arabia have produced characteristic modes of thought, feeling, and action among a large percentage of the world's population. In other words, Islam has played a large part in the development of a particular type of human culture, so much so that one historian writes of "Islamicate" civilization.[13] Similarly, we may think of Christendom or of Buddhist civilization or Navaho culture.

4. "... with respect to problems of ordering and understanding existence." Recall the earlier discussion of definitions that stress the function of religion in addressing issues of suffering and death. Our definition stresses the way in which notions of sacred reality are related to these and other problems (for example, the ordering of political or economic life).

What are the strengths and weaknesses of this definition? In some sense, that is for others to judge. We think this proposal provides a way to distinguish religious ways of viewing the world from nonreligious ways. To return to our original example, the intuition expressed by the tour guide (yourself) that there is a difference between a religious service and a political rally rests in some sense on the connection of the former with a notion of sacred reality. We think, further, that our proposal helps to explain the ordinary uses of the terms "religion" and "religious," particularly when we keep in mind the distinction between noncontroversial and controversial cases. Important borderline cases remain, such as those presented by certain forms of Buddhism and Marxism; the reference to notions of sacred reality helps to explain how it is that the former seem to be religious, the latter not. Finally, the definition is comprehensive with reference to the breadth of religious phenomena and experience.

IN CONCLUSION

In subsequent chapters, we further explain and illustrate the various parts of our definition. In closing, however, two questions remain. First, we note that tying a definition to the use of terms in a particular culture (as we have done) can raise questions about the applicability of the definition to other cultures. We might ask: What right do we have to impose our understanding of religion on other cultures? Should we not first seek to understand what other cultures regard as an example of religion, then proceed to study it?

In a sense, this seems an admirable goal. Part of the study of religion does involve an attempt to understand other cultures. And yet, admirable goals may be unrealistic. The answer to the question raised is as follows: The very attempt to ask someone from another culture "What do you count as religion?" *already presupposes* our understanding of the term. If we ask a citizen of a Muslim country what she counts as religion, either we must suppose she is familiar with Anglo American uses of the term, or we must explain it to her. Alternatively, if we try to ask the question in her terms (for most Muslims, that would involve words or phrases in Arabic, Persian, or Urdu), we must make a translation that involves selecting the best approximation between her language and our own. In either case, we cannot escape our presuppositions about the term "religion." We may, of course, find our understanding enriched through dialogue with persons from other cultures. We may find, at the least, that there are practices and beliefs associated with religion that are different from those with which we are familiar. But we cannot avoid starting with the understanding of terms that is a part of our own cultural and linguistic heritage.

The second question is this: Can we ever say that one definition of religion is "right"? By now it should be clear that the answer to this question is complex. We have tried to indicate some of the possible definitions of religion and the issues involved in constructing and evaluating them. In addition, we have advanced a proposal that we think is justifiable and helpful, as it clarifies the considerations that lie behind the distinctions people in our culture draw between religion, politics, and other terms. Remembering the warning of William James cited at the outset of this chapter, and recognizing the expansive number of definitions proposed by scholars of religion, we close on the following note. Definitions, although unavoidable, do their best work while in the background. A definition of religion is not religion itself. For that, we must turn to more concrete concerns of the religious life—the sacred quest.

NOTES

1. William James, *The Varieties of Religious Experience* (New York: Modern Library, 1929), p. 27.
2. Friedrich Schleiermacher, *The Christian Faith*, trans. H. R. Mackintosh and J. S. Stewart (Philadelphia: Fortress, 1928), especially pp. 12–16.
3. Rudolf Otto, *The Idea of the Holy*, trans. John W. Harvey (London: Oxford University Press, 1936).
4. Alfred North Whitehead, *Religion in the Making* (New York: New American Library, 1974), p. 16.

5. Emile Durkheim, *The Elementary Forms of the Religious Life*, trans. Joseph Ward Swain (London: Allen & Unwin, 1964), p. 419.

6. Immanuel Kant, *Critique of Practical Reason*, trans. Lewis White Beck (Indianapolis, Ind.: Bobbs-Merrill, 1956), p. 134.

7. Mark 8:36 and parallels.

8. J. Milton Yinger, *Religion, Society, and the Individual: An Introduction to the Sociology of Religion* (New York: Macmillan, 1957), pp. 8–10.

9. From *Buddhist Scriptures*, selected and trans. by Edward Conze (Middlesex, England: Penguin, 1954), p. 186.

10. Paul Tillich, *Theology of Culture* (New York: Oxford University Press, 1959), p. 8.

11. Mircea Eliade, *Patterns of Comparative Religion*, trans. Rosemary Sheed (Cleveland and New York: World, 1958), p. xiii.

12. This term is taken from a famous essay by Clifford Geertz, entitled "Religion as a Cultural System." This essay has been printed in a number of places, the most accessible being Clifford Geertz, *The Interpretation of Cultures* (New York: Basic Books, 1973).

13. Marshall G. S. Hodgson, *The Venture of Islam*, vol. 1 (Chicago: University of Chicago Press, 1974).

THOUGHT EXPERIMENTS

1. In the entry on "religions, definitions of" in the *HarperCollins Dictionary of Religion* (1995), religion is defined as a "system of beliefs and practices relative to superhuman beings." In the light of this chapter's discussion, critique that definition either positively or negatively.

2. There have been some recent court battles over the posting of the Ten Commandments in courtrooms or in public schools. Those who favor their inclusion argue that the Ten Commandments are a moral code that underpins general public morality. The question is whether posting them favors a specific religious tradition and, as such, violates the constitutional separation of church and state. How would you judge this debate? In order to make sense of the argument, read Exodus 20:1–16 in the Bible as background for your discussion.

3. Look up the word "religion" in a sampling of commonly used dictionaries. Do the definitions pass the test of inclusiveness? Do they adequately account for the complexity of religion as you understand it?

SUGGESTIONS FOR FURTHER READING

ALSTON, WILLIAM P., "Religion." In *The Encyclopedia of Philosophy*, vol. 7, ed. Paul Edwards. New York: Macmillan and Free Press, 1967. A concise survey of the basic problems in the definition of religion. Alston proposes that a conception of "religion-making characteristics" lies behind the use of the term and that ways of viewing the world are more or less religious according to the ways they reflect these characteristics.

CONNELLY, PETER, ed., *Approaches to the Study of Religion*. New York: Cassell, 1999. A series of essays outlining various approaches to the study of religion.

GEERTZ, CLIFFORD, "Religion as a Cultural System." In Clifford Geertz, *The Interpretation of Cultures*. New York: Basic Books, 1973. Difficult going for the beginner, but a very influential essay by a leading anthropologist.

KING, WINSTON, "Religion." In *The Encyclopedia of Religion*, vol. 12, ed. Mircea Eliade. New York: Macmillan, 1987. A concise and helpful discussion of a number of issues connected with the definition of religion.

LITTLE, DAVID, and SUMNER B. TWISS, JR., *Comparative Religious Ethics: A New Method*. San Francisco: Harper & Row, 1978. For the ambitious student. This study develops definitions of a number of terms important to the comparative study of religious ethics, including "religion," "morality," and "law."

MCCUTCHEON, RUSSELL T., *Manufacturing Religion*. New York: Oxford University Press, 1997. McCutcheon argues strongly that definitions of religion, and indeed various approaches to the study of religion, necessarily reflect the realities of power in social and political life.

SMART, NINIAN, *Dimensions of the Sacred*. Berkeley: University of California Press, 1996. A study that emphasizes the various aspects of religious practice such as doctrine, myth, ritual, and so forth to outline the essential contours of religion.

SMITH, WILFRED CANTWELL, *The Meaning and End of Religion: A New Approach to the Religious Traditions of Mankind*. New York: New American Library, 1963. An interesting argument *against* the use of the term "religion" in the field of religious studies. According to Smith, there is no such entity as "religion." Rather, there are religious persons who find meaning through the experience of faith. A good contrarian effort to get away from the difficulties of defining the term "religion."

2 *The Nature of the Sacred*

THE COMPLEX CHARACTER OF THE SACRED

The early Israelites were instructed: "Observe the sabbath day to keep it holy."[1] A popular Christian hymn begins "Holy, holy, holy, Lord God almighty!" Islamic tradition refers to Jerusalem as *al-quds*—the holy city, or the city set apart.

In various cultures around the world, we find notions of the sacred. It is that which is "set apart," different from the ordinary. The biblical psalmist depicts sacred reality in personal terms in this prayer.

> O God, You are my God; I shall seek You earnestly; My soul thirsts for You, my flesh yearns for You, In a dry and weary land where there is no water. Thus I have beheld You in the sanctuary, To see your power and your glory. Because your loving kindness is better than life, My lips will praise You. (Psalm 63:1–3)

A different image of the sacred is found in the Bhagavad Gita.

> Thou [God] art the Imperishable, the supreme Object of Knowledge, Thou art the ultimate resting-place of this universe; Thou art the immortal guardian of the eternal right; Thou art the everlasting Spirit. . . .
> Without beginning, middle, or end, of infinite power, Of infinite arms, whose eyes are the moon and sun, I see Thee, whose face is flaming fire, Burning this whole universe with Thy radiance.
> For this region between heaven and earth is pervaded by Thee alone, and all the directions; Seeing this Thy wondrous, terrible form, The triple world [heaven, earth, and sky] trembles, O exalted one! (11:18–20)

Yet another image, this time describing a sacred realm or state of being, is spoken of in a Buddhist discourse on "The Nature of Nirvana."

> King Milinda said: "I will grant you, Nagasena, that Nirvana is absolute Ease, and that nevertheless one cannot point to its form or shape, its duration or size, either by simile or explanation, by reason or by argument. But is there perhaps

some quality of Nirvana which it shares with other things, and which lends itself to metaphorical explanation?"

"Its form, O king, cannot be elucidated by similes, but its qualities can. . . . As the lotus is unstained by water, so is Nirvana unstained by all the defilements. . . . As cool water allays feverish heat, so also Nirvana is cool and allays the fever of all the passions. . . . As medicine protects from the torments of poison, so Nirvana from the torments of the poisonous passions. . . . Nirvana and medicine both give security. . . . As a mountain peak is unshakeable, so is Nirvana. . . ."[2]

In short, there are many notions of the sacred. In that sense, the sacred is an abstraction that has many concrete expressions. Our task is to examine some of these, but we also have to give an account of the concept of the sacred. What is it that allows one to describe the God of the Bible, the "Imperishable" of the Bhagavad Gita, and Nirvana alike as "sacred"?

THE CONCEPT OF SACRED REALITY

We may begin with the statement of Mircea Eliade: "The first possible definition of the sacred is that it is the opposite of the profane."[3] At least we might say that the sacred is "distinct from" the profane. The Latin *sanctus* refers to something separated or set apart from other things, as do the related terms from Greek (*hagios*) and Hebrew (*kadosh*). In the Bible God is preeminently sacred or holy, and everyone else and everything else is holy or sacred only in relation to God. In ancient Rome, *sanctus* applied as much to the place of certain activities as to the activities themselves. Those acts that were sanctified were performed in the *fanum* or temple; other acts were *pro fanum*, that is, performed in front of or outside the temple. By contrast, the Hebrew Bible uses *kadosh* to describe God and things set apart by God's choice: the people of Israel, the land they live in, types of food, modes of human relations. There is nothing special about such things except that they are chosen by God or are in some kind of relation to God.

> For you [people of Israel] are a holy people to the Lord your God; the Lord your God has chosen you to be a people for his own possession out of all the peoples who are on the face of the earth. The Lord did not set His love on you nor choose you because you were more in number than any of the peoples, for you were the fewest of all peoples, but because the Lord loved you and kept the oath which He swore to your forefathers, the Lord brought you out by a mighty hand, and redeemed you from the house of slavery, from the hand of Pharaoh king of Egypt. (Deuteronomy 7:6–8)

Of course, one wants to go beyond the notion that the sacred is "distinct." Eliade further characterized the sacred in terms of "the real." In its various forms, the sacred stands for that which provides absolute and objective authority to an otherwise relative and subjective existence.

The sacred belongs to or consists of an entirely different order than the ordinary life of human beings, yet it becomes manifest through objects that are integrally connected with ordinary existence. Stones, trees, the sky, bodies of water, various people—all these may be the vehicles of the sacred and thus share in its distinctive reality. The sacred can never be reduced to these things alone, but they serve as mediums or vehicles for its power.

To speak of the sacred as "the real" points directly to its various manifestations—a topic that is the focus of Chapter 3. We can, however, formulate a more general concept of the sacred in the following way. We recognize a notion of sacred reality wherever we can describe a particular manifestation of the real (the form may vary) in terms that indicate it is (1) specially distinctive or "set apart" from everything else in the world, (2) to some extent, beyond the volitional control of human beings, (3) specially prominent with respect to human welfare, and (4) properly determinative of various aspects of human existence.[4] In what follows, we illustrate each of these characteristics of sacred reality.

Specially Distinctive

To be specially distinctive or set apart from everything else in the world is, we have noted, the most basic quality of the sacred. Whether we think of Christianity's "God and Father of our Lord Jesus Christ," of Shinto's various *kami*, or of the "bullroarer" of various aboriginal tribes, we are dealing with a notion of a reality distinct from all else, and thus sacred. Such realities are "not us."

In some sense, "distinctive" implies "different." But how? There is no one answer to that question. The various religious traditions offer quite diverse notions of sacred reality, a diversity that extends not only between traditions but to some extent within them. For example, Judaism, Christianity, and Islam are sometimes characterized as religions of *transcendence*, meaning that they present notions of sacred reality as "going beyond" or "standing over" ordinary existence. Hinduism, Buddhism, and the various religions of China and Japan then are described as religions of *immanence*, meaning that in their notions of sacred reality there is less of a divide between the sacred and the natural world.

There is certainly something to such classifications. It is difficult to think of Judaism, Christianity, and Islam without the notion of an all-wise, all-powerful God who lives and reigns eternally and who surpasses human understanding. Isaiah 55:8–9 expresses this well.

> "For My thoughts are not your thoughts, Neither are your ways My ways," declares the Lord. "For as the heavens are higher than the earth, So are My ways higher than your ways, And My thoughts than your thoughts."

Similarly, the chapter of the Qur'an called "The Sincerity" exhorts:

> Say: He is Allah, the One! Allah, the eternally Besought of All! He begetteth not nor was begotten. And there is none comparable unto Him. (112)

In comparison, if we consider certain elements of Asian religions, the notion of the sacred as connected with or even dwelling in the world of nature seems clear. In Shinto tradition, the origins of Japanese society are tied to stories relating the activities of the various *kami*, or spirits. The kami include powers of regeneration and growth, natural phenomena, and ancestor spirits. Of particular interest is the sun goddess *Amaterasu Omikami*, whose descendants come to rule Japan and establish a dynasty, which (according to tradition) continues to this day. All Japanese are in some sense the children of the kami; through the forces of nature and especially the person of the emperor, the sacred is connected with the world of ordinary experience.

Conceptions of sacred reality as immanent appear also in aspects of Hindu or Buddhist tradition. For example, the Chandogya Upanishad presents a discussion between a Hindu sage and his son on the nature of reality. The sage begins,

> "Fetch me from thence a fruit of the Nyagrodha tree."
> "Here is one, Sir."
> "Break it."
> "It is broken, Sir."
> "What do you see there?"
> "These seeds, almost infinitesimal."
> "Break one of them."
> "It is broken, Sir."
> "What do you see there?"
> "Not anything, Sir."
> The father said: "My son, that subtle essence which you do not perceive there, of that very essence this great Nyagrodha tree exists.
> "Believe it, my son. That which is the subtle essence, in it all that exists has its self. It is the True. It is the Self, and thou, O Svetaketu, art it." (6:12)

This identification of the sacred with the essence of the world and especially of human beings is not dissimilar to the way that certain types of Buddhism speak of the "Buddha-nature" of human beings. Zen Buddhism especially stresses this as the true nature of all persons. The Buddha-nature of human beings may be clouded by ignorance or wrongful desire, but it nevertheless exists and may be drawn out through meditation.

However, characterizations of transcendence and immanence may fall short when we attend to the complexity of religious traditions and their notions of sacred reality. Thus, in Christianity, the God who is immortal, invisible, and all-wise is revealed through *Jesus* of Nazareth, the *Christ* or anointed one. Historically, most Christian teaching has understood Jesus to be the *incarnation* or manifestation "in the flesh" of the eternal God. The Gospel of John begins:

> In the beginning was the Word, and the Word was with God, and the Word was God. He was in the beginning with God. All things came into being through Him; and apart from Him nothing came into being that has come into being. In Him was life; and the life was the light of men. . . . And the Word became flesh, and dwelt among us, and we beheld His glory. . . . No man has seen God at any time; the only begotten God, who is in the bosom of the Father, He has explained Him. (1:1–18)

Among Western religions, the Christian doctrine of the incarnation presents a radical notion of the sacred as immanent. Yet Judaism and Islam also have elements of immanence in their notions of the sacred. For the former, the *Torah* is God's Word, teaching humanity the will of God and serving as the medium of God's presence: ". . . two that sit together and are occupied in words of [Torah] have the Shekinah [presence of God] among them. . . ."[5] Similarly, the Qur'an declares that God is close to humanity:

> We verily created man and We know what his soul whispereth to him and We are nearer to him than his jugular vein. (50:16)

The Qur'an itself, say the Muslims, is the speech of God. For the historical majority of Muslims (*Sunnis*) this can be qualified further. The Qur'an is God's uncreated speech. It represents the purest form of God's eternal message to humanity, which is that human beings should recognize their position as creatures of God and submit. As such, the Qur'an brings God close or makes the sacred immanent.

Just as the religions of transcendence are not without elements of immanence, many of those traditions that seem to stress immanence contain elements of transcendence. It is difficult to think of Hinduism, for example, without considering the picture of Krishna in the Bhagavad Gita. In the midst of conversation, the warrior Arjuna discovers that his confidant, his charioteer, is in fact the Lord Krishna, who says to Arjuna:

> Hear my highest message. . . . The throngs of gods know not My Origin, nor yet the great seers. For I am the starting-point of the gods, And of the great seers, altogether. I am the origin of all; From me all comes forth. . . . I am the soul. . . . That abides in the heart of all beings; I am the beginning and the middle Of beings, and the very end too. I am gambling of rogues, I am majesty of the Majestic, I am conquest, I am spirit-of-adventure, I am courage of the courageous. Moreover, whatsoever of all beings Is the seed, that am I, Arjuna; There is none such as could be without Me, no being moving or unmoving. There is no end to My marvelous Supernal-manifestations, scorcher of the foe; But I have declared by way of examples The extent of my supernal-manifestation. Whatever being shows supernal-manifestations [i.e., supernatural power], Or majesty or vigor, Be thou assured that in every case Is sprung from a fraction of My glory. I support this entire World with a single fraction (of Myself). . . . (10, selected verses)

As the source and origin of all, sustaining "this universe with only a small part of" himself, Krishna transcends the world of ordinary experience, even as he fills it and manifests himself through it. Similarly, Buddhist notions of Nirvana suggest transcendence; and the Shinto spirits, in many cases identified with natural powers, are nevertheless "high" or "lifted up"—such is the implication of the word "kami." The sacred may be characterized as transcendent or immanent, or (in most traditions) by the interplay between these conceptions. In any case, it is counted as specially distinct and is set apart as an object for various forms of worship and devotion.

To Some Extent, Beyond the Volitional Control of Human Beings

For many scholars, the biblical story of Uzzah and the ark of the covenant (II Samuel 6) provides a classic illustration of notions of the sacred. We cite it here as an example of the second aspect of our definition of sacred reality. It would be useful to read the biblical account in order to follow the explanation of what follows.

The story really begins in I Samuel 4, when the Israelites suffer a devastating loss at the hands of their archenemies, the Philistines. In the course of the fighting, the people of Israel decide to bring the ark of the covenant to the battlefront, hoping it will ensure their success. The ark, mentioned at various places in the Hebrew Bible, was a sign of God's presence with the "chosen people" and thus a highly sacred object. The disaster of defeat at the hands of the Philistines is heightened by the fact that, according to I Samuel 4:11, the ark is captured and taken away from the people of Israel. When the high priest, Eli, hears the news, he understands it to be a judgment on Israel; he falls backward, breaking his neck, and dies. His pregnant daughter-in-law gives verbal form to Eli's feeling: As she dies in childbirth, she gives her newborn son the name Ichabod, meaning "no glory," and comments, "The glory has departed from Israel, for the ark of God was taken" (4:22).

Subsequent chapters (I Samuel 5, 6, and 7:1–2) relate incidents involving the ark, which lead the Philistines to rid themselves of it. For example, at 5:1–5 the ark is brought into the temple of Dagon, one of the Philistine deities. When the Philistines return to the temple, they find the image of Dagon on the ground in a position of submission before the ark, the hands and head severed from the trunk. The Philistines decide to place the ark in a cart drawn by two cows (that is, without a driver) and send it wherever it will go. The ark makes its way back among the Israelites, eventually standing in the house of Abinadab, where it remains for twenty years.

In II Samuel 6, David has become king and desires to bring the ark to Jerusalem, his capital. He and his men go to the house of Abinadab, where they place the ark on a cart and begin to move it, with Abinadab's sons Uzzah and Ahio leading the way.

> So they brought [the cart] with the ark of God from the house of Abinadab, which was on the hill; and Ahio was walking ahead of the ark. Meanwhile, David and all the house of Israel were celebrating before the Lord with all kinds of instruments made of fir wood, and with lyres, harps, tambourines, castanets, and cymbals. But when they came to the threshing floor of Nacon, Uzzah reached out toward the ark of God and took hold of it, for the oxen nearly upset it. And the anger of the Lord burned against Uzzah, and God struck him down there for his irreverence; and he died there by the ark of God. And David became angry because of the Lord's outburst against Uzzah, and that place is called Perez-uzzah [that is, the "break-through" or "breaking out upon" Uzzah] to this day. So David was afraid of the Lord that day; and he said, "How can the ark of the Lord come to me?" (II Samuel 6:4–9)

The story continues as the ark is left at the house of Obed-edom. When David hears that Obed-edom has prospered with the ark nearby, he ventures to bring it up again, and this time succeeds. No explanation is given for the judgment against Uzzah; but commentators have frequently noted the way the entire cycle of the story of the ark in I and II Samuel stresses the sovereignty or independence of the ark, and thus of God. "[God] goes where God wants" is a clear implication of the story, and one could add that God does so when God wants to. The sacred is not subject to the will or desires of human beings.

It is important to say that the story of Uzzah represents an extreme version of the independence of the sacred. Other notions of the sacred (and, indeed, other depictions of the sacred in the Hebrew Bible) do not always present such an emphasis on sovereignty. In some cases, prayer or sacrifice may be seen as an attempt to influence the sacred. In certain contexts, the sacred always responds to a ritual performed rightly, and the ability to so perform is the chief sign of being gifted spiritually. For example, the role of the *shaman* is, in many religious contexts, to perform rituals involving chanting, dancing, and perhaps prayers and sacrifices in such a way that various spirits or powers will respond in a certain way. The *kut* rituals of Korean folk religion provide an interesting example in which the shaman (usually a woman) performs a ceremonial dance, often accompanied by male musicians. A part of the performance involves attracting the presence of largely male inhabitants of the spirit world by means of elaborate feminine costumes—worn in many cases not only by the shaman but also by her male assistants—and the provocative dance. If this part of the ceremony is successful, the shaman is united with the spirits and enabled to perform extraordinary feats, such as dancing on the blades of sharpened swords. If the ceremony is further successful, then observers go away feeling that their goal has been achieved: Either the presence of good spirits and their accompanying blessings is guaranteed, or evil spirits have been exorcised.

In such contexts, in a sense the shaman may be said to "control" the spirits through her actions. Her power and prestige rest on the notion that she is able to make the spirits present and to influence their behavior. Yet even here, the sacred is not entirely subject to human control. In the Korean context, as in most traditions in which the role of the shaman is recognized, the shaman's spiritual power is first established because the spirits have chosen her. The phenomenon of "spirit-sickness" comes upon certain women, often at the onset of middle age, and establishes their shamanistic potential. They may resist the calling of the spirits but will then (according to popular lore) suffer repeated attacks of the sickness and, eventually, death. A woman who experiences the calling of the spirits attaches herself to an older shaman, who then teaches her the ways of spiritual performance.

In considering this second aspect of our description of sacred reality, then, it is important to keep in mind both the idea that the sacred is "beyond the volitional control of human beings" and the qualification "to some extent." This allows for the fact that the extent to which the sacred is independent of human considerations varies considerably among and within religious traditions.[6]

Specially Prominent with Respect to Human Welfare

In the chapter called "The Opening," the Qur'an speaks of God as the "Owner of the Day of Judgment" or the "Master of the Day of Doom" (1:4). The Qur'an foresees a time when people will be called upon to give an account of their actions, and God will render judgment. As such, it provides a good illustration of the third aspect of our description of sacred reality.

Various chapters of the Qur'an begin with gripping images of the message of the Day of Judgment. The wicked will suffer burning and the torments of hell; the righteous, on the other hand, will receive their reward in the cool and beauty of Paradise. According to the chapter called "The Overwhelming":

> On that day (many) faces will be downcast, Toiling, wary, Scorched by burning fire, Drinking from a boiling spring, No food for them save bitter thornfruit Which doth not nourish nor release from hunger. On that day other faces will be calm, Glad for their effort past, In a high garden Where they hear no idle speech. Wherein is a rushing spring, Wherein are couches raised, And goblets set at hand, And cushions ranged, And silken carpets spread. (88:2–16)

Such judgment is, according to the Qur'an, the point of God's creation of the world. God did not create the world for sport, says 22:16–17: "If we wished to find a pastime, We could have found it in our presence. . . ." Rather, the point of God's creative activity is to put humanity to the test. "He [God] it is Who created the heavens and the earth in six Days . . . that He might try you, which of you is best in conduct" (11:7). It is to warn humanity of this that God sends Muhammad and other messengers.

The Qur'anic notion of judgment is not confined, however, to the "last day" or to an afterlife. The judgment of God is plain even now for those who reflect. In particular, history is filled with signs that astute persons should heed: for example, the story of the "folk of Lot," recounted at 26:160–175 (compare the biblical story of Sodom and Gomorrah in Genesis 19). In the story of Lot, which recounts the destruction of the wicked by a "dreadful" rain, the Qur'an proclaims there is a sign for all humanity—a sign of God's judgment of the human race.

With respect to the concept of sacred reality, the central message of the Qur'anic verses on judgment is the affirmation that God's actions and decisions have a tangible impact on the welfare of human beings, for good or for ill. In fact, in the case of Islam and certain other traditions that speak of a day of judgment, one may say that the prominence of the sacred with respect to human welfare is absolute. All plans, all desires, the ultimate fate of humanity are the province of sacred reality.

Such ultimacy is not a universal aspect of the sacred's relation to human welfare, however. Some traditions, while suggesting the prominence of the sacred in the attainment or frustration of security and happiness, do not suggest that the sacred's importance is absolute. The religion of the Navaho Indians, for example, presents a notion of "sacred people" who are in some sense the architects of the world and the creators of the Navaho. The various sacred people, who may be classified according to their willingness to help or harm the Navaho, are definitely set apart and are, to some extent, not subject to the will of human beings. Yet their action and their teaching are not the absolute determinant of human welfare. Rather, their point is to guide the Navaho in maintaining a relationship of harmony among all things. This is particularly so with respect to those sacred personages who are willing to help the Navaho: They are teachers as much as powerful aids, and the Navaho must choose to attend to their teaching in order to attain help. Certainly one finds evidence in Navaho religion that the sacred is especially prominent with respect to human welfare; but the prominence is somewhat weaker than that depicted in the Qur'an.

Properly Determinative of Various Aspects of Human Existence

The fourth aspect of our description of sacred reality follows from the discussion of "special prominence." In various ways, religious traditions express the idea that the prominence of the sacred is legitimate. Further, they suggest that persons and groups ought to order their lives in certain ways that are consonant with particular notions of sacred reality. This is not just because the sacred is specially powerful, or able to confer benefits and inflict burdens, but because such ordering is proper, the right or good thing to do.

Buddhist teaching presents an important example. Buddhism points humanity to the sacred realm, Nirvana, as that which is specially distinct, to some extent beyond the volitional control of human beings, and specially prominent with respect to human welfare. "As cool water allays feverish heat, so also Nirvana is cool and allays the fever of all the passions . . . as medicine puts an end to sickness, so Nirvana to all sufferings."

Nirvana is also properly determinative of various aspects of human existence. In particular, human beings are to order their lives according to the Buddha's teaching (*dharma*), which constitutes the path to Nirvana. It is at this point that one of the characteristic emphases of Buddhist teaching becomes apparent, for the Buddhists believe that the attainment of Nirvana involves a recognition that there is no self.

We can summarize the Buddha's teaching in the Four Noble Truths: Life is painful and filled with suffering; the root of suffering is craving or desire; Nirvana, or the cessation of this craving, is also the cessation of suffering; and the way to attain Nirvana lies in following the Noble Eightfold Path—the cultivation of right views, right intention, right speech, right action, right livelihood, right effort, right mindfulness, and right concentration. According to traditional interpretations, the second of the Noble Truths in particular leads to the conclusion that there is no self. The image of a "person," in particular of an eternal aspect of the self that is in some sense immortal or indestructible, is an illusion and leads to pain. Beings who cling to it, and thus wish at some level to continue to exist, get their wish. Through the process called "co-dependent origination," such beings will be "reborn"—at least, their deaths will be followed by the birth of another that is, in some sense, linked with them. But such rebirth is an empty thing, because it leads only to more experience of suffering. The way of liberation, the path to Nirvana, involves the realization that there is no self.

The practice of Buddhism involves the observance of moral precepts, adherence to right beliefs, and the development of a mind-set reflective of the "no-self doctrine." Why should one engage in such practice? The answer is simple, even if the doctrine is not. One practices Buddhism in order to attain Nirvana. That sacred realm is the thing most to desire, because it is "a happy state." But it is also the thing most right to desire, because it is the one reality. All else—the experience of pain, the heat of desires—is in one sense an illusion, and it rests on the ultimate falsehood: that there is a self. To attain Nirvana is to see the truth, and thus one properly orders his or her life around the search for it.

A number of religious traditions make the claim that the way in which a notion of sacred reality leads believers to order their lives is in accord with the truth about human nature. Judaism, Christianity, and Islam, for example, all contain ideas that focus on the connection between human nature and true religion. Classical rabbis spoke about the Noahide covenant, according to which there are seven precepts that all human beings are obligated to observe: no idolatry, no blasphemy, no bloodshed, no sexual sins, no theft, no eating from a live animal, and the duty to establish a legal system.[7] In a similar vein, Muslims stress the idea that Islam is the "natural" religion of humanity, according to such Qur'anic passages as 7:172, in which God makes a kind of "primordial covenant" with the human race.[8] In this respect, the Christian doctrine of the Incarnation may also be interpreted as establishing the rightful claim of the sacred to affect and order human existence. According to classical teaching, Jesus the Christ is "true God and true man."

SUMMARY

In subsequent chapters, we shall return to issues raised by this description of sacred reality. Here, the point has been to explain the concept of the sacred in a way that will answer the question: What is it that enables us to speak of the various teachings presented by diverse religious communities as so many "notions of sacred reality"? We recognize that this concept of the sacred is somewhat abstract but it provides us with a way to think of the reality that is so central to all religious experience. Beginning with the statement that the term "sacred" implies something specially distinctive or "other," our discussion has attempted to specify the unity-in-diversity of sacred reality as "set apart" from everything else in the world; to some extent, beyond the volitional control of human beings; specially prominent with respect to our welfare; and properly determinative of various aspects of our existence.

Such characteristics are by their nature rather formal. The examples presented here suggest that, within the form of the sacred, there is an extraordinary richness that requires further discussion. To address that richness and to begin to think about its import for the study of religion, we will attempt, in subsequent chapters, to talk about specific ways in which the sacred is manifested in religion.

NOTES

1. Deuteronomy 5:12.
2. From *Buddhist Scriptures*, trans. Edward Conze (Middlesex, England: Penguin, 1954), p. 156.
3. Mircea Eliade, *The Sacred and the Profane*, trans. Willard R. Trask (New York: Harcourt Brace Jovanovich, 1959), p. 10.
4. With slight modifications, these characteristics are drawn from David Little and Sumner B. Twiss, Jr., *Comparative Religious Ethics: A New Method* (New York: Harper & Row, 1978), especially pp. 59–61.

5. *Pirqe Aboth* 3:3, page 43 in *Sayings of the Jewish Fathers*, ed. Charles Taylor (New York: Ktav Publishing House, 1969).

6. On this point, see Little and Twiss, *Comparative Religious Ethics*.

7. Steven S. Schwarzschild and Saul Berman, "Noahide Covenant," in *Encyclopedia Judaica*, ed. Cecil Roth (Jerusalem: Keter, 1972), vol. 12, pp. 1189–1191.

8. The term "primordial covenant" is Fazlur Rahman's, used in his *Major Themes of the Qu'ran* (Chicago: Biblioteca Islamica, 1980).

THOUGHT EXPERIMENTS

1. In the Bible look up four or five psalms to search out words such as "holy," "exalted," or "majestic." When you find such words, think about what concept of the sacred they suggest.

2. Look up the article on the sacred in the *HarperCollins Dictionary of Religion* (1995). The author of that article suggests that the concept of the sacred may have outlived its usefulness as a theoretical model. What arguments are advanced to support that idea?

3. Some people speak about their personal relationships as "sacred," or talk about the "sacredness of life." What precisely do you think such usages are trying to convey? Do you consider this kind of language as "religious"?

SUGGESTIONS FOR FURTHER READING

BUSH, RICHARD C., et al., *The Religious World: Communities of Faith* (3rd ed.). New York: Macmillan, 1993. A solid, basic text in world religions. Provides useful information relative to the discussion in this chapter.

CONZE, EDWARD, *Buddhism: Its Essence and Development*. New York: Harper & Row, 1959. One of the best surveys of Buddhism available.

EARHART, H. BYRON, *Religions of Japan*. New York: Harper & Row, 1984. Provides basic information about Shinto and other Japanese traditions.

GAMMIE, JOHN, *Holiness in Israel*. Minneapolis, Minn.: Fortress, 1989. A classic biblical study with much information on the nature of holiness.

OTTO, RUDOLF, *The Idea of the Holy*, trans. John W. Harvey. Oxford: Oxford University Press, 1981. Otto's classic work focuses on what he calls the nonrational character of religious experience. The sacred involves, for him, an experience of the "numinous," which gives rise to feelings of fear, awe, wonder, and love.

SMART, NINIAN, *The World's Religions* (2nd ed.). New York: Oxford University Press, 1998. A standard survey text; good on the notion(s) of the sacred.

ZAEHNER, R. C., *Hinduism*. New York: Oxford University Press, 1966. A survey of the Hindu tradition.

3 *The Appearance of the Sacred*

We may recall for a moment one of the major features of a phenomeno-logical approach to the study of religion. We begin by collecting data or observing religious phenomena in a variety of settings. Then we try to identify patterns—themes, ideas, or types of action that occur again and again within the rich interplay of religious traditions.

In the last chapter, we focused on the nature of sacred reality. Religious traditions present a great variety of notions of the sacred, so much variety, in fact, that it is difficult to describe precise patterns. The concept of sacred reality itself provides certain guidelines: Sacred reality is always considered specially distinctive; to a certain extent, beyond human volitional control; specially prominent with respect to human welfare; and properly determina-tive with respect to the beliefs, attitudes, and acts of human beings. Within these rather formal guidelines, the diversity of notions of the sacred is extremely rich and complex.

In this chapter, we turn to the appearance of the sacred. Technically, this chapter is about the ways in which the sacred is manifest in the world of human experience. How do people experience sacred reality? The appearance of the sacred is technically called a *hierophany* from the two Greek words that mean "to reveal the Holy." Again, at first glance the diversity of claims about such appearances is overwhelming.

Consider the following examples. First, here is a Muslim tradition recounting the beginning of the revelation of the Qur'an.

Ramadan was the traditional month of retreat, and it was one night towards the end of Ramadan, in [Muhammad's] fortieth year, when he was alone in the cave, that there came to him an Angel in the form of a man. The Angel said to him: "Recite!" and he said: "I am not a reciter," whereupon, as he himself told it, "the Angel took me and whelmed me in his embrace until he had reached the limit of mine endurance. Then he released me and said: 'Recite!' I said: 'I am not a reciter,' and again he took me and overwhelmed me in his embrace, and again when he had reached the limit of mine endurance he released me and said: 'Recite!,' and again I said 'I am not a reciter.' Then a third time he overwhelmed me as before, then released me and said:

'Recite in the name of thy Lord who created! He createth man from a clot of blood. Recite; and thy Lord is the Most Bountiful, He who hath taught by the pen, taught man what he knew not.'"[1]

The story continues with Muhammad, shaken by his experience, fleeing to his home, when he hears a voice saying, "O Muhammad, thou art the Messenger of God, and I am Gabriel" [the angel of God]. Thus begins the story of the prophecy of Muhammad. It is a story of God, the merciful and compassionate Creator and the "Owner of the Day of Judgment," who calls humanity to submission through the revelation of the Qur'an, "the speech of God."

Now, compare the following account of the enlightenment of *Siddhartha Gautama*, the *Buddha*. The Buddha, having great skills in meditation, puts himself into a trance. He is intent on comprehending the truth about all things and also the ultimate goal of existence. In his trance, the Buddha "sees" all his former lives; he also "sees through" the ordinary, historical existence of human beings and understands that it is not "substantial," that is, not ultimately real.

Then, as the *third watch* of that night drew on, the supreme master of trance turned his meditation to the real and essential nature of this world: "Alas, living beings wear themselves out in vain! Over and over again they are born, they age, die, pass on to a new life, and are reborn! What is more, greed and dark delusion obscure their sight, and they are blind from birth. Greatly apprehensive, they yet do not know how to get out of this great mass of ill." He then surveyed the twelve links of conditioned co-production, and saw that, beginning with ignorance, they lead to old age and death, and, beginning with the cessation of ignorance, they lead to the cessation of birth, old age, death, and all kinds of ill. When the great seer had comprehended that where there is no ignorance whatever, there also the *karma*-formations are stopped—then he had achieved a correct knowledge of all there is to be known, and he stood out in the world as a Buddha.[2]

Thus begins, in some sense, the story of the Buddha. It is a story of an extraordinary man who discovered the secret of enlightenment and spent the remainder of his life teaching humanity the way to achieve Nirvana— "the cessation of birth, old age, death, and all kinds of ill."

These are two accounts of the appearance of the sacred—of ways in which that which is specially distinctive becomes manifest in the world of human experience. What can we say about them? Is there anything in these stories, and in the phenomena of sacred appearances, besides great diversity?

TYPES OF SACRED APPEARANCE

In this chapter, we consider two ways of talking about the variety of hierophanies. The first focuses on sacred *media*. With this focus, we characterize hierophanies according to the particular vehicle of a sacred appearance. In particular, we discuss examples of sacred persons, objects, time, and space.

It will soon be clear, however, that there are certain patterns within each of these categories. To say that a number of religious traditions understand certain persons to be vehicles of sacred reality, for example, does not indicate the variety of ways in which such persons are in fact "sacred." It is important to note the various modes of relation to sacred reality, even within a general category of "sacred persons." Thus it will prove useful to refer to a second way of thinking about hierophanies, which focuses on the recurrence of certain patterns within the general phenomenon of sacred appearances. Here, we shall speak of three patterns: the prophetic, the sacramental, and the mystical. The first, identified primarily with Judaism and Islam, focuses on a person (the *prophet*) who receives a revelation that deals in various ways with historical events in the life of a community. The second—most apparent in certain forms of Christianity, in Shinto, and in various tribal religions—emphasizes the presence of the sacred through aspects of material reality and stresses the role of *priests* or shamans in the community. The last considers the importance of a certain state of being or consciousness in the quest for enlightenment or union with the sacred and is most characteristic of certain types of Buddhism and Hinduism.

A brief qualification is in order here: We should note that the terms "identified primarily with," "most apparent in," and "most characteristic of" indicate that examples of each of these patterns may be found in many, if not most, of the religions of the world. Many religious traditions present a mix of these patterns, especially if we consider their development over time. We return to this point in some concluding reflections on the complex nature of sacred appearance in religious traditions.[3]

VARIETIES OF MEDIA

Sacred Persons

The association of the sacred with certain persons is a characteristic of numerous religious traditions, most obviously those whose history points to a "founder" or great figure at the beginning of the tradition. Moses, Jesus, Muhammad, the Buddha, Confucius, and Lao-tzu have all been identified as founders of religious traditions at one time or another. The precise historical status of such persons, their actual relationship to the beginnings of a religious tradition, may be open to question. For the study of religion, however, that is less important than the fact that believers associate them with the foundation of particular movements or communities and thus with sacred reality.

Moses, for example, is the great prophet of Judaism—not the only prophet, to be sure, but nevertheless distinctive. The word "Prophet" means one who speaks with the authority of another, in the case of biblical prophets, one who speaks for God. The book of Deuteronomy ends with the story of Moses' death and comments: "Since then [that is, the time of Moses] no prophet has risen in Israel like Moses, whom the Lord knew face to face" (34:10).

Moses' connection with sacred reality is, in one sense, the point of many of the stories told in the biblical books of Exodus, Leviticus, Numbers, and Deuteronomy. The book of Exodus, for example, begins with an account of the difficult existence of the people of Israel in Egypt. Oppressed and afflicted in various ways, the children of Israel "sighed because of their bondage, and they cried out. . . ." (Exodus 2:23b). We are then told that God "heard their groaning, and remembered His covenant with Abraham, Isaac, and Jacob" (2:24). The result is the call of Moses.

> Now Moses was pasturing the flock of Jethro his father-in-law, the priest of Midian, and he led the flock to the west side of the wilderness, and came to Horeb, the mountain of God. And the angel of the Lord appeared to him in a blazing fire from the midst of the bush; and he looked, and behold, the bush was burning with fire, yet the bush was not consumed. . . . When the Lord saw that [Moses] turned aside to look, God called to him from the midst of the bush and said, "Moses, Moses." And he said, "Here I am. . . ." [God said] "I am the God of your father, the God of Abraham, the God of Isaac, and the God of Jacob." Then Moses hid his face, for he was afraid to look at God. (Exodus 3:1–6)

The story continues with the directive that Moses speak to the ruler of Egypt (the Pharaoh) and lead the people from Egypt to the "promised land." And, with many twists and turns, that is what Moses does. His death, related at the end of Deuteronomy, occurs as he brings the people to the borders of Canaan.

In the biblical stories, Moses' primary role is as a spokesman for the "Holy One of Israel." In particular, he brings to the people of Israel the Torah or instruction he receives from God. At Exodus 20, and also Deuteronomy 5, we read the "ten words" or "commandments," which are perhaps the best-known portion of the Torah. But the Torah attributed to Moses is far more extensive than the Ten Commandments and includes directives for the construction of a place of worship (the Tabernacle, Exodus 35–39); instruction for the priests' performance of various sacrificial rituals (the book of Leviticus); and rules for dealing with a variety of contracts, criminal acts, and economic exchanges.

In later Judaism, Moses becomes the archetype of all those who keep and understand the Torah, and the first rabbi ("teacher"). He receives from God not only the written Torah of the various biblical commandments but also the oral Torah by which to interpret these commandments. In the end, Moses is regarded as the best of all humanity. According to one popular legend, God granted a special distinction to Moses at the latter's death. And this was "well merited, for Moses outweighed all other pious men." Greater than Adam, Noah, Abraham, Isaac—greater than all those famous in the history of Israel—Moses "not only surpassed all other human beings, he surpassed also the entire creation that God had brought forth in six days. . . . When, therefore, God laid all the objects of creation on one side of the scales, and Moses upon the other, Moses outweighed them." Indeed, "Moses was justly called 'the man of God,' for he was half man and half God."[4]

Moses is sacred as a spokesman for God, and this establishes his place in Jewish understanding. By contrast, the Buddha is sacred as the teacher of the truth about human existence, or as the sage who, having attained enlightenment, is able to guide others to the experience of Nirvana. Like Moses (or Muhammad), the Buddha has a message to proclaim. But the message of the Buddha is not the "instruction" of God. Rather, it is the insight of a master of meditation into the essential nature of all things.

This much has already been indicated, in the account of Siddhartha Gautama's coming to enlightenment. Some further information about the story of the Buddha is helpful in discussing his role as a sacred person, however, as is some discussion of his place in later Buddhism.

The story of the Buddha is, in essence, one of seeking and finding. In one sense, the story begins with his birth as Siddhartha Gautama (ca. 563 B.C.E.), eldest son of a noble family and heir apparent to his father's wealth and power. In another sense, the story begins with the "former lives" of the Buddha. During one of those lives, the one who would be born as Siddhartha swore to become a Buddha:

> Long is the time before this vision could arise, Long is the time before Tathagatas [i.e., Buddhas] appear. Long is the time before my vow shall be fulfilled: A Buddha I'll become, there is no doubt on that![5]

Eventually, this "vision" is fulfilled, and Siddhartha becomes the Buddha. But not without struggle. As a youth, Siddhartha is sheltered from all of life's troubling aspects. But at age twenty-nine, a series of experiences leads the young prince to flee from his comfortable life and to take up a life of spiritual discipline. In brief, Siddhartha is exposed to old age, disease, and death. Troubled by these sights, he beholds one who has renounced the world for the sake of attaining "that most blessed state" in which old age, disease, and death are unknown. Siddhartha makes his decision: He, too, will seek release. For a number of years, he lives in austerity.

> In his desire for quietude he emaciated his body for six years, and carried out a number of strict methods of fasting, very hard for men to endure. At meal times he was content with a single jujube fruit, a single sesame seed, and a single grain of rice. . . .[6]

In the end, however, Siddhartha comes to the conclusion that such severe self-denial is not the key to insight. The way to enlightenment (as he would call it) is a "middle way," a way given neither to sumptuous living nor to extravagant self-discipline, but to the contemplation of the Four Noble Truths (see Chapter 2). As the Buddha, Siddhartha gives the remainder of his life to teaching this *dharma*, or doctrine.[7]

The Buddha's connection with the sacred has to do with this dharma, to a great extent. He is *Sakyamuni*, that is, the sage or wise man of the Sakya clan. His importance lies in the wisdom that he is able to impart to seekers of the truth.

The Buddha is also a model, however. His life of seeking and finding is an example to believers, as is his compassion in teaching the dharma to suffering humanity. He teaches anyone willing to listen, and he has useful advice to offer no matter how far short one is of the ultimate goal. For those ready to renounce all in pursuit of Nirvana, Siddhartha holds out participation in the *sangha* or order of monks and nuns. For those less far along, he offers basic spiritual practice, including the "five precepts": Avoid taking life (animal or human), stealing, illicit sexual relations, lying, and intoxicants.[8]

The compassion of the Buddha becomes especially important in later Buddhism, setting the context for the various doctrines and legends associated with the *bodhisattva*. Especially associated with the *Mahayana* or "great vehicle" tradition in Buddhism, the term "bodhisattva" refers to those who, like Siddhartha, attain enlightenment but put off complete enjoyment of their "Buddha-hood" in order to help suffering humanity.[9] Indeed, in Mahayana tradition, the bodhisattva becomes a kind of savior who, by virtue of his or her meritorious deeds, is able to bring believers into the paradise of a "Buddha land" where all people live in the bliss of nonattachment. It is this aspect of Mahayana teaching that gives credence to the name "great vehicle"; that is, the possibility of a savior makes it possible for a greater portion of humanity to attain enlightenment and salvation. Siddhartha is one bodhisattva, but there are many more who, like him, perceive the truth and teach out of compassion for humanity.

It is clear by now that the general description "sacred" need not imply sameness, at least as applied to sacred persons. Moses and the Buddha are quite distinct in their roles and in their relationship to sacred reality. As a final example of sacred persons, consider the place of Jesus in Christianity.

Modern scholarship makes it clear that the various books of the New Testament present a complex picture of the relationship between Jesus and sacred reality. For example, the synoptic gospels (Matthew, Mark, Luke), the letters of Paul, and the Gospel of John all make the claim that Jesus is, in some way, the fulfillment of a divine plan that began with the history of Israel (including Moses). According to the book of Deuteronomy, Moses said that God "will raise up for you [Israel] a prophet like me from among your countrymen. . . ." (18:15). Over the long history of Israel, this text and others like it had been joined together into a belief in the expectation of the *messiah*, literally an "anointed one" (in Greek: *christos*—hence the title "Christ") who would come as God's servant to make Israel secure from her enemies and to establish the rule of justice and equity. According to the New Testament writers, this expectation is fulfilled in Jesus, a teacher from the hill country of Galilee in Judea. Thus Jesus is the *Christ*—a Greek word that approximates the Hebrew *messiah*. But Jesus may also be called "son of God," "son of man," and "son of David." The precise meaning of these terms is much debated and may vary somewhat from one writer to another. For example, when Paul writes that "when the fulness of time came, God sent forth His Son, born of a woman, born under the Law, in order that He might redeem those who were under the Law. . . ." (Galatians 4:4–5a), the term "Son" (of God) seems to be very close to "Christ"—that is, Jesus is the anointed servant of God whom Hebrew tradition had led people to expect. On the other hand, when the Gospel of John says that "God so loved the world, that He gave His only begotten Son, that whoever believes in Him should not perish, but have eternal life" (3:16), the reader cannot help but think of the statements made in the prologue to the Gospel, statements that indicate that Jesus is the incarnation or embodiment of the eternally existent *logos*, or "word," of God:

> In the beginning was the Word, and the Word was with God, and the Word was God. All things came into being through Him; and apart from Him nothing came into being that has come into being; And the Word became flesh, and dwelt among us, and we beheld His glory, glory as of the only begotten from the Father, full of grace and truth; No man has seen God at any time; the only begotten God, who is in the bosom of the Father, He has explained Him. (John 1:1–18)

We might express the unity of the New Testament writers this way: One who meets Jesus meets God. Their diversity appears in the various ways they understand the identification of the former and the latter.

The classical Christian position on this matter actually developed over several centuries. The Nicene Creed, recited to this day in many worship services of Christian churches, reflects the "official" Christian position on the doctrine of God—or, in the terms used in this book, the Christian notion of sacred reality. According to this creed, Christians believe in one God, who is described as "Father" and "Almighty." This God is the "maker of heaven and earth." Further, Christians believe in

> one Lord, Jesus Christ, the only begotten Son of God; born of the Father before time began; God from God, light from light, true God from true God; begotten, not made; one in essence with the Father, and through whom all things were made.[10]

The creed continues that this eternal Son of God "came down from heaven, took flesh of the Virgin Mary by the action of the Holy Spirit, and was made man" in order to accomplish the salvation of humanity. To that end, he was crucified by the authority of Pontius Pilate, the Roman governor of Judea from 26 to 39 C.E., then was raised from the dead on the third day. This section of the creed concludes: "He [Jesus the Christ] shall come again in glory to judge the living and the dead; and His kingdom shall have no end."

Classical Christian doctrine, then, views Jesus as something different from a prophet or sage. In his life, death, and resurrection, God is incarnate, or present "in the flesh." Traditionally, many Christians hearing the stories of Jesus from the gospels have understood them to be mirrors or signs of the divine nature. That Jesus performs healings, for example, is a sign of God's power over sickness. Perhaps it is also a sign of divine compassion. That Jesus teaches people, as in the Sermon on the Mount (Matthew 5–7), or calls *disciples* (followers) to learn from him, is a sign of God's willingness to guide a confused humanity. That Jesus proclaims forgiveness of sins is a sign of God's forgiveness. Finally, that Jesus raises people from the dead, and is himself raised after being crucified, is a sign of God's power over death. As the apostle Paul put it, the resurrection of Jesus leads believers to say: "Death is swallowed up in victory. O Death, where is your victory? O death, where is your sting?" (I Corinthians 15:54–55). Whatever is accomplished in the story of Jesus is, according to Paul, a kind of "first fruits" that points to the final intention of God for all creation. Jesus is, in the words of one Catholic theologian, the Christ—the "sacrament of the encounter with God."[11]

Sacred Objects

Our brief discussion of sacred persons already implies certain characteristic tendencies within the phenomenon of sacred appearance: Moses represents the prophetic tendency, Jesus the Christ the *sacramental*, the Buddha the *mystical*. A brief discussion of sacred objects furthers this impression of diversity within common forms.

By sacred objects, we mean a number of material items that have, or have had, importance in religious contexts: for example, books, statues, relics, foods. Some communities have perceived sacred reality in rocks, trees, or animals; others have focused on the sky, the earth, or the sun.

Muslims think of Islam as a religion "of the book," that is, founded on a revelation "sent down" from God, given to a prophet who then declared the message to humanity. According to Islam a number of religions share this characteristic. In particular, Judaism and Christianity are religions of the book. They are the result of the work of prophets who, like Muhammad, proclaimed the oneness of God and the coming Judgment, and whose message was set down in a Scripture—that is, in a book preserved by and for believers. From the Muslim point of view, the Qur'an, as the message given to

Muhammad, does not contradict the message given to earlier prophets. As a normative matter, the Torah of Moses and the Gospel of Jesus contain, in their essentials, the same message as the Qur'an. Where there are differences, they are due to corruptions in the text of the earlier messages or to corrupt understandings of the message of the earlier prophets. The Qur'an is then the "decisive criterion" by which disputes between the peoples of the book can be settled.

Is the Qur'an a sacred object? Not if by that one means that it is to be worshiped. Yet the Qur'an is the "speech of God," and according to the consensus of the majority of Muslims, is "uncreated." Of course, the paper on which the words are written is created, as is the ink that is used, and the person who recites the Qur'an is similarly a creation of God. The point of the idea of an "uncreated Qur'an" is this: When someone hears the Qur'an recited, he or she hears the word of God. There is no other word like it.

Because of this, the Qur'an occupies a unique place in Muslim understanding. It is recited in worship; it is an object of ongoing and intensive study; it is the first source for Islamic thinking about law, theology, and ethics. The most impressive act of piety in Islamic circles is the memorization of the Qur'an; one who achieves this feat bears the title *hafiz*. The Qur'an is thus understood as a vehicle for the manifestation of sacred reality; in the terms we are using, it is a sacred object.

Consider a somewhat different example. The practice of Zen Buddhism is sometimes characterized as "meditation." In fact, that is how *Zen* is often translated. There is a sense, however, in which one might better speak of "concentration." The point of Zen is to free oneself from a focus on nonessentials. The ultimate aim is to "see" the one thing that is essential: that which lies at the "bottom" of the self, which is variously called "Buddha-nature," "nothing," the "great empty circle." All ordinary reality is, in a sense, illusory. That which is truly real is sacred, distinct, set apart. With this in mind, it is curious to note that the practice of Zen often begins with the performance of certain acts, and concentration on particular objects: meditation, with concentration on breathing; archery, with concentration on the target; martial arts, with concentration on the opponent; or most strikingly in terms of sacred objects, the preparation and drinking of tea.

Can tea be a vehicle for the appearance of sacred reality? Practitioners of the tea ceremony think so. Attentiveness to every detail of the preparation and drinking of tea is the chief characteristic of this ceremony. The tea serves not so much to refresh oneself; if that were the purpose, tea would be like any other drink. Rather, tea serves as the focal point for concentration. If a person can focus on tea, bringing all his or her mental powers to bear on the immediate act of preparing and drinking it while eschewing other, less important matters, he or she is on the way to enlightenment. Tea is not sacred in itself; it can be, however, a vehicle for the attainment of that state of consciousness that Zen Buddhists call Nirvana.

Christian tradition presents a number of examples of sacred objects, not least the bread and wine of Holy Communion. Nearly all Christians find religious meaning in this observance. The connection of the elements of bread and wine with sacred reality is most clear, however, in those communities which think of the communion meal as a sacrament in which material elements become vehicles of grace.

In Roman Catholicism, for example, Communion takes place in the context of the *sacrifice* of the Mass or, as it is also called, the Eucharistic Liturgy. The elements of bread and wine, set apart through prayer and consecrated by a priest, serve as the principal symbols in the reenactment of the sacrificial death of the Christ. At one moment in the ceremony, the priest elevates the elements for all to see. Later, as people go to communion, the priest offers the consecrated elements saying: "the body of Christ," "the blood of Christ." The terminology is justified, according to Catholic understanding, because during the Liturgy the bread and wine are transformed into the broken body and shed blood of the Christ.

As with the relation of Christ and God, the relationship between the bread and wine and the body and blood of Christ is subject to varying interpretations by Christian communities. The traditional Catholic understanding has been that the bread and wine are altered in substance, so that they remain bread and wine to the senses, but are in fact the body and blood of Christ. To provide a full explanation of this position, known as *transubstantiation*, would take us far afield. For our purposes, what is important is the way that foods that are common in one setting may become sacred vehicles of grace in another. At various times, Catholic piety has so emphasized the element of transformation that the sacred "host" (the bread) has been placed in the front of the church for purposes of adoration. Believers kneel as they enter the church, to show awareness of the presence of the Blessed Sacrament and thus to honor God in Christ.

Sacred Time

It may be difficult to think of time as sacred. In ordinary conversation, there is much to suggest that time is a commodity: We "waste" it, "lose" it, even "kill" it. We can also "save" time. In so many ways, the implication is that time is something human beings use. It is a tool, a thing to be handled, useful for certain ends. It is hardly a thing "set apart" or "specially distinctive."

And yet, there are ways we may speak about time that suggest a somewhat different view. Thinking of death, some might say, "When my time comes, I hope I can accept it." Similarly, conceptions of "Father Time" suggest ways in which time may be a force that is, to some extent, beyond the volitional control of human beings. In such conceptions, time is something given, and human beings must respond to it. One "marks" time or perhaps prays for it to be meaningful. Thus, the writer of Psalm 90 reflects:

> As for the days of our life, they contain seventy years, Or if due to strength, eighty years, Yet their pride is but labor and sorrow; For soon it is gone and we fly away. . . . So teach us to number our days, That we may present to Thee a heart of wisdom. (10–12)

If time is a given, something human beings must deal with, it may be connected with sacred reality. What do religious traditions say concerning the reality of time?

Once again, examples of a common phenomenon reveal certain diverse tendencies. If we consider those traditions most associated with a prophet, time appears as the creation and, in a sense, the "field of revelation" for sacred reality. The overall conception of time is *linear*: Time has a beginning, and it will have an end. Consider the first verse of the Hebrew Bible: "In the beginning God created the heavens and the earth" (Genesis 1:1). Much contemporary discussion of this verse, and of those that follow, focuses on the question "Can these stories be taken literally?" We shall return to this question in Chapter 4. But the mistake in emphasis evident in such a question is worth mentioning even at this point. No doubt, the ancients who told the story of the world's creation wanted to explain the origin of things. But their interests were not "scientific," in the modern sense of the word. They were more interested in what a modern intellectual might call *cosmology*, that is, in considering the relationships among various aspects of their existence. For such people, the notion of God as the great and sovereign lord of time was already a crucial aspect of self-understanding. To say that the origin of things was connected with God was simply a logical extension of previously held ideas.

What were these previously held ideas? They were primarily that (1) God had chosen a particular group of people to do God's will and obey God's law, and (2) the story of this group pointed to God's power to carry out God's purposes. The story of ancient Israel really begins, not in Genesis 1 with the creation of the world, but in Genesis 12, where God says to Abram (eventually, Abraham):

> Go forth from your country, And from your relatives And from your father's house, To the land which I will show you; And I will make you a great nation, And I will bless you, And make your name great; And so you shall be a blessing; And I will bless those who bless you, And the one who curses you I will curse. And in you all the families of the earth will be blessed. (1–3)

As the story continues, the life of Abraham, the birth of Isaac, the struggles of Jacob (or Israel) and Joseph, and ultimately the career of Moses all point to the purpose of God. God has chosen the people of Israel and eventually will redeem them (and through them, all the world). The structure of time is indicated by the important points in the story of the people: the creation of all things, the revelation of the Torah, and, finally, the redemption of the world. Thus time is the "field" in which God acts; or, we may say, time is a vehicle of sacred reality.

In some religious traditions, a *cyclical* view of time prevails. If a linear view of time implies a story with a beginning, middle, and end, a cyclical view focuses on repetition, implying a story of slow yet ceaseless movement around a central point. To say only this about cyclical views, however, is misleading. For the nature of repetition, as well as the relationship between time and the sacred, varies considerably when we compare the cycle of time in different religious traditions.

For example, in the great religions of India, historical existence is characterized by the term *samsara*. This term may be translated "migration"; it implies the cycle of birth, death, and rebirth that is characteristic of all beings. Coupled with the notion of karma, or the moral "weight" of one's actions, samsara indicates a highly developed set of beliefs about personal and historical existence in which time is a medium of the sacred.

Almost as soon as we say this, however, we must note that samsara mediates the sacred in a complex way. Both Hinduism and Buddhism support the idea that appropriate behavior can result in positive karma, thus improving one's spiritual status in successive lives. In this respect, we might consider the relationship between samsara and Nirvana as complementary. Believers will think of samsara as the cycle of time and Nirvana as the fixed point around which all else revolves, and they will consider that the former provides endless opportunities to move toward the latter. Over the long stretch of time (the religions of India think in terms of very long stretches), one can make progress toward the ultimate goal.

At the same time, however, some aspects of Hinduism and Buddhism suggest that, if samsara is a medium of the sacred, it is a negative one. This is especially true with respect to certain mystical tendencies in these traditions. Recall the saying of the Buddha:

> Alas, living beings wear themselves out in vain! Over and over again they are born, they age, die, pass on to a new life, and are reborn! What is more, greed and dark delusion obscure their sight, and they are blind from birth. Greatly apprehensive, they yet do not know how to get out of this great mass of ill.[12]

The "great mass of ill" is samsara, and it is ultimately an illusion. To make time the focus of existence is self-defeating. The point is to see through historical time to the still point that is Nirvana. In a sense, we can still use the analogy of the cycle and the fixed point at its center. In another sense, the fixed point is so different from the cycle that the two seem unrelated. To attain the center is not a matter of progressive movement from the lower stage (the cycle) to a higher one. It is rather a radical shift from the world of birth, death, and rebirth to a reality that cannot be grasped in words. Thus Hinduism and Buddhism speak finally of *moksha*: "liberation" or "release" from samsara.

This complex approach to sacred time, especially the idea that time is a negative reality, is quite different from the notions of time that prevail in religious traditions that depict the sacred as an "earth goddess." The myth of Demeter (honored as the goddess of grain in ancient Greece), for example, suggests that the movement of the seasons itself is a manifestation of divine or sacred power. In ancient Greece, the months from June to October were a time when the sun scorched the earth, making agriculture impossible. Following the structure of Demeter's myth, these months signify the time Persephone, the daughter of the goddess, must spend "beneath the earth" with her husband Hades, lord of the underworld. The remainder of the year makes up the time of renewal or rebirth, when Persephone is reunited with her mother—the time of fertility and growth, and of the harvest reflecting the joy of Demeter in her daughter's presence.

The myth of Demeter is but one of many traditions in which the movement of the seasons is identified as a manifestation of the sacred. In other settings, gods may bear the names of the seasons, or the seasons may demonstrate the relations between Sky and Earth (Father and Mother). The interest of the pattern here is in terms of the conception of time implied— that the change in seasons is itself a mirror of sacred reality.

In Chapter 5, we will return to this theme, in particular with respect to the various rituals by which human beings might be said to participate in sacred time. For now, however, it will be enough to note that, even though the tribal conception of time is cyclical, its view of the relationship between time and the sacred is quite distinct from Hindu and Buddhist notions of samsara. The latter, as has been shown, implies ultimately a negative medium of the sacred. The point is to see through the illusion of historical time; such seeing is the result of the mystical experience characteristic of enlightenment. The myth of Demeter and related traditions, on the other hand, view time as a positive manifestation of the sacred, and participation in the change of the seasons is a way of participating in the very life of sacred reality. Such a focus is suggestive of the sacramental tendency to view aspects of material reality as vehicles for sacred appearance.

Sacred Space

When one considers the meaning of sacred space, he or she might think first of places that have been set apart for worship or for the performance of sacred rituals. An American might think readily of churches or synagogues as examples of such places; if he or she considers the phenomenon more deeply, it might be that one place of worship stands out above others as sacred. Many Christians or Jews might think of places in Jerusalem, the "holy city" in the Holy Land: for example, the Church of the Holy Sepulchre, which is said to mark the tomb in which the crucified Christ lay, or the Wailing Wall, which is all that remains of the great temple destroyed in 70 C.E.

Most religious traditions exhibit the phenomenon of sacred space, but again, the meanings attached to such places vary. A few examples will indicate once more the various patterns previously identified as prophetic, sacramental, and mystical.

Muslims may speak of any number of sacred places. Every mosque is sacred, in that it provides the place of gathering for communal worship and a special place of prayer for Muslims at any time. Jerusalem, sacred to Jews and Christians, is also of import in Islamic tradition. In Arabic, Jerusalem is *al-Quds*, the "holy" city, which contains two of the most important mosques in Islam. The famous Dome of the Rock dominates the skyline of old Jerusalem; according to Islamic tradition, it marks the place where Abraham undertook to sacrifice his son in obedience to God's command. Equally significant is *al-Aqsa* mosque, associated with the story of Muhammad's nocturnal journey and ascent into heaven. Among Shi'i Muslims, dominant in Iran, the tombs of great *imams* or leaders are holy sites, and one who prays at such places can count on the intercession of holy people.

By far the most important places in Islam, however, are the holy cities of Mecca and Medina, in the Arabian peninsula. These are the places where the foundational events in Islam took place: the call of the Prophet, the revelation of the Qur'an, the formation of the Islamic community. And near Mecca is the holiest of holy places, the shrine called the *Ka'ba*. In one sense, the Ka'ba seems rather ordinary. It is a cubical structure that, if it were not the object of special attention and adornment, would seem quite plain. The only extraordinary aspect of its appearance is the presence of a black stone, perhaps a meteorite, embedded in one of the walls. Worn concave from generations of touching by devout worshipers, the stone is a remnant of the religion of Arabia prior to the revelation of Islam. It was the sign of Allah, "the god," known to the Arabian tribes as the creator of the world, yet worshiped as one only among many other divinities. After the triumph of Islam, the stone remained as a testimony to the uniqueness of Allah.

The Ka'ba does not need to be extraordinary in its appearance to be sacred, however. Its distinction is its association with the story of Islam, especially (though not exclusively) the story of Muhammad. According to the Qur'an, the Ka'ba is the sanctuary built by Abraham and his son Ishmael to worship Allah. They did so in submission to God, and thus proved themselves Muslims (those who submit).

Even so, Muhammad submits to God and recites verses that establish that Muslims are to pray in the direction of the Ka'ba.

> We have seen the turning of thy face to heaven (for guidance, O Muhammad). And now verily We shall make thee turn (in prayer) toward a *qiblah* [direction of prayer] which is dear to thee. So turn thy face toward the Inviolable Place of Worship, and ye (O Muslims), wheresoever ye may be, turn your faces (when you pray) toward it. Lo! those who have received the Scripture know that (this Revelation) is the Truth from their Lord. And Allah is not unaware of what they do. (Qur'an 2:144)

According to Islamic tradition, building on the implication of the surrounding verses of the Qur'an, Muhammad and his community had been praying, facing in the direction of Jerusalem in order to demonstrate solidarity with the Jews of Medina. When the Jewish tribes refused to support Muhammad or, from the Muslim point of view, when they acted treacherously toward him, the verses of the *qiblah* were revealed. In one sense, it made no difference which direction one faced while praying: "Unto Allah belong the East and the West" (Qur'an 2:142). The point of a qiblah in the story of Muhammad is submission to God. Today, Muslims continue to face toward Mecca and the Ka'ba when they pray, and as they do, they remember the story of Muhammad and the revelation of the Qur'an.

Shinto shrines present a very different conception of sacred space. The graceful *torii* marks the entrance to the territory of a kami or superhuman being. It may be that the original impulse for identifying such territories rested in perceptions of beauty or majesty. It is hard to look at Mount Fuji, for example, without a sense of its awesome beauty. Such perceptions could easily be associated with the presence of the sacred and did not need to be formalized.

Over time, however, it became important to identify the most auspicious of such sites as the dwelling place of particular deities. While the most important of these would be Amaterasu Omikami, the sun goddess and ancestor of the Japanese imperial clan, a variety of nature deities, clan ancestors, and such abstract deities as growth, thought, and others might be worshiped as well. In terms of sacred space, the importance of Shinto conceptions lies in the obvious sacramental implications. Space is sacred, not because it fits into the story of a prophet but because it is the dwelling place of a deity.

As a final example of sacred space, consider the *stupa* or "burial mound" of Buddhism. According to tradition, the Buddha told his followers to deal with his remains in the manner customary for a "universal monarch." In the Indian context, this meant that he was to be cremated, his ashes deposited in a golden urn and set in a mound constructed at the crossing of four well-traveled roads. Believers could then make offerings of flowers, incense, food, and music at the sacred place.

As Buddhism spread throughout India and Asia, new stupas could be constructed either by bringing a portion of the Buddha's remains (genuine or not) or through a similar burial for others who had achieved enlightenment through following the Buddha's teaching. According to Buddhist teaching, one who makes offerings at a stupa or who enters it (actually, one enters a temple constructed around a stupa) is confronted with the great challenge of the Buddha: his teaching or dharma. This idea was signified through the use of art, which presented the stories of the Buddha in visual form.

In one sense, the stupa is reminiscent of any number of manifestations of sacred space. The use of the Buddha's remains as relics, for example, recalls traditions important in Roman Catholic or Eastern Orthodox settings. Yet the central aspects of the Buddha's teaching can give a significance to the stupa that is quite different from such contexts. In Catholic or Orthodox Christianity, relics mediate divine power. The sacramental implications of such a notion are obvious. Insofar as Buddhism stresses the mysticism inherent in the Buddha's teaching, however, the importance of the stupa is that it is conducive to the attainment of enlightenment. In this regard, the stupa mediates sacred reality in the same manner as the Buddha—by pointing the way.

SACRED APPEARANCE AND THE COMPLEXITY OF TRADITIONS

The identification of patterns in the appearance of the sacred suggests that there are characteristic "types" of religion. Judaism and Islam, we have said, may be identified with prophetic tendencies; certain aspects of Hinduism and Buddhism fit into the mystical pattern; some forms of Christianity may be characterized as sacramental, as may Shinto and various tribal religions. Such classifications are helpful, as long as they are not pushed too far. Especially if one thinks of the long history of particular religious traditions, he or she is likely to find much evidence of the mixing of various patterns. Many religious traditions make complex claims about the appearance of sacred reality.

An example is the sacramental tendencies of Christianity, which can hardly be denied. Yet there are also strong prophetic trends in the Christian tradition, most apparent in the Protestant focus on the Word of God preserved in the Bible and proclaimed by the preacher. But prophetic tendencies are also present within Catholicism. A linear conception of time, for example, is dominant in the great creeds of the Church: Creation is the beginning of the story, the incarnation is the midpoint, and, in the end, Christ "will come again in glory to judge the living and the dead, and His Kingdom will have no end." This is joined to a cyclical view that resonates with other sacramental conceptions. The Church year with its liturgical calendar, for example, not only recalls the mighty acts of God in history but also relates to the change in seasons. The great festivals of Christmas and Easter represent a kind of Christianization of older celebrations tied to the movement of nature.

Similarly, the mystical tendencies so characteristic of the religions of India do not stand alone. Hinduism in particular presents strong sacramental motifs. The great god Vishnu, it is held, makes himself present at crucial times in the history of the world through an *avatar*. In this way, Vishnu becomes incarnate in human or animal form and is able to instruct and preserve humanity. One of the most notable avatars of Vishnu is Krishna, the divine charioteer in the Bhagavad Gita (see Chapters 1 and 2). Followers of Vishnu honor the god by participating in a sacred meal with him at a shrine or altar, usually in the home. And they trust him, in the end, to deliver them from the cycle of endless birth and rebirth (samsara).

If we consider the long history of many religious traditions, such complexity is not surprising. Remembering that religion can be related to almost every facet of human experience, we expect religious traditions to prove adaptable to a variety of human needs and interests. This brings us to a final consideration: To what extent are notions of the sacred, and indeed of sacred appearances, human creations? Does the sacred "break through" to human beings, or do human beings "create" vehicles of the sacred?

From a phenomenological perspective, the answer to both questions must be "yes." For example, if we think of sacred space and the example of the stupa or burial mound in Buddhism, it seems obvious that we are dealing with a human creation. Empirically, the stupa is a product of Indian culture. One problematic aspect of death has to do with the disposition of remains; the stupa is only one of so many ways of dealing with such remains, and historically it was used for the burial of significant persons. In this sense, the stupa is one result of the creative capacity of human beings. Similarly, we may speak of the Ka'ba, or of linear and cyclical conceptions of time, as products of human culture.

If we think of the intentions of Buddhists (or Muslims or other religious persons), however, to speak of the stupa (or Ka'ba) as a human creation does not suffice. Such phenomena are vehicles of sacred reality. That is, persons perceive in and through the stupa that which they consider specially distinctive, to some extent beyond the volitional control of human beings, specially prominent with respect to human welfare, and properly determinative of various aspects of human existence. In this sense, a burial mound, recognized as having the significance of sacred space, is no longer simply a burial mound. It has been transformed by an experience of sacred reality. We may analyze the history of such an experience; we may explore its relation to a variety of aspects of human thought, feeling, action, personal and social existence, and the recognition or expression of values. The appearance of the sacred cannot, however, be adequately described in any one of these aspects of human experience, or in any combination of them, without ceasing to be "religious."

Shall we say then that persons who claim an experience of sacred reality are telling the truth? A desire to examine the phenomenon of religion does not commit us to any particular answer to this question. Indeed, it would seem that there cannot be any "global" answer. It has been the burden of this chapter to discuss the richness and diversity of sacred appearances, and to draw out of this richness several characteristic patterns. To answer questions about the truth of claims to an experience of the sacred would require a more complete analysis of the various types of claims religious people make. The claim of Muslims that Muhammad received the Qur'an through divine inspiration is different from the claim of Buddhists that Siddhartha Gautama "saw" the truth about human existence as he meditated during the "third watch" of the night. To evaluate the truth of each requires that we attend not only to their unity (as claims about sacred appearances) but also to their diversity (as claims about particular appearances and about distinct notions of sacred reality). To say this another way: In speaking about Muhammad or the Buddha, Muslims and Buddhists use diverse forms of religious language. To deal with questions about the truth of their claims, we must become sensitive to the various types of language Muslims and Buddhists use. Considerations of truth thus presuppose an understanding of sacred language, which is the subject of the following chapter.

NOTES

1. Martin Lings, *Muhammad: His Life Based on the Earliest Sources* (London: Allen & Unwin and the Islamic Texts Society, 1983), pp. 43–44.
2. *Buddhist Scriptures*, trans. and ed. Edward Conze (Middlesex, England: Penguin Books, 1954), pp. 49–50.
3. In pointing to the three patterns of prophetic, sacramental, and mystical, we draw on the suggestion of William Alston in "Religion," *The Encyclopedia of Philosophy*, ed. Paul Edwards (New York: Macmillan and Free Press, 1967), vol. 7, pp. 140–145.
4. From Louis Ginzberg, *The Legends of the Jews*, trans. Paul Radin (Philadelphia: The Jewish Publication Society of America, 1911, 1939), vol. 3, pp. 479–481.
5. Conze, *Buddhist Scriptures*, p. 22.
6. Conze, *Buddhist Scriptures*, p. 46.
7. According to tradition, Siddhartha died at the age of eighty. This would be approximately 483 B.C.E.
8. For members of the *sangha*, add: no food after noon, no worldly amusements (dancing and so on), no luxurious seats or beds, no handling of gold or silver, no idle talk.
9. The descriptive Mahayana was especially formulated to counter the claims of the Theravadin school to greater antiquity as the Buddhism "of the elders." For Mahayanists, the Theravadin school was in effect *Hinayana*—a term that means "lesser vehicle," in the sense of less accessible to the mass of people and in effect containing less truth.
10. Following the translation in *Liturgies of the Western Church*, selected and introduced by Bard Thompson (New York: World, 1961), pp. 63–64.
11. Edward Schillebeex, *Christ the Sacrament of the Encounter with God* (New York: Sheed and Ward, 1963).
12. Conze, *Buddhist Scriptures*, p. 50.

THOUGHT EXPERIMENTS

1. Follow the story of a character in the Bible (for example, Abraham) and identify various appearances of the sacred in his or her life. What media serve as vehicles of sacred reality? Are there implications of prophetic, sacramental, or mystical patterns in the appearances you identify?

2. For several days, make a point of entering a number of the different buildings used for religious purposes in your community (churches, synagogues, mosques, Buddhist temples, etc.). Are there any aspects of the various forms of architecture that indicate the existence of sacred space? Are there any features of the buildings that characterize different notions of sacred space—for example, is there anything about a Catholic Church building that reveals that it is Catholic?

3. Spend one day paying close attention to the various ways you think of time. As you move through the day, do you experience a greater sense of story associated with linear views of time, or of repetition associated with cyclical views?

4. Are there places (space) or times that are most important for you? Does that importance have anything to do with your sense of the sacred? Where would you go or at what time do you think you would most likely have some experience of a hierophany?

SUGGESTIONS FOR FURTHER READING

Articles on "Sacred Space," "Sacred Time," "Sacred and Profane," and other topics may be found in *The Encyclopedia of Religion*, 12 vols., ed. Mircea Eliade. New York: Macmillan, 1987. They may be found also in the *HarperCollins Dictionary of Religion*. San Francisco, Calif.: HarperCollins, 1995.

DUPRE, LOUIS, *Symbols of the Sacred*. Grand Rapids, Mich.: Eerdmans, 2000. Excellent but difficult study of how symbols mediate the Transcendent.

ELIADE, MIRCEA, *Patterns in Comparative Religion*, trans. Rosemary Sheed. Cleveland and New York: World, 1958. Eliade's work is basic to discussions of the phenomenology of religion. It is especially relevant to the topic of sacred appearances.

PORTERFIELD, AMANDA, *The Power of Religion*. New York: Oxford University Press, 1998.

4 The Language(s) of the Sacred

Throughout this book we have insisted that the religious person is one who affirms that there is a dimension of reality beyond the world of immediate experience, yet with which human beings can have contact. We use the term "sacred" to refer to that reality, although it is obvious that the diverse religious traditions have quite distinctive notions about the sacred, and quite specific names for it: God, Brahman, Nirvana, Heaven, the kami. What is common to all religions is the conviction that the sacred is somehow "set off" from ordinary experiences and relations that are "merely" customary. When the great sixteenth-century Spanish mystic, John of the Cross, attempted to describe his sense of God, he used the paradoxical phrase *Todo y Nada* (everything and nothing). When Hindu mystics are asked to describe the ultimate principle of the universe (Brahman), they say, in Sanskrit, "*Neti, Neti*" (neither this nor that). In both of these instances, there is an obvious attempt to say implicitly that the sacred somehow defies language and that it is unlike other realities. Saint Thomas Aquinas, in the very first question of the *Summa* (article 9), argues that God's relevation comes to us in metaphorical language adequate to express the reality of God. Thomas further argues that it is easier to say what God is not than what God is.

Religious traditions do not always use paradoxical language to describe the sacred. They might call God, for instance, Father or Mother or Lord or King in order to set out an analogy with something that, while "ordinary," seems helpful in describing the object of their devotion. When we look at religious language, in short, we find something very close to poetry: Believers (and poets) use ordinary words, yet they want to convey a sense of something that they consider larger, more profound than the ordinary referents of the words.

We can get some sense of the ways religious language develops by performing a small experiment. Think of the happiest moment in your life (or, if you wish, the saddest) and recollect the feelings that were present then. Try to set out, in a limited number of words, a description of that moment that will communicate to a sympathetic audience something of those feelings. Those who are genuine poets may carry off this assignment with ease, but for many it will prove difficult. The same thing happens in religion: Words strain to give meaning.

The origins and difficulty of much religious language are very similar. Such language attempts to convey to persons the experiences of people of faith. The Bible presents numerous and varied examples: narratives (e.g., the gospels), poems and hymns (e.g., the Psalms), proverbs, legal codes, sermons, letters, stories of beginnings and endings, parables and ethical reflections, chronicles and histories. Interestingly, what one does not find are rigorously philosophical or scientific texts—although Jews and Christians responding to the Bible in diverse contexts have certainly developed such texts. Generally, the biblical answer to questions of philosophy or science seems to be a story of some sort.

The entire question of religious language is frighteningly complex. Philosophers ask about the meaning and truth of religious language; experts in interpretation try to establish methods for understanding texts; language scholars attempt to penetrate the exact meaning of words and the reliability of translations from one language to another. This chapter attempts a much simpler task. In the pages that follow we set out some of the ways in which language is used in religion and then reflect on the character of religious language.

MYTH

We begin with the language that may be the oldest and most widespread form of religious discourse. The word "myth" has a distinctly premodern ring; it is associated with stories that "are not true" or are fanciful. In the field of religious studies, however, myth has a somewhat different meaning. For the purposes of this chapter, the following will serve as a summary definition: *Myth* indicates a narrative concerning sacred reality and its relationship to humanity. Many scholars would add to this: In its concern with sacred reality, myth is designed to disclose the ultimate truth about crucial human questions—for example, the origin of the cosmos or the final destiny of the world and its inhabitants. Other topics include how evil got into the world, what the world was like at its beginnings, and how the world will eventually end and what will come after that ending.

There are many types of myths, to be sure. But it is interesting to note that all religions, wherever they fall in the typology developed earlier in this text, attempt to answer the question: How did everything and everyone begin? How did it all start—and why? Answers to this question are nearly always cast in the form of a story. The Bible provides such a story in the opening chapters of the book of Genesis; that story is repeated, though in piecemeal fashion, at various places in the Qur'an. Other religions tell of great struggles between the gods and a primordial chaos, or see the world as hatching from a great cosmic egg; still others depict the creation of the world as similar to the unfolding of a long drama flowing from the creative force of the absolute. There are obvious and important differences among these stories, but at this point the interesting fact is that so many of them have similarities and that they occur in almost every culture.

In modern, scientifically oriented societies, the relationship between creation myths and historical or scientific "fact" is of great concern. The ongoing debate in the United States over the teaching of evolution in public schools bears witness to this. And yet, to focus exclusively on the question of whether God in fact created the world in six calendar days (as many think the opening chapter of the book of Genesis suggests) would be to ignore important aspects of the religious dimensions of creation myths.

In examining such stories, the great question of religious studies is this: What basic premise(s) lie behind such language? What notion(s) of sacred reality, and of its relation to human beings, is reflected in the imaginative language employed in a particular myth? We might say, at a minimum, that every creation myth reflects a tacit assumption that the world is not self-explanatory; the world is dependent on a sacred "other" from which it derives its significance. If we turn again to the biblical and Qur'anic story of creation, it seems clear that the story affirms at least the following: (1) God is not only independent of the world but "stands outside" it as its effortless creator; (2) the world is created as good—it is not evil, nor is it an illusion; (3) at the center of creation, both as apex and as steward, stand the primordial man and woman, Adam and Eve. The story thus stands as a vehicle for Jews, Christians, and Muslims to express some of their deepest feelings about the origins and purpose of the world and of human beings.

Should we view the story as a rival or alternative explanation of, for example, the "Big Bang" theory of contemporary physicists? Undoubtedly the story may be read this way—at least, it *is* read this way in certain religions, especially in Christian communities. But for most communities that refer to the story, it functions as myth: That is, it discloses their perceptions of the ultimate truth concerning cosmic and human origins.

We should underscore the point that creation myths are never the product of an individual. These, and indeed all religious myths, come out of the collective experience of a people. The stories related by American Indians or Australian aborigines of the origin of the world are not statements of personal opinion. They express the perception of a community concerning the relation of the world, including itself, to the sacred. Such myths serve as frames of reference for a particular community's notions of reality. They define the community and its relationship to the world. It may well be that some*one* created the story, but its power comes from the fact that it is remembered and re-created in a community.

It is worth noting that a myth, rather than being a harmless story, is a powerful vehicle for life and action. That fact can be demonstrated through an example of a myth turned to degenerate usage. In the 1930s, Nazi ideology resurrected old myths of Germanic purity, stories of blood and national identity, and dressed them in a whole range of ritual and symbolic gestures in order to instill in the German population a sense of social cohesion and a contempt for others (Slavs, Jews, Gypsies, etc.) who were not a part of the "master race." This dimension of myth—its power to energize a community for evil, in particular—shows how naive a dismissal of myths as "fairy tales" or "tall stories" can be.

There is a final point. It is alleged that myth has now been replaced by rationality in modern culture. Scholars like to point to the philosophers of ancient Greece (sixth century B.C.E.) as forerunners of modern science because they were the first to attempt an account of the world without reference to myths of origins. Although the evidence of certain dialogues of Plato, in particular the *Timaeus*, which contains a myth of origins, would seem to count against this, it is undoubtedly true that modern science owes much to Greek "rationalism." And it is undoubtedly true that most people in industrial societies look to science for an explanation of world origins. Nonetheless, the persistence of mythic thinking in modern culture is an unassailable fact. Myth, after all, is narrative that conveys perceptions of deep and abiding truths about the human condition.

Mircea Eliade argued that, although there are persons in modern society who live without reference to mythic patterns of thought, they constitute a very small and exceptional minority. Eliade's words, written more than a half a century ago, still hold true:

> A whole volume could be written on the myths of modern man or the mythologies camouflaged in the plays he enjoys, in the books he reads. The cinema, that "dream factory," takes over and employs countless mythical motifs—the fight between hero and monster, initiatory combats and ordeals, paradigmatic figures and images (the maiden, the hero, the paradisical landscape, hell, and so on). . . . Whether modern man "kills" time with a detective story or enters such a foreign temporal universe as is represented by any novel, reading projects him out of his personal duration and incorporates him into other rhythms, makes him live in another "history."[1]

STORIES

Myths, of course, are stories, but they are stories of a certain kind. Myths deal with "cosmic" questions: the origin of the world; the creation and meaning of human beings; stories of a lost paradise or golden age; stories about the end of the world and the manner of that end. Beyond those great mythic reconstructions are other stories, narratives embedded in the historical religious experience of the people. The God of the Bible, for instance, is often described as the "God of Abraham, Isaac, and Jacob"—that is, the God who did marvelous things for those patriarchs whose stories are central to the evolution of the people of Israel. In a similar fashion, we should remember that large parts of the New Testament are made up of stories either about Jesus or about the experiences of his earliest followers or stories that Jesus himself tells.

Every great religious tradition has its official stories (in Hinduism, for example, the great Mahabharata is an epic poem),[2] but we should note that every religious tradition also produces stories of believers who witness to, in their narrative, the significance of their personal encounter with the sacred. It is worthwhile noting that autobiography begins in Western culture with the publication of Augustine of Hippo's *Confessions*—an attempt to account for his slow coming to Christian faith—in late antiquity. The taste for religious autobiography continues to this day both in its written form and in the oral tradition of those who testify how their faith was born, sustained, and matured over time.

Why is story so central to religion? We can begin by noting that story is central to the fact of being human. When one person asks another, "Who are you?" and wants something more than a name and Social Security number, the answer includes a story. How much the one giving the answer reveals depends a great deal on the degree of intimacy he or she shares with the inquirer. The fact that one person tells another about personal desires, longings, and disappointments is often a sign of trust, one of those benchmarks of friendship and love between persons. Stories, in short, are forms of disclosure and revelation. They are meant to alter relationships (usually, for the good).

Michael Novak once defined religion as the "acting out of a vision of personal identity and human community—it is the living out of an intention, an option, a selection among life's possibilities."[3] To paraphrase Novak: Religion is *my* story being shaped by another (religious) story. For a Jew this means that his or her story is shaped by the larger story of God's covenant with Israel. We should be very clear about this point. Apart from some minor chronicles, the normative stories of a religious tradition are not told simply to hold on to a history but to disclose a notion of the sacred to people. For example, when the biblical writers reveal their purpose in writing, they indicate it is to "build faith" in the revelation of God. Many scholars have called the first twelve chapters of the Gospel of John the "book of signs" because of the writer's repeated use of the term "sign" with reference to the stories he tells of Jesus' words and deeds. At the close of the gospel, the writer makes it clear that his purpose is not to record a history but to make a disclosure that will enable faith:

> Now Jesus did many other signs in the presence of the disciples which are not written in this book; but these are written that you may believe that Jesus is the Christ, the Son of God, and that believing you may have life in his name. (John 20:30–31)

What are the central functions of religious stories? First, and most simply, the stories are a kind of discourse that passes on information, insights, lessons, and instruction. In this sense, religious stories are like histories, novels, and other pieces of literature because they contain material that people think is worth remembering. Such stories give shape to religious *tradition* (i.e., that which is "handed down"). Thus Buddhists keep alive the stories of the Buddha's journey toward enlightenment because they believe that the memory of his seeking and finding retains value across generations.

Second, religious stories recall paradigmatic moments and/or persons. A paradigm is a blueprint or model. Religious stories thus are not simply "handed down"; they provide models to emulate. Early on, pious Muslims began to collect reports of Muhammad's words and deeds. The motivation of such activity was in part simple love and admiration for the Prophet and his memory, but such stories also provided a normative example for submission to the will of God. Hence they were (and are) collectively known as the *sunna*—the "beaten path" provided by the Prophet's example.

Third, religious stories are vehicles for disclosure or *revelation*. Such stories may recount events that could be called "ordinary," but for the believing community they mediate sacred reality. What, for example, could be more ordinary than the traditional Chinese story of a meeting between the founders of Confucianism and Taoism? According to the story, Confucius entered into the presence of Lao-tzu and paid him homage—a simple enough act, because Lao-tzu would have been the elder. But told from a Taoist point of view, the story indicates the superiority of Lao-tzu and thus of his way. It discloses the connections between Lao-tzu's teaching and ultimate truth.

In many traditions, of course, such stories (and usually, other material) are set down in a written text and receive an official form. In such cases, the text itself may become a disclosure of the sacred. The book(s) take on the character of a repository of what we can say about the divine. Thus, Jews enshrine the scrolls of the Torah in an ark in their synagogues; many Protestants display an open Bible in their churches or homes; Catholic priests kiss the Scriptures after the solemn reading of the Bible at their worship; Muslims regard the memorization of the Qur'an as a supreme act of piety. One of the more dramatic examples of the sanctification of a written text occurs in the worship of the Orthodox churches. Before the gospel for the day is read, the deacon or the priest cries out to the assembled people: "Wisdom! Let us be attentive." He then comes in procession before the congregation with the gospel book (usually lavishly ornamented on its cover) in order to read aloud. The symbolism is patent: It is from hearing the story that one gains not just knowledge, but wisdom, the Wisdom that is God's Word.

It is also worth noting that the religious character of persons and societies is almost always described in terms of a story simply because there is a narrative character to human life. A person is who he or she is, religiously speaking, because there is a history, a story behind the person that is either accepted or rejected (for example, the religion of his or her family). The personal religious experience is most commonly interpreted in a way that emphasizes the contribution such experience makes to one's growth as a person. Religious people tell stories because they wish to demonstrate the way(s) religion gives shape to their lives.

STORY AS PARABLE

Thus far we have discussed two kinds of religious language: myth and story. One division of the latter, however, deserves special attention: the parable.

Parables are to be distinguished from allegories. *Allegories* are stories, usually fictional, in which the various characters and incidents actually represent figures and events not a part of the story as such. George Orwell's *Animal Farm* is an allegory: It is a story about barnyard animals and their problems, but each animal (and the barnyard itself) actually represents something quite outside the story.

A *parable*, by contrast, is a story, usually fictional, in which the narrative thrust is to make a point (often, though not always, religious) but the elements of the story do not, in each and every instance, stand for something else. The point to be grasped arises from the story in its own right.

The parable is meant to arrest the hearer or reader in such a way that he or she must think of things in a new and unaccustomed manner. The parable has a certain element of the puzzling or the outrageous that carries with it a kind of "shock value," which calls into question comfortable assumptions. The gospels depict Jesus as a teller of parables—a technique that is also common in rabbinic literature. When Jesus tells parables, his audience often does not understand the stories or is upset by them. In Luke 10:35–47, Jesus tells the story of the "good Samaritan" in response to the question of a scholar of Torah: "Who is my neighbor?" The parable as told is a rebuke to the scholar, for the Samaritan (regarded commonly as ritually impure and doctrinally aberrant in the Judaism of first-century Palestine) acts as a neighbor to a person in need, while a priest and a Levite (religious leaders, like the scholar) fail to do so. To make such a person as the Samaritan a hero presents a challenge to a certain way of thinking about love. It is the acts of a person and not his social status that determine who the true neighbor is. The parable is meant to shock the reader into realizing this new insight.

Unlike the myth, which deals with great, cosmic issues such as origins, the parable deals with immediate, existential realities: for example, awareness of one's neighbor and the proper response to his or her need. In that sense parables belong to that broad class of religious language called "wisdom" speech. Like proverbs and allegories, the parable hopes to move people beyond conventional understandings to a deeper engagement with realities conceived to be sacred. Here is an excellent story told of the Buddha. It is a short dialogue in question-and-answer form between a seeker and the Buddha that underscores the fact that the path of the Buddha leads to spiritual enlightenment:

> "Are You a god or a magician?"
> "I am not a god or a magician. I am awake."

THE PRESERVATION OF SACRED LANGUAGE

Although people do not often reflect on it, language has in it a power that alters and shapes the way they perceive the world and the way they live. This is generally recognized only on those solemn occasions when language is used in a formal manner. One may say what one wants with respect to the truth; when he or she utters the words of an oath to tell the truth in a law court, the language used effects a change. Not to tell the truth after repeating that oath is not simply a moral wrong; it is a felony called perjury. With similar formulas the relations between two people may be altered (as, for example, with the marriage vows) or persons may be inaugurated into public office. In all of these instances words carry power.

For many religious people words have a peculiar power because they point to and/or reveal the sacred dimension of reality. That is why religious stories, myths, and so on are preserved within religious communities; they constitute the peculiar memory and the accumulated power of a given religious tradition. In fact, one way different kinds of religions may be distinguished is according to the manner in which they effect this preservation: Some have an oral culture, others a written one. Let us say a few words about each.

Oral Cultures

Examples of oral cultures abound among the indigenous or aboriginal peoples of various parts of the world: the Indians of North, Central, and South America; the tribal cultures of Africa; the aborigines of Asia, Australia, and New Zealand. Among all these peoples there are religious traditions that involve myths and stories of various types. The point of distinguishing such traditions here is that they transmit the stories orally, from one generation to the next. This transmission may be the special task of certain families or designated "wise persons," or certain stories may be taught to the young of the tribe at appropriate times (for example, at the onset of sexual maturity). These stories or myths, furthermore, are told only at certain occasions or at certain times; they are sacred and, more to the point, sacred for specific reasons and specific times.

It is not hard to see the functional benefit of such transmission to particular communities. The stories thus communicated provide historical identity to the tribe. The retelling of important myths links the young with the old, and ultimately places all the living in relationship with the ancestors and the gods and goddesses of the tribe. The transmission of myth, in short, ensures cultural and social identity. Further, cultures that focus on oral techniques of transmitting myths store in such myths ways of acting that ensure their survival. The Hopi Indians, for example, tell stories that emphasize the great importance of corn, in particular, its origin and its use for the tribe. By learning such myths, the younger generation imitates the past and learns how, when, and under what circumstances they should plant corn in the semiarid lands in which the Hopi live. The oral transmission of sacred stories maintains and ensures both the social sense of the people and their relationship to the world of nature.

Scriptural Cultures

The word "scripture" comes from Latin and means simply "that which is written." Many of the great religions of the world preserve their inherited past and their religious language in writing. In fact, it is common to refer to the three great religions of the West (Judaism, Christianity, and Islam) as "religions of the book" because of their emphasis on the written word. We should also note, however, that written records of religious language are also important for the great religions of the East.

More technically, *scriptures* indicates those writings that, by reason of their particular authority, are considered privileged and normative for a particular tradition. These writings are called *canonical*. *Canon* (from the Greek word meaning a "list") refers to a particular set of books or a single book that is authoritative for a religious community. In Christianity the canon of scripture (the Bible) is the list (canon) of texts read in public worship. Thus, for example, in Christianity there are many religious writings, ranging from the classical treatises of great theologians to certain treasured devotional works; in Theravada Buddhism numerous works systematize and comment on discourses of the Buddha. Only the writings in the Bible (for Christianity) or the collection of texts known as *tripitaka* ("three baskets"; Buddhism), however, are authoritative or canonical.

What is the function of written scriptures? Of course, there are variations among the several traditions related in large part to their view of the nature of scripture. But certain functions occur across the lines of diverse traditions, such as those discussed here.

Scriptures serve as the yardstick (another meaning for the word "canon") against which the truth of certain ideas or the rightness of certain practices can be measured and judged. Nobody, for example, can be considered a Muslim if that person openly contradicts the teachings of the Qur'an. Conversely, a pious Muslim will appeal to the same book as the norm for how he or she should relate to God and live in the world. Thus one may say that a scripture has normative power.

Scriptures evoke the presence of the sacred. The classic, Vedic rituals of ancient Hinduism constitute only one of the many examples in which scriptural materials form an integral part of religious worship. In the *srauta sacrifice*, a group of specialists contributed to the performance of rituals that invoked the presence and favor of sacred beings, each specialist being a reciter of selected sections of the Rig-Veda, a group of hymns praising the various virtues of gods and goddesses. Scriptures reveal the sacred, not in the Western sense that they come from God, but in the sense that through their use in reading, meditation, and ritual, the sacred is revealed. As unique words, scriptures possess power and act as a repository of material for the spiritual life of believers.

As in the oral traditions discussed earlier, scriptures define a community. In that sense the scriptures have a symbolic function that testifies to who a person and/or a community is. Because all scripture appeals back to a revelation or ancient, sacred wisdom, it serves to connect contemporary readers with the community's traditions. When contemporary Jews read the accounts of the Passover meal in the book of Exodus, they affirm, in that reading, that there is a connection between themselves and the events of which Exodus tells. They become, as it were, contemporary with the text.

Finally, scriptures function in a way parallel to the stories of oral cultures in that both act as a means of preservation for the traditions of particular communities. In both cases, myths of origins and destiny are preserved and can continue to communicate a tradition's worldview to those who listen to or read them. Such preservation, and more precisely the memory it engenders, founds and sustains the world (to paraphrase Mircea Eliade). Scriptures provide a framework for the religious life of the believer.

A SUMMARY AND SYNTHESIS

It should be obvious by now that there is a close connection between the various topics discussed in this chapter. Myths, stories, and parables are all part of the larger phenomenon called religious language. The focus of this discussion on these few categories does not even touch such genres as law codes and sacred poems. These also have a part in the religions of the world and are reflected in both oral and scriptural cultures.

We might summarize this section by asking and responding to a final question: What motivates religious people to hold on so deeply to sacred stories and other forms of religious discourse? We can frame an answer by recalling Joseph Campbell's explanation for the persistence of myth. Campbell, a lifelong student of the world's religious myths, cited four reasons:

1. Sacred stories are a means of connecting with the sacred dimension of existence. Through such stories believers get a sense of the otherness of the sacred and a glimpse into the world or realm of the sacred. For the person who does not believe, sacred stories might be "great poetry" or "great literature"; for the believer, they are vehicles for the disclosure of sacred reality.
2. Religious stories "order the cosmos." The basic purpose of myth is to provide coherence to the world in which the believer lives. Religious stories act as a buffer against the notion that there is no direction, purpose, or meaning to the world. That is why, as Mircea Eliade points out in many of his books, chaos plays such an important role in creation mythologies. Creation is often described in terms of a struggle or a victory over the forces of chaos and disorder. The Bible begins with an account of how the world came to be and ends with an account of the final days. From Genesis to the Revelation, there is a framework that gives shape to the human journey, from its origins to its final destiny.

This ordering of the cosmos is, at its root, an attempt to give meaning to life. At this level the telling of religious stories corresponds to those deep theological questions that stand behind every religious tradition: Who am I? Where did I come from? What does my life mean? How will I (and everything else) end? If the first purpose of religious language is to provide a disclosure of the sacred, its second purpose is to account for the world.

3. With respect to the communal or social aspect of religion, stories give shape to memory; they sustain and nourish a tradition. A Christian is a Christian precisely because the story of Jesus has a pertinence and reality that goes beyond the historical record; a Muslim is a Muslim because what Muhammad recited in the Qur'an is applicable now; a Buddhist is a Buddhist because he or she recalls the story of Gautama's enlightenment and, in that recollection, finds meaning and clues for his or her own enlightenment.
4. Also in connection with the communal aspect of religion, stories serve an ethical function. Believers measure behavior, style of life, attitudes, and patterns of living against the paradigms provided in the tradition. One is identified as part of a certain tradition precisely because one patterns his or her life after important stories. The recollection of such stories encourages approved behaviors and provides a standard of judgment for the

community in dealing with persons who act in ways that are dissonant with its tradition.

THE LANGUAGE OF THEOLOGY

For purposes of this chapter, one can think of a theologian as a believer who reflects on the fact of personal and communal faith in such a way as to clarify it and/or to argue that such faith is worthy of consideration by those outside his or her community. One who "bears witness" to the importance of faith in his or her life acts as a theologian, as does one who engages in the systematic study of and reflection on the importance of faith, although the latter is obviously more professionally and explicitly so.

The basic point here is that much of theology is "second-level discourse." The theologian attempts to set forth, systematically and conceptually, the meaning of the stories of a particular tradition. Thus, in Matthew's Gospel, Jesus' early message is summarized as follows: "Repent, for the kingdom of heaven is at hand" (4:17). These words are "first-level discourse" for the tradition; that is, they are part of the scriptural record that transmits the sacred stories of Christian faith.

Now, the theologian—whether "simple believer" or professional—formulates conceptions of the meaning of these words. He or she must consider the import of the command "repent," and the sense of the phrase "the kingdom of heaven is at hand"; he or she may also judge the truth or falsehood of the words and perhaps be willing to provide reasons for the judgments that result. A professional theologian, for example, might use knowledge of ancient languages and insights from biblical studies and the psychology of religion in order to translate the words of Jesus into a modern idiom. He or she might point out that Jesus demanded a radical change of life prompted by a keen sense of the impending end of history, and then go on to suggest that the attitudes engendered by such a message help the believer maintain a sense of tension between the world "as it is" and the world "as it might be." When the theologian does this, he or she is engaging in "second-level discourse." That is, the theologian tries to interpret the story by moving toward statements that are less in the form of narrative, more like propositions, and framed in a language that a person who lives after biblical times might comprehend. One of the most useful definitions of *theology*, formulated by Anselm of Canterbury in the middle ages, is "faith seeking understanding."

The theologian's task is to transform story into doctrine. This may involve a number of steps, some of which are as follows:

Exegesis. This term refers to the process by which texts are explained and explicated. The theologian as exegete requires a range of skills: knowledge of languages, history, archaeology, cultural history. The task of *exegesis* is to indicate the range of meanings that a text may have.

History. Tradition is an essential element in religion. The theologian as historian attempts to understand the development and meaning of particular aspects of a community's tradition.

Systematic Thinking. The theologian as systematician attempts to develop the relations between various aspects of the community's tradition and to give a comprehensive account of the community's faith.

Apologetic Discussion. As apologist, the theologian tries to answer the questions and critiques of the community's faith offered by outsiders.

Critical Thinking. As critic, the theologian provides a thoughtful perspective on the community's current faithfulness (or lack thereof). He or she may also examine political, literary, social, or scientific affairs from the viewpoint of the community's faith.

Ethics. Religion is not only a matter of believing but of behaving. As ethicist, the theologian elucidates the practical teaching of the community in an attempt to show its implications for human behavior.

As a closing observation, we note that it is wrong to think of the theologian as a detached commentator. Although theological discourse necessarily occurs at a "second level," and is slightly removed from the "first level" of a tradition's stories, theologians are believers—often, passionately so. For that reason it should not be surprising that some of the greatest theologians also contribute to their communities through other forms of discourse. Great theologians have also been great writers of hymns, poetry, stories, and prayers.

THE VISUAL LANGUAGE OF RELIGION

To this point the discussion has focused on verbal language—whether transmitted orally or in writing. But there is another stream of religious language that we ought to mention: the use of painting, sculpture, architecture, and the other arts as a means of conveying a sense of the sacred. Indeed, long before writing became the primary vehicle for communication, people used visual images to communicate and preserve their religious traditions. The oldest examples of religious language available are paintings (for example, the cave paintings of neolithic peoples) and manufactured images (the ancient "Venus" figures of female deities from prehistoric sites). Sacred sites, whether of temples or shrines, should be understood not simply as buildings but as expressions of religious belief. The point is this: A careful study of religious art is, at its base, a study of a particular kind of language (a symbol system) that reflects an apprehension of the holy.

The ways in which this kind of art is used are many and varied. Some religions view the artwork as a direct vehicle that lets one "see" into the world of the sacred. Thus, in Orthodox Christianity, the *icon* (Greek for "image") is a window through which the believer is led to the sacred mysteries of Christ and the gospels. Sacred buildings may serve as an "anteroom" to the world of the divine. When people enter a temple or a church, it is as if they are passing from the profane world to that of the sacred. It is worthwhile remembering that *profane* means "outside the temple."

Sacred art also serves a didactic, or teaching, purpose. The great cycles of biblical stories in the stained glass windows of medieval cathedrals were often called the Bibles of the poor. In an age in which literacy was limited to a small class and books were a luxury for the rich, the ordinary person could look at the windows and "read" the great stories of biblical history. The great sculptural programs that adorn Hindu temples were an attempt to set out in stone what might otherwise be available only to the few who could read the sacred texts.

Visual representations also serve as a form of religious statement. On any large American university campus, students wear around their necks a cross or a star of David as if to say visually, "I am a Christian" or "I am a Jew." We often see, in the yellow pages of the telephone book, the advertisement of a firm with a stylized fish as a sign that its owners are "born again" Christians, just as a food store might use the Hebrew letters for "kosher" to indicate that it observes the Jewish dietary laws in the handling and preparation of food.

Paradoxically, even in religious traditions that are strongly *aniconic* (against images), there is, nonetheless, a strong visual quality to religious practice. Quakers, for example, avoid religious decorations, but the very austerity and simplicity of their meeting houses testify to their strong belief in the spiritual nature of God and the movement of God's spirit. Similarly, Islam prohibits images, equating them with idolatry, an affront to the absolute otherness and transcendence of Allah. As a consequence, Muslims traditionally decorate their mosques with abstract, nonrepresentational art and with highly stylized calligraphy (from the Greek for "beautiful writing"), utilizing verses from the Qur'an. Anyone viewing such mosques understands the motive of such artistic work: to present ordered beauty while insisting that the ultimate source of beauty cannot be represented by human hands or conceived by the human imagination.

The basic point to be made is this: There is in religious art more than decoration or beautification or solemnity. A complex language is being used. With patience, care, good will, and intelligence, a reading of that language is possible. Such a reading is as helpful for understanding religion as is an acquaintance with either the oral or written language of a given tradition.

When one travels on highways it is not uncommon to see white crosses with flowers or souvenirs that mark the location of a fatal traffic incident. We have seen the same phenomenon at other scenes of tragedy, such as the area near ground zero after the 9/11 attack. Those "shrines" are a form of religious language that express a whole range of feelings: sadness, hope, courage, and so on. More often than not the "shrines" are constructed from traditional religious artifacts, for example, crosses, or burning candles. These displays constitute a religious language also.

LANGUAGE AND TRUTH

A question emerges from the discussion of such a wide series of religious stories and types of religious language. Are the stories true? Or better, is any one of them more true than the others? If so, which? Shall we accept the Buddhist story or the Islamic one?

Obviously, we cannot test the truth of religious stories with the same ease that we test for measles. It is true that philosophers and theologians argue that the truthfulness of certain religious claims can be proven (for example, the existence of God), but by and large, many religious claims are likened to other commonly held beliefs that are not fully subject to "proof." Can we really "prove" that a mother loves her child? We might say that her actions indicate the kind of caring associated with love, or do not—we might, in other words, give reasons for a considered judgment that she does or does not love her child—but does that "prove" the point? Can we, in fact, really identify such a thing as "mother's love"?

Some have argued, usually citing the thinking of philosopher Ludwig Wittgenstein, that religion is a "language game." One enters the game by using the language and plays according to the rules of that particular game. Within the limits of the rules, everything makes sense and has its place. In this way, we can say that every religion is true for those who play the game and false for those who do not, unless they also wish to join the "game."

An obvious objection occurs: We ought to be able to ask questions about the various games to be played or choices to be made. Why should we play the Buddhist game as opposed to the Islamic? The Christian as opposed to the Jewish? It ought to be possible to answer questions about the justifiability of playing one game rather than another. Many people make such judgments. Many people do in fact argue that their religion is true—even that it is the only true faith. Others, a bit more modest, say that some of the truths of their religion are verifiable, and thus they have a closer connection to human nature and experience.

In approaching religion from the more descriptive, phenomenological point of view, should we be drawn into such questions? In one sense, questions of truth and falsehood seem contrary to the spirit of the phenomenological approach. And yet, can students with inquiring minds avoid such questions? Here, we offer four tentative observations.

First, most traditions attempt, at some level or another, to answer questions of the truth or, at least, justifiability of their faith claims. Indeed, something of that has already been indicated in the discussion of theology as religious language.

Second, such attempts may certainly be evaluated by students of religion in terms of their coherence, consistency, and accuracy. Particularly in cases that make claims of fact, historical and/or scientific tests may be applied to religious statements, at least in principle. We add this qualification because of the importance, in many religious traditions, of claims concerning very ancient events in which the data necessary for historic and/or scientific evaluations may be difficult to come by. The Jain tradition of India (*Jainism*), for example, which is a very small though important one in relation to Hinduism and Buddhism, makes certain claims about its chief exemplars, the "ford-crossers"—persons who, through ascetic and meditative discipline, achieved "release" from the world of matter. The most recent of these is thought to have lived during the sixth century B.C.E., but according to Jain tradition he was the twenty-fourth in a long series stretching back into prehistoric times. How does one test such claims?

Third, we must also say that not all the claims of religious traditions are "factual" in the ordinary sense of the word. Earlier in this chapter, we indicated that a too narrow focus on the "factual" accuracy of the Genesis creation myth can obscure the importance of other dimensions of the story: its view of human nature in relation to the sacred, for example. That human beings were created "good" and subsequently "fell" into evil is a claim indicating certain tensions in human nature, in particular its propensity for evil in relation to its desires for and intuitions of goodness.

Finally, from a phenomenological point of view it is of crucial importance that we not ask such questions too soon. The point of a phenomenological approach is not so much evaluation as understanding. In examining the claims of Jains concerning the ford-crossers, for example, a phenomenological approach leads us to be concerned more with the meaning of certain expressions in the context of particular traditions, and thus in the general history of religion, than in their precise correspondence to truth. We can ask, "Is it true?" but only after dealing with such questions as "What is being said?" and "Does the language of one tradition have affinities with others?" From this perspective, it is of greater interest to know how religious thinkers and communities have tried to justify their claims than to think about theories of truth.

NOTES

1. Mircea Eliade, *The Sacred and the Profane* (New York: Harper Torchbook, 1961), p. 205.
2. This is also true of ancient Greek and Roman religion. Modern persons tend to read the *Iliad* as a piece of literature; the ancients read it as a religious text.
3. Michael Novak, *Ascent of the Mountain, Flight of the Dove* (New York: Harper & Row, 1971), p. 2.

THOUGHT EXPERIMENTS

1. It has been said that the most graphic examples of myth available to Americans today can be found in such classic movies as the "Lord of the Rings" trilogy or even the Harry Potter films. Consider one of these (or another similar film), and explain why it might be called "mythic." For example, what views of humanity, the world, and the sacred seem to be present as underlying themes?
2. Can you think of a story, fictional or not, that carries some profound truth for you personally? Can you articulate what the power of the story consists in and what the truth means for you as a person?
3. Try to think of the various ways in which you have seen or heard of the Bible being used as a sacred text. Include in your summary both the "handling" of the Bible (as a keepsake, precious family treasure, and so forth) and as a sacred text. Why do we "swear on" the Bible?
4. Pick out a piece of religious art (or an architectural monument) and try to describe its religious language; what is the monument or artwork "saying"?
5. Can you, from your experience, describe the difference between theology and religious story? What mode of discourse conveys greater power for you?
6. Think of a proverb you have learned. Where did you learn it? Do you have any idea how old it is? The study of proverbs tells us a good deal about the transmission of oral wisdom.

SUGGESTIONS FOR FURTHER READING

APOSTOLOS-CAPPADONA, DIANE, ed., *Art, Creativity, and the Sacred*. New York: Crossroad, 1984. An important anthology of texts and studies.

DE HAMEL, CHRISTOPHER, *The Book: A History of the Bible*. New York: Phaidon, 2001. A brilliant illustrated history of the Bible as artifact.

DENNY, F., et al., *The Holy Book in Comparative Perspective* (2nd ed.). Columbia: University of South Carolina Press, 1993. Essays on the sacred book in the religions of the world. Important source for this chapter.

ELIADE, MIRCEA, *Myth and Reality*. New York: Harper & Row, 1963. Important for an understanding of myth in religion.

———, *From Primitives to Zen*. New York: Harper & Row, 1967. A fine anthology of mythic texts from the world's religions.

NEVILLE, ROBERT, ed., *Ultimate Realities*. Albany: State University of New York Press, 2000. Explorations of how the major religions attempt to speak of the transcendent.

WILLIAMS, PETER, *Houses of God*. Champaign: University of Illinois Press, 2000. An excellent book (now in paperback) on how architecture teaches different ways in which American religion has expressed itself.

5 *Ritual*

One often hears people say they want a simple religion, free from "ritual and mumbo jumbo." The popular denigration of ritual in religion overlooks a very important point: No person who lives in human society is free from some form of ritual. Ritual is one of the signposts of human living.

At this point, we may define ritual in the manner of the dictionaries: A *ritual* is a ceremonial act or a repeated stylized gesture used for specific occasions. When we think of ritual in terms of this definition, we see immediately that life is filled with such gestures. People shake hands as a sign of mutual trust; stand to indicate honor to another; indeed, make untold numbers of small formal gestures during each day. Such gestures are stylized and full of symbolic significance. In fact, many ritual gestures are so familiar and so frequently used that their significance is overlooked until someone fails to perform them or, as a kind of antiritual, does the opposite of that which is expected—for example, refuses to shake hands or to stand in honor of a particular person. Such failures or refusals often make us aware of the importance, otherwise obscured by ordinariness, of customary rituals.

Alongside such personal rituals as shaking hands, we find numerous examples of civic rituals. Making the ritual gesture of raising the right hand, swearing on the Bible, and uttering an oath signifies that one is bound to tell the truth in an American court. In some sense, the ritual surrounding the task of bearing witness in court deepens the obligation to speak truly. Failure to do so is not merely a lie, it is a felony given the formal name of perjury and can result in criminal penalties. Other civic rituals similarly involve gestures having broad consequences that are recognized by the law; any person who has been married knows the truth of this.

It seems obvious that ritual plays an enormous part in every religious tradition. Such traditions as Roman Catholicism or Russian Orthodoxy are certainly famous for their ritual character, but even those religious traditions that are noted for resistance to ritual do not really escape it. The Sabbath meetings of the Society of Friends (or Quakers) are known for their absence of ritual and their emphasis on silence and simplicity. However, the very action of sitting in a plain and unadorned room is a stylized form of behavior peculiar to the Quaker meeting and hence can be seen as ritual behavior, even if it is deliberately "plain."

The varieties of ritual and ritual behavior are so great that it would be impossible even to catalog them here. Rituals may be as simple as the "body language" a believer uses when praying, or as elaborate as the official sacrifices of early Hinduism, which required priestly experts to perform rites over a span of several days. For the purposes of this chapter, we focus on describing a few forms of rituals and then discuss several generalizations about the relationship of ritual and the sacred.

MYTH(OS) AND RITUAL

One of the most common forms of ritual involves acting out or dramatizing religious stories. Mircea Eliade notes, in a number of his books, that in many tribal societies people not only remember the tribal myths but also live them and act them out. Creation stories, for example, may be ritualized through dance and gesture at particular times of the year so that people reenact the first deeds of gods and goddesses. Typically such ritual activity occurs in the spring, when the world is "reborn" or "re-created" after its winter "death." In this case, the conjunction of myth and ritual serves as a way for people to participate in the creative power of the sacred.

Of course, such ritual enactment of myths is not peculiar to tribal societies. The origins of both Greek tragedy and modern drama derive from religious ritual, in the former case in the worship of the god Dionysius, and in the latter case, in the acting out of the Easter story in the liturgy of French monasteries in the Middle Ages. Further, both Judaism and Christianity preserve examples of the conjunction of myth and ritual at the heart of their traditions, as in the Passover (from Judaism) and Holy Communion or the Eucharist (from Christianity) in which biblical traditions are reenacted.

The Passover

Every spring (the date varies from year to year, based on the lunar calendar) Jews all over the world gather in their homes to share a formal meal involving the eating of symbolic foods, various readings and prayers, and a number of blessings. The meal is orchestrated by the head of the household, who conducts it according to well-established traditions. In fact, the *Passover* meal is also called the *seder*, a Hebrew word that means "order" or "arrangement."

Passover commemorates the meal eaten by the Jews the evening before they left Egypt and the enslavement of their people in order to journey toward, and eventually reach, the Promised Land. Central to the Passover meal, then, are those great events described in the Bible in the book of *Exodus*. One of the high points of the meal comes when the youngest person present at the table asks why the meal is eaten. The response comes in the form of a reading from the *haggadah* (from the Hebrew meaning "narrative") about the great events recounted in Exodus.

We should underscore what is being played out at the Passover meal. Jews celebrate an ancient story in their tradition by reenacting the story in a highly ritualized fashion. The purpose is basically to affirm that there is a continuity between past and present; that God did singular things for the ancient Jews; that there is a solidarity between contemporary Jews and those ancestors who were called out of slavery into freedom: "And you shall tell your son on that day, 'It is because of what the Lord did for me when I came out of Egypt'" (Exodus 13:8). Such a celebration is not merely a historical remembrance. For Jews participating in the Passover meal there is a deep admixture of memory, worship, and hope.

Holy Communion (The Eucharist)

Holy Communion in Christianity functions in ways that are analogous to the Passover in Judaism. In fact, Holy Communion has its roots in the Passover meal. The various Christian communities give diverse interpretations of the significance of communion and they celebrate it with varying frequency (for example, Baptists may celebrate the "ordinance" of the "Lord's Supper" a few times a year, while Catholics may celebrate the *Eucharist* or "thanksgiving" every day). Yet all Christian groups agree that when they celebrate the communion meal, they are reenacting events connected with Jesus of Nazareth. The gospels of Matthew, Mark, and Luke, as well as the letter of Paul known as First Corinthians, describe a ceremony involving the use of bread and wine, which are given significance through words attributed to Jesus. According to the apostle Paul:

> The Lord Jesus, on the night he was betrayed took bread, and when he had given thanks, he broke it, and said, "This is my body which is given for you. Do this in remembrance of me." In the same manner also the cup, after supper, saying "This cup is the new covenant in my blood. Do this, as often as you drink it, in remembrance of me." (I Corinthians 11:23–25)

As in the Passover celebration, a religious story (the mythos) is reenacted long after the event it narrates, not because it tells a particular moment in history, but because it carries a meaning that the community of believers, long after the event itself, wishes to restate. The reenactment puts believers in touch with the origins of their community, while at the same time it expresses certain religious convictions that are viewed as having enduring significance.

The conjunction of myth and ritual is characteristic of many of the most important ceremonies of religious traditions. In *Shi'i Islam*, the "passion plays" of the month of *Muharram* reenact the martyrdom of Husayn at Karbala in 692 C.E. and draw members of the Shi'i community into an eternal drama in which good suffers in its struggle with evil. In Shinto, the rituals performed at shrines throughout Japan reenact the conflict between Amaterasu (the sun goddess) and Susanoo (the god of storms), and enable participants to feel themselves a part of the struggle to bring order to the world. Such rituals allow people to step outside ordinary time in order to become one with long-past events. The stories provide data and/or symbolic memories, which the rituals bring into the present. Rituals, we may say, are ways of entering the realm of the sacred. They enable believers to participate in remembered moments of a sacred past, and thus they illumine the present.

RITES OF PASSAGE

"Rites of passage" is a technical term, first popularized and thoroughly studied by the anthropologist Arnold van Gennep. Rites of passage describe those ceremonies associated with the transitional moments in a person's life. More specifically, van Gennep and others were interested in those ceremonies that marked the transition from childhood to adulthood in traditional societies. Students of religion have long observed that all religions provide rituals and/or theological rationales to commemorate such moments. Indeed, nominal believers who feel no great need to observe most of the customs of a tradition may still turn to religion for rites of passage. Thus, a nominal Jew or Christian might ignore the weekly demands of synagogue or church but still have a child circumcised or baptized in infancy or turn to the synagogue or church for a ritual of status change (bar mitzvah or confirmation; marriage) or to observe rites for mourning or death. For some people, such situation-specific rituals are what are most important in religion.

Apart from the specific meanings invested by a religious community in such rituals, it is not difficult to see why such moments and their celebration are important for people. No matter how technologically advanced a culture might be, a sense of awe and risk still surrounds human birth, just as there is fear and bewilderment about the reality and inevitability of death. Even the most unsentimental or secular person approaches a marriage with a sense of ceremony and symbol. These great, transitional moments in people's lives touch persons as individuals and as social beings.

Let us say a few words on specific rites of passage.

Birth Rituals

Although some traditional cultures actually ritualize the moment of birth, "birth rituals" usually refer to rites connected to the newborn and its parents. Some of these rites, for example, circumcision and baptism, are profoundly social in their implications. By circumcision a male child becomes a member of the Jewish people (and note that circumcision serves a similar purpose among Muslims), with the circumcision itself seen as a sign of the biblical covenant between God and the Jews: "You shall be circumcised in the flesh of your foreskins, and it shall be a sign of the covenant between Me and you" (Genesis 17:11). Through *baptism*, a child becomes a member of the Christian church; in some Christian communities baptism is *the* ceremony that distinguishes the Christian from the non-Christian. Other Christian groups emphasize the naming of the child or its dedication to God as the central point of baptism. Through ritual feeding, a Hindu family initiates a male child into the duties of its caste. Similar meanings are given to birth rituals in the various religious traditions, even though the forms are quite diverse. People celebrate the safe passage of the infant from the womb into the world; they welcome him or her into the family; they give the child a name; they pay homage to the creative power of the sacred.

Rituals of Initiation

It was this complex of rituals that first attracted the attention of Arnold van Gennep. He focused his study on those rituals celebrating and symbolizing the passage of a person from childhood into adulthood. In those settings studied by van Gennep, this began typically for females at menarche (the onset of menstruation) and for males at the onset of puberty. In either case the ceremonies signified the passage from childhood to the responsibilities of adult life, especially those attached to marriage and parenthood. While the specifics of this rite varied in different cultures, the outlines of the ceremony remained rather constant: ritual segregation from the larger group and some form of testing followed by the actual ceremonies of initiation, then reentry into the group as a recognized adult. Every member of a sorority or fraternity or anyone who has been in the military will recognize the pattern immediately: pledge or recruit status, initiation ceremonies after testing, acceptance as a full-fledged brother or sister or trooper.

The importance of this type of rite in signifying the passage from childhood to adult status is perhaps less clear in modern, industrialized cultures because of the extending of the period called adolescence. Even though many young people go through a traditional rite of passage (for example, a *bar* or *bat mitzvah*, or confirmation) the "adults" are, in fact, economically dependent on their parents for some time after their "passage."

The great ritual of initiation in postmodern cultures is marriage. Even when the ceremony is contemporary, certain elements in the marriage rite hearken back to ancient traditions. The practice of the bride not seeing (or really, not being seen by) the groom before the ceremony, the symbolic colors (for example, white for purity), the use of flowers, the separation of the newly-weds from the larger group (for example, through a honeymoon), even the horseplay of soaping the car and throwing the rice—all of these things reflect ancient feelings about the mystery of sexuality, its generative power, and its promise of offspring. This sexual undertone to the ceremony parallels the symbolism of moving from a parental home to a new and independent one.

Rituals of Mourning and Death

If there is one moment in the human journey that speaks most compellingly of mystery and sacredness, it is the moment(s) of dying, death, and burial. Even in the most secularized cultures, the transitions from the death watch to death itself to the funeral are all freighted with awe. Death, while an intensely personal reality, is also social. Hence the universal sadness (and, in some cultures, horror) at the prospect of dying alone or of not giving someone a "proper" burial.

Different religious traditions ritualize the mourning process in various ways. Taoist rites include an elaborate ritual involving an enactment of the soul's journey into the underworld and its rescue and delivery into heaven by ancestral spirits. The ceremony, which may require months of preparation, features the acrobatic actions of various acolytes (attendants), directed by a priest trained in Taoist traditions of ritual performance. By comparison, Muslims and Orthodox Jews bury the dead within a day, marking the occasion with only very simple ceremonies; the bereaved family and community subsequently observe a designated period of mourning.

Many burial rites symbolize the relationship of human beings to the natural world. Pious Hindus in India cremate their dead and consign the ashes to the river Ganges as a sign of the never-ending cycle of life and death. Christians bury their dead as a sign of committing the body back to the earth from whence it came: Humanity was created from the "dust of the earth," according to the book of Genesis. A careful analysis of these and other kinds of funeral rites provides clues about beliefs concerning life after death, notions of personal immortality, and the like. Certain funeral rites are intended to aid the spirits of the dead to journey through the afterworld either by providing symbolic gifts for them (as in the practices of the ancient Egyptians or the native peoples of North America), by providing living "guides" for them (see the example of Taoism mentioned earlier), or by helping the souls of the dead to purge sin, as in the practice of praying for the dead in Roman Catholicism and Orthodoxy.

TEMPORAL RITES AND CELEBRATIONS

Rites of passage mark the human journey from birth to death. They are intensely personal; at the same time, they have obvious and explicit social implications. This human journey takes place in the world of time and seasons. The observance of cycles of time has been a central characteristic of most, if not all, historic religious traditions. The point of such observance, and even more its symbolic force, is altered by the conditions of modern industrial societies. Most people in such societies are of course aware of the changing of the seasons (is there anyone who does not welcome the arrival of spring?), but they do not see the change as crucial for their existence. We can easily imagine, however, the wonder and mystery attached by persons in more agricultural or pastoral societies to the arrival of spring each year. For them it is not just a "season," but a power, warming the earth for planting, providing the first shoots of green for animals to graze, nurturing the first buds of fruit-bearing trees, bringing to birth the young of animals. Spring meant the promise of life and the mark of a time when things could grow and mature before the killing frosts and snows of winter came—winter, the power of death—a time of waiting for spring to break forth once more.

For people who hunted, gathered, or planted, this cycle was crucial to life. Food came, not from markets, but from the earth and tangible, natural sources. Its growth (not its production) depended on the orderly cycle of nature, time, and ultimately the fertile power of the *cosmos*. The importance of the cycle explains in part the prevalence of the ancient vision of earth as a great, pulsating maternal principle impregnated annually by the paternal principle identified with the sky. In this vision the earth went through a cycle of insemination in spring, gestation in summer, birth in the harvest of autumn, and death in winter—with the cycle repeating itself again the following year.

With this primordial background in mind, we can understand why, even in modern industrial societies, many of the great festivals continue to take place in conjunction with the change of the seasons (though with alterations in meaning and, even more, in symbolic force). Easter provides a case in point. *Easter* is, of course, a specifically Christian feast day (Christians see it as *the* feast day in the church) celebrating the resurrection of the Christ. As such, it is a high point in the worship cycle of the Christian church and (according to Christian belief) (marks the decisive point in God's dealings) with the world. At the same time, many people who are not Christians (and, in fact, many who are) celebrate this springtime festival with a range of customs and gestures that bear little or no resemblance to or connection with the story of the resurrection. By and large these customs are best understood as reflections of the primordial religious imagination. They reflect the sense that spring is a period of fertility, rebirth, and the awakening of nature after its winter death. The symbolism of the "Easter bunny," the widespread use of the egg, the predominance of flowers, and the custom of wearing new clothes all link Easter to the more ancient observance of the spring festival. Perhaps most tellingly, the very word "Easter" probably derives from the Norse name for the spring season, *Eostur*,[1] and the Saxon goddess of Spring, *Aestre*.

The North American Thanksgiving, which is not linked to any particular religious tradition but to a kind of "civil religion" (see Chapter 6), centers on a ritual meal intended to express gratitude for a bountiful autumn harvest. A solemn meal and ceremonies of thanksgiving are combined in commemoration of familial and national good fortune. Interestingly, even though North American society is highly industrialized, the symbolism of Thanksgiving remains strongly agricultural: the haystack, the dried corn, the overflowing cornucopia. Although the feast as observed is a rite of recent invention, purely North American, it has many analogues in the religious traditions of the world.

Besides the nearly universal custom of ritual observances in spring and fall, it is important to note one other time that is invested with ritual significance: the New Year. Although the time is variously computed (for example, the Christian New Year begins with the four Sundays before Christmas, while the Jewish New Year varies according to a lunar calendar, and neither corresponds to the January 1 date familiar in Western cultures), all the major religious traditions begin a new year with celebrations. From the Chinese custom of fireworks to the North American custom of parties and noisemakers, a new year is a time to remember, to make amends for past mistakes, and to look forward to new possibilities. That is why religious observances of a new year often combine celebration with rites of penance and purification.

THE RELIGIOUS MEANING(S) OF RITUAL

This brief survey of various kinds of ritual—some of which reenact myths important to given traditions, whereas others sanctify certain times in the lives of individuals or recognize the power of natural cycles—should make it obvious that all rituals are commemorative, inasmuch as they recall events, persons, and ideas at particular times and places. Rituals are conservative in the sense that they involve repetition. The same actions are done time after time, generally at fixed times and in a designated manner. Imagine bringing out Christmas decorations in July or celebrating Independence Day in January—such deviations from habitual practice would be jarring, to say the least. In the realm of ritual, all things have their time and season.

It was noted earlier that there is a historic link between religious ritual and the rise of drama. We underscore the fact that rituals have a certain theatrical or dramatic quality about them, in that they follow a pattern or a script. This is especially true of rituals within the framework of the various religious traditions. Words are spoken, vestments or clothes are worn, gestures are made, ceremonies are performed according to a set standard that everyone within the tradition recognizes as "right." In fact, in many instances in the history of religions, new movements begin in arguments over seemingly trivial differences—trivial to the outsider, but to believers, such disputes may involve the very structure of sacred reality. Some Protestant groups, for example, have been born out of disagreements over the correct mode of baptism or the role of musical instruments in church. There was a schism in the Russian church in the early modern period over, among other things, the correct mode of making the sign of the cross. Rituals emphasize continuity, and innovations that threaten continuity are often resisted.

What do believers see as the relationship between ritual activity and the sacred? How does ritual activity relate to the absolute or the real?

Ritual is so closely identified with formal worship that one can say generally that the ends of ritual are the ends of worship. Traditionally speaking, worship promotes one of these four ends or purposes, or a combination of them: adoration, thanksgiving, petition, and penance/purification.

Adoration

Basically, *adoration* means acknowledgment of the sovereignty of the sacred over the person. Adoration means the acknowledgment that one is not self-sufficient, but dependent. For those religions with a strong sense of a personal, transcendent God, there are basic ritual gestures assumed in moments of prayer that dramatically illustrate the concept of adoration. Bowing the head, kneeling down in prayer, or prostrating oneself in prayer (as in Islam) are all gestures of adoration. It is interesting to contrast such gestures with the quite different ones common in those traditions that do not emphasize a transcendent deity having personal characteristics. In Buddhism, for example, the typical image of the Buddha is that of a seated person, eyes half open, quietly and serenely meditating. This follows from the emphasis on the search for enlightenment, understood in terms of an inward journey to discover the truth about oneself and the world. Hence the primary gesture is a meditative one. Although it is of course true that there are varieties of Buddhism and that some of these involve rather complicated strategies for adoring gods and goddesses, it remains the case that the central ideal of Buddhism is to discover, not the one God sovereign over all, but the truth; that is, to attain Nirvana.

Thanksgiving

Because one of the basic insights of many religious traditions is that the world and all its bounty flow from the world of the sacred, it is only fitting that such traditions emphasize the need to acknowledge that gift. In one sense that is an act of adoration, but it is also a specific act of thanksgiving (the two acts are often hard to disentangle). The most common form of thanksgiving is through the ritual act of giving a gift. Such donations may run from the formal act of a sacrifice, to the leaving of a gift at an altar or shrine, to decorating a holy place with adornments or flowers. In all such gestures there is, implicitly, the notion of a return of favors done or given. At times, either in a regular cycle or after some particular peril is overcome, people may organize a formal ritual ceremony for thanksgiving.

The most common gesture combining both adoration and thanksgiving is the short ritual that many call "grace before meals." Whether that ritual is done with a set formula or an improvised prayer, the act combines both elements discussed thus far: the bowing of the head (signifying submission and adoration) and words giving thanks for the food and fellowship that the participants are about to enjoy. That simple act is a microcosm for all the more elaborate acts of worship emphasizing adoration and thanksgiving.

Petition

The third way in which ritual is used to connect with the sacred is to *petition*—to ask or beg favors of either a spiritual or material nature. The springtime rituals of traditional societies were specifically designed to persuade the gods and goddesses of the tribe to ensure the continuing fertility of the earth. The prayers offered in churches, synagogues, or mosques for a good harvest or for rain at crucial times of the year (for example, during a drought) continue this old petitionary process.

To make petitions in times of crisis is such a familiar gesture that many see it as *the* characteristic of religious practice, one that many otherwise non-religious persons turn to in times of trouble. Is it not true that the most unmindful believer or the most convinced secularist instinctively turns to petition in moments of duress? How many stories abound of persons saying in a critical moment: "Please let my mother get well; please let me pass calculus; please let me get out of this mess"?

Penance/Purification

It is well to remember that the root meaning of the word holy is "that which is separate." In the Bible and the Qur'an God is holy *par excellence*, and everything that is called holy is so only to the extent that it is close to God and thus separate from the profane.

A very deep instinct exists in many religious traditions to be worthy of closeness to the sacred; that is the origin of the dialectic of the sacred and the profane. One should remember that profane literally means "that which is separated or distinct from a sacred place." To approach the sacred often requires the making of a ritual gesture of separation from the profane: Muslims perform a ritual *ablution* or washing prior to prayer; a Catholic may "bless" himself or herself with holy water prior to entering a sanctuary. These and many similar rituals signify the desire of the person to be worthy of addressing the divine or of coming into the presence of the sacred.

The notion of ritual *purification* is common in the religions of the world. That notion is also akin to the widespread sense that one must be ethically pure in order to stand close to divinity. There is obviously a close connection between certain human behaviors and worthiness to be in the presence of the sacred.

The connection between human behavior and ritual worship can take many forms. A person may be required to avoid certain kinds of behavior in order to worship, or he or she may be required to make certain preparations that purify the self. Likewise, many religions prescribe rituals of *penance* to make up for or absolve persons from the guilt of transgressions against particular moral precepts. All of these rites indicate a felt need for a kind of symmetry between the moral/religious character of the worshiper and the worshiped.

RITUAL AS A PROBLEM

It has been noted that the deep power of ritual can be seen by the reaction of observers to deliberate reversals or parodies of particular rites. Religious believers often resent the protest or, alternatively, lack of reverence they identify in such behavior, and they typically use a powerful vocabulary to describe it: Such behavior is blasphemous or a desecration. Such reversals or parodies are considered inappropriate—as, for example, the painting of swastikas on synagogue walls.

In cases of blasphemy or desecration, the power of ritual is challenged, but in a sense it is also reaffirmed. Sometimes, however, a ritual loses its power. When the meaning traditionally carried by a ritual becomes separated from the ritual, then the latter becomes an empty or automatic gesture. The history of religions shows that when a particular community insists on elaborate ritual (usually requiring a specially trained and somewhat exclusive class of priests) people often become alienated, seeing less and less meaning in the traditional gestures. This in turn brings a reaction in which there is a tendency to reject or drastically modify existing rituals, accompanied by an emphasis on practices focusing on the feelings or faith of believers and their moral reform.

One very conspicuous example of this kind of reaction would be the Protestant Reformation of the sixteenth century. The early reformers (e.g., Martin Luther) and indeed many critics who continued to be identified as Roman Catholics (e.g., Erasmus of Rotterdam) shared a perception that the late medieval church put too much emphasis on processions, veneration of *relics*, multiple celebrations of the Mass, statues, medals, and so on. The Reformation critique of these practices was that they had degenerated into forms of superstition in which things were done, rituals performed, or practices repeated with the belief that such gestures would bring about God's favor apart from personal commitment and a sense of faith. Allied with this criticism was the feeling that such practices demanded an elaborate group of professionals who held power over such rituals and, as such, exercised enormous power over the common people. The reaction came in the form of an emphasis on faith over works, a denial of the sacramental power of visible things such as medals and statues, and a determination to preach about the need for inner personal renewal. The sixteenth-century struggle over ritual is a casebook example of the perception that ritual can lose its power if it becomes separated from its original meaning.

Authentic ritual involves the acting out of perceived and experienced religious conviction; it is the making visible of faith. Less authentic forms of ritual result when the actions are done simply as a matter of form or, as is more common, when people think that particular gestures exercise the kind of power associated with "magic." It is at this level that ritual turns into superstition.

The desire to purify religious ritual to make it meaningful is part of the dynamic of many religious traditions. To cite one more example, the Hebrew Bible contains many texts in which prophetic writers warn against the empty ritualism of temple observances unaccompanied by a commitment to social justice. Although it would be an overstatement to say that there is a dichotomy between temple or priestly religion and prophetic religion in the Hebrew Bible, it is nonetheless true that the *prophetic* writings are critical of ritual practice devoid of true conviction. That is the clear import of words such as these, taken from the book of Jeremiah:

> The word that came to Jeremiah from the Lord: "Stand in the gate of the Lord's house and proclaim there this word and say: Hear the word of the Lord, all you men of Judah who enter these gates to worship the Lord. Thus says the Lord of Hosts, the God of Israel: Mend your ways and your doings, and I will let you dwell in this place. Do not trust in these deceptive words: This is the temple of the Lord, the temple of the Lord, the temple of the Lord." (7:1–4)

This chapter began with the observation that many people speak of ritual as mindless and/or superstitious. Let it now be said that such views offer a legitimate critique in the history of religions.

RITUAL AS A SYSTEM

In closing, we should emphasize a point that has been implicit up to now. Rituals should not be thought of as discrete or atomistic gestures, but as a kind of system within a given religious tradition. In fact, it would not be too much to say that rituals constitute something like a language for the communication of particular notions of the sacred.

This becomes clear when one thinks of particular religious traditions. Some rituals are associated with personal devotion; others are observed in family contexts; still others relate to communal gatherings; finally, in some rituals an entire community affirms its corporate identity.

When we think of rituals as an interconnected system of symbolic meanings (to be likened, for example, to a language), we can begin to understand that a system of rituals defines who a group is, what it stands for, what it searches for, and what it ultimately desires to express. It is for that reason that anthropologists such as Victor Turner have emphasized the dialectic of separation and reentry into community as one of the basic movements of rituals of status and rites of passage. Confirmation and bar mitzvah not only have meaning for the individuals who undertake them, they are vehicles through which young persons are introduced into the common ritual language of a group.

Rituals, from the most intimate (family members bowing their heads to say grace before meals) to the most elaborate (funerals or weddings), are markers that intrude into the daily round of life to signal the relationship of persons to, and their awareness of, the place of the sacred in their lives. In that sense rituals are ways in which people "take note" of some larger reality that transcends the ordinary routine of their lives. In that sense, too, rituals are forms of culture. Human beings shape and make additions to the biological imperatives of their lives. That is what culture is. A jungle is nature; a garden is culture. Ritual systems are specific forms of human culture that can communicate particular notions of sacred reality.

The penchant for ritual activity is so deeply rooted in history that it creates one of those insoluble questions that tease the minds of scholars: How did ritual begin? What, ultimately, are its roots? The answer to that question is as elusive as that other great puzzle: How did language begin? Thus far, no one can answer. What can be said with assurance is this: Ritual, symbol, and language are all attempts to frame, interpret, and give meaning to the world. They are ways of responding to particular notions of sacred reality. This point is so basic that it seems appropriate to end this chapter with a statement that sets the matter with clarity and conviction:

> Human life is not lived as the lives of animals are. Life is enacted; it is drama that follows the script that culture has written. . . . It provides us with a set of values and larger perspectives that tell us who we are, where we fit, and what

our purpose is. The way we live is but one of many ways we have found workable in dealing with reality. This life is our interpretation of how to live, of human existence, of what the meaning and purpose of life are. People disagree on which interpretations are more accurate, which are human inventions and which are based on divine guidance, but they are all interpretations.[2]

NOTES

1. John F. Baldovin, "Easter," in *The Encyclopedia of Religion*, ed. Mircea Eliade (New York: Macmillan, 1987), vol. 4, pp. 557–558.
2. Michael Barnes, *In the Presence of Mystery* (Mystic, Conn.: Twenty-Third, 1984), p. 203.

THOUGHT EXPERIMENTS

1. Follow the ritual activity of a person who belongs to a religious community with which you are familiar. Would it be possible for you to generalize about the ritual "language" of that religious community in any meaningful manner? Can you detect the emphases of that religion?
2. Suppose you are called upon to organize a nondenominational celebration on the occasion of some event for which a community wishes to express thanks. What kind of setting would you provide? What readings? Speakers? Ceremonies?
3. What ritual experience, religious or not, have you yourself had that made a deep impression on you? Can you explain why?
4. People react to highly ritualized religious services in different ways. Can you describe your own preferences for the kind of religious services that most attract and/or repel you?
5. Do you have any personal habits that might be described as rituals that have degenerated into superstitions (for example, always wearing a lucky shirt to a sports event)? Whether you do or not, can you speculate a bit on the fascination of people with superstitions and the hold they have on some people?
6. How would you like your own wedding to be conducted? Analyze the ritual "language" (gestures, symbols, setting, etc.) that you wish to employ. Why have you made your choices? You may also wish to consider how you would like your own funeral to be conducted. What would you want the ceremony to "say" about you, your family, and your friends not only in words but in gestures?

SUGGESTIONS FOR FURTHER READING

BELL, CATHERINE, *Ritual: Perspectives and Dimensions*. New York: Oxford University Press, 1997. (Together with the same author's *Ritual Theory, Ritual Practice*, New York: Oxford University Press, 1992, constitutes a monumental contribution to the study of this topic.)

DOUGLAS, MARY, *Natural Symbols*. New York: Pantheon, 1970. This work is by one of the most creative thinkers in the area of the anthropology of religion. A somewhat difficult but very important work.

GRIMES, RONALD, *Beginnings in Ritual Studies*. Lanham, Md.: University Press of America, 1982. Introduction to ritual studies as a field.

HUIZINGA, JOHANN, *Homo Ludens*. Boston: Beacon Press, 1955. This classic work, first written in the 1920s, studies the human propensity for play. Play is, of course, a form of ritualized behavior, as any person who watches baseball understands.

(JOURNAL OF RITUAL STUDIES.) The scholarly outlet for all academic studies of ritual.

RAPAPORT, ROY. *Ritual and Religion in the Making of Humanity*. Cambridge: Cambridge University Press, 1997.

TURNER, VICTOR, *The Ritual Process*. Chicago: Aldine, 1968. This is a classic work on ritual; a very influential work by a world-class anthropologist.

VAN GENNEP, ARNOLD, *The Rites of Passage*. Chicago: University of Chicago Press, 1960. The fundamental work on this topic. This chapter is much in debt to van Gennep's work.

6 *Sacred Communities*

North Americans, with their inherited sense of tolerance and individualism, tend to approach religion from a very personal point of view. We often hear people say that religions are different but, in the end, they all point to the same end. Or people say, as a variation, that we have respect for all religions and that what one believes is a personal matter into which others should not make inquiries.

It is undoubtedly true that what one believes is an intensely personal matter. After all (as people say), it is *my* belief and I have a right to it. Furthermore, unless I am a very intolerant person, I believe that others should be allowed to believe what they want to believe. And it seems to follow that religious belief is a matter of taste or choice or upbringing.

The burden of this chapter will be to look at religion from a somewhat different perspective. We shall argue that, when we look at religion as a worldwide phenomenon, we see that religiosity most often expresses itself not in terms of beliefs chosen (or not chosen) by individuals but in terms of notions of the sacred that define particular communities. In fact, one of the melancholy facts of the human story is that religious groups can find such powerful forms of identification in the force of the sacred that they may see the sacred as legitimating all sorts of conflict with other communities whose sense of the sacred is different from their own. Although religion is rarely the sole explanation for such conflicts, it certainly plays a role in many of them, for example, in Northern Ireland, where Protestants and Catholics continue to struggle over political power and economic justice. In 1948, to cite another famous example, India gained its independence from Great Britain; but in order to deal with the fears of Muslims, in particular, there had to be a partition of that subcontinent into a Muslim state (Pakistan) and a predominantly Hindu one (India). In India today there are still explosive conflicts among Hindus, Muslims, and Sikhs. Such conflicts rage throughout the world. One reads in the daily papers similar stories of conflicts in the Philippines (Muslims versus Christians), in Sri Lanka (Buddhists versus Hindus), and in the former Yugoslavia (Orthodox Christians versus Catholic Christians versus Muslims). It is an old story. In order to make sense of it, one needs to pay close attention to the relationship between notions of the sacred and religious communities.

THE SOCIAL CHARACTER OF RELIGION

In 1912, the French sociologist Emile Durkheim published a landmark book entitled *The Elementary Forms of the Religious Life.* In that work, Durkheim argued that for many societies religion was the collective expression of what people thought their society was, how it was to be governed, how they related to it, and what its sanctions were. The god(s) were the symbolic expression of society. For Durkheim the explicit content of religious ideas was not that important; religion expressed not theological but sociological reality.

It is not necessary to accept Durkheim's analysis completely to admit that he makes a very important point. When we look at tribal societies, we see clearly that religion provides a kind of "glue" that holds the tribe together. Navaho religion, for example, centers on the concept of sacred reality related in the "emergence myth," which tells the story of "how the Navaho came to be." The story also relates certain values and rituals that provide sanctions for certain kinds of behavior and explain how the Navaho "fit" in the world. The basic point is this: Navaho *religion* defines the Navaho *people.* Navaho religion is different from that of other tribes (say, the Hopi) in part because the Navaho tribe is different. One would not try to persuade a Hopi of the "truth" of Navaho religion, or vice versa. The religious systems of the various tribes are simply givens, part of the identity of the tribes. Navaho religion tells who a Navaho is, how the Navaho lives, and what the relationship is between the Navaho and his or her ancestors and the spirit world. The same is true of Hopi religion.

In other cases, religion may be essential in defining the life of a nation. In a country such as Saudi Arabia, not only is Islam the official religion of the state but also—and this is the crucial point—the state itself is defined as Islamic. Hence, the laws of economics and justice are derived, not from secular theories of the market or law enforcement, but from the religious law of Islamic tradition. The state institutionalizes a particular religion. This is a much closer identification between a particular religion and political struc-ture than, say, in the system found in Great Britain, in which the Anglican church is state supported (the clergy are paid by the state; the bishops are appointed by the state; the monarchy belongs to the church of England) but the church has no direct role in secular governance or the shaping of state policy.

In democratically pluralistic cultures such as the United States, people (and the groups they belong to) may identify themselves in terms of their religion but resist the notion of a state religion. U.S. law expressly forbids the establishment of any one religion as "official," though it may be important to speak of the "civil religion" of America. According to a number of scholars, there is an overarching, though ill-defined, religious underpinning to U.S. institutions that leads Americans to use the phrase "under God" in the Pledge of Allegiance, to inscribe the phrase "In God We Trust" on the currency, to celebrate a day of Thanksgiving, and to open legislative sessions with a prayer—all supposedly without connection to any specific religious tradition. One might say that American culture sanctions a secular state, but also a religious nation. Thus, while there can be no "state church," there is evidence for a "civil religion" that overarches particular denominational differences to express a sense that the American people are united under the governance of a provident God who watches over their destiny and fortunes.

All these examples make a single point: Religion can, and in many cases, actually does, serve to hold a social unit together. Conversely, religion(s) can also tear communities apart if they become sources of conflict. We thereby underscore Durkheim's point: There is an inescapable social dimension to religion.

RELIGION AND SOCIAL RESISTANCE

The examples used in the preceding section all pointed to religious systems that were connected with the social values of a given group, either to the point of identification (as in tribal religion) or as a vehicle to reinforce social ideals (as in American "civil religion"). But other forms of religious societies seem to be at loggerheads with the majority culture. Either such groups may stand apart from the common values of a society as a respected, though minority, alternative, or their values may seem antagonistic to the majority, and the group may become the object of discrimination and/or active persecution. One way of understanding the relation of religion to culture is to look at those religious groups that seem to be in tension with a society.

At this point we introduce a famous distinction between church and sect, formulated by the German scholar Ernst Troeltsch in his now classic study, *The Social Teachings of the Christian Churches* (1912). By *church*, we mean to indicate a religious community of some social standing that invites all members of a society to take part in its activities, has a stake in the well-being of the larger social community, and claims to be the custodian of religious truth. A *sect*, by contrast, tends to demand more conformity in its members, is exclusive in its membership, distances itself from the concerns of the larger society, and also claims to be the bearer of religious truth.

Troeltsch, as a German, had the European scene in mind when he made this distinction. For him, the primary examples of churches were the state-supported churches of Europe (for example, the church of England or the

Evangelical Church in Germany) and the sects were those dissident groups that, because of their religious beliefs, were somewhat cut off from the larger cultural life of the country (the Nonconformists or the Quakers in England, for example).

In the United States, those making use of the church/sect distinction usually point to religious groups such as the Methodists and Presbyterians who seem "comfortable" with the predominant culture and call them churches. These are distinct from groups such as the Amish who separate themselves from the larger culture in order to be faithful to their religion. The Amish are pure sectarians.

The fact is that the church/sect distinction, at least in North America, is not always a neat one. Although it is clear that there are examples of church-type religion in the United States (one could add Anglicans and Reform Jews to the earlier examples) and that the Amish (and probably Hasidic Jews) are sectarian, it is also true that many American communities manifest characteristics of both church and sect.[1] Here are two very different examples that illustrate this point. Roman Catholicism is a church-type religious community. But within its tradition, Roman Catholicism allows for those who wish to experience a sectarian separation from the world to join a monastery. Monasticism has all of the sociological characteristics of a sect. In a somewhat different manner, among some fundamentalist groups (such as Independent Baptists) one may find a section of the group that is very comfortable with the culture and another part that is separatist and sectarian. Thus, for example, at Virginia's Liberty University (founded by the Reverend Jerry Falwell) or South Carolina's Bob Jones University the tone is proAmerican, proflag, profree enterprise, but Hollywood is frowned upon, steady dating discouraged, drinking and smoking absolutely forbidden, and a "born again" experience is considered normative. Deviation from doctrinal standards (at least, among faculty) is not tolerated. Thus, one finds both sectarian and church characteristics in the movement.

The final meaning of sect is to be found in the attitude of particular groups toward the larger culture. When we say that a religious community is sectarian or that a group is a sect, we mean, in essence, that it is exclusivist, inward looking, and in some tension with the larger culture in which it finds itself.

Is there a difference between a sect and a *cult*? The two terms are often used interchangeably but they have technically different meanings. A cult has three characteristics, which we list in descending order of importance:

1. A cult is founded by a charismatic leader, whose powerful personality is the focus of his or her followers. It is through that person that the cult's religious message is delivered.
2. A cult normally claims that it has had a new revelation from God or a new insight into the sacred that either perfects or changes an older religious tradition or invigorates it.

3. Cults, at least in their beginnings, are viewed with extreme suspicion by the older, more established religious communities; the latter usually regard the "new revelation" as heretical or sacrilegious or blasphemous.

A classic example of an American-founded cult is the Church of Latter-Day Saints, better known as the *Mormons*: Established by a charismatic leader (Joseph Smith), who claimed a new revelation beyond that of the Bible (codified in the *Book of Mormon*), they were a despised and much abused religious minority. Indeed, they are strong in Utah today because they fled west after persecution (including the killing of Joseph Smith) in the eastern United States.

Most Americans no longer think of the Mormons as a cult because, as often happens if a cult survives, the original charisma of the founder was institutionalized (into the hierarchy of the Mormon church), and the movement, in time, became larger and more acceptable in the larger society. That is a very important point to keep in mind. History gives perspective.

We note that Christianity itself had all the classic characteristics of a cult in its beginnings. Now that Christianity has become the majority religion of Western culture, it is somehow difficult to remember that originally it was considered a dangerous, antisocial movement that merited the scorn of the Jewish religious establishment and the official condemnation of the Roman Empire, which saw it as a destabilizing factor in civil society.

Thus far, the discussion has focused on the relationship of religious communities and the larger cultures in which they exist. Sect and cult have been defined in terms of antagonism or resistance to the majority culture. Now we turn to a discussion of religious groups as anticultural agents or refuges against the real or perceived threats of the larger culture.

Even a cursory reading of the daily news provides evidence of religious communities that stand as resisting forces in a given culture. In the recent past, in once Marxist-controlled Poland, for example, the people identified strongly with the Catholic Church because historically it has been the vehicle of Polish language, culture, and nationalism. Apart from genuine religious motives, the greatest attraction of the Catholic Church for many Poles was its availability as an "alternative" organization. Poles who gave allegiance to the Catholic Church offered a rebuke to the power of the Soviet Union and to the Marxist government in Poland itself; they also protested against a certain cultural and linguistic imperialism that was characteristic of Soviet relations to Poland long before the communists came to power. Further, Poles who identified with Catholicism became a part of an organization that, in their minds, symbolized devotion to truth and justice against an official, ruling party widely seen as decadent, corrupt, and under the thumb of the Soviets. If religious fervor declines in contemporary Poland (there is some evidence of that), it is an indirect confirmation that the church was seen as a cultural force as much as an assembly of faith.

In the Iranian Revolution of 1978, many people, not all of whom would count themselves as strongly religious, identified with the uprising led by the late Ayatollah Khomeini. In doing so, they acted on the traditional Shi'i and Iranian principle that certain religious leaders are guardians of the Islamic community. In cases of extreme corruption and injustice, such leaders are to speak out against the "powers that be"—in the Iran of 1978, the Shah. Khomeini's speeches and writings indicated that the Shah was not so much viewed as religiously problematic—say, a heretic or unbeliever. Rather, he failed to keep faith with the Iranian people, allowing Western (especially American) interests to dictate the policy of Iran in matters such as the price and distribution of oil or relations to Israel. Iranians saw themselves as taking a stand against "west-struckness," as one popular book put it.[2] Khomeini's revolution provided a way to stand for the Iranian nation, its culture, and its language against imperialism and official corruption. In a different way, current unrest in Iraq is a very similar situation.

Religious groups provide refuge from the pressures and fears (real or imagined) of social change and/or disruption. The close bonds of such groups set up a kind of umbrella under which people can feel secure. At times, such groups manifest the worst elements of a cult or sect: rigid authoritarian structures, absolute reliance on a leader, manipulation of the lives of people, and so on. It is that kind of charge that is often brought against new religious movements. For example, in the North American context, the last two decades have seen a great deal of interest (usually negative) in groups such as the Unification Church (popularly known as "Moonies"), the Church of Scientology, the Hare Krishna movement, and other countercultural movements. Fears about such groups gained greater credibility when a bizarre pseudo-Christian cult led by the Reverend Jim Jones committed suicide *en masse* in the jungles of Guyana and after the tragedy of the followers of David Koresh and the Branch Davidians in Waco, Texas. Further reports focus regularly on cases in which cultish fundamentalist sects abuse children or coerce members through force.

What can we say about such phenomena? We make three points:

1. All cults/sects must be seen in the light of their place in history. Most cults and sects begin as social groups at odds with the prevailing culture. That is true of the Hare Krishna movement today, as it was of the Methodists in the eighteenth century and of Christians in the first century. The simple point is this: All cults and sects are capable of generating hostility from the larger culture.

2. The fact that a cult or sect is unpopular does not mean that it loses its right to constitutional protection in the United States. Snatching people in order to "deprogram" them is a hysterical reaction to unpopular religions. If a cult or sect is doing something against the rights of a person to life, liberty, or property, the proper course is to pursue such matters through the application of criminal law.

3. The emergence of cults and sects in large numbers is often a symptom of social dislocation and in that sense serves as a barometer indicating the cultural health of a society. In other words, one might learn a good deal from the appeal of such groups. Their existence and their attractiveness should not be written off as only some form of "lunacy." They should be understood as manifestations of various forms of cultural distress.

HERESY/SCHISM/DIVISION

Those notions of the sacred that signify the religion of a particular community provide a strong symbolic system (what Peter Berger has called, in a nice phrase, a "sacred canopy") that gives coherence to life. For tribal societies this bond is so strong that when those societies confront modernity not only do the traditional tribal structures fail, but meaning itself—the cohesion that bonds people together—begins to fail. Changes in the "life situation" of a tribe—say, forced migration from its traditional territories or forced changes in its socioeconomic lifestyle—may undermine the power of its religious system. Many Native Americans, for example, believe that the problems of reservation life (especially alcoholism) derive from a lost identity: Native Americans no longer possess their own traditions, and they have only imperfectly absorbed those of the whites. These final words of the book *Black Elk Speaks*, reflecting on the meaning of the defeat of the Sioux at Wounded Knee in the 19th century, are a sad and pathetic example of this loss of identity:

> And so it was all over.
> I did not know then how much was ended. When I look back now from this high hill of my old age, I can still see the butchered women and children lying heaped and scattered all along the crooked gulch as plain as when I saw them with eyes still young. And I can see that something else died there in the bloody mud, and was buried in the blizzard. A people's dream died there. It was a beautiful dream. And I, to whom so great a vision was given in my youth—you see me now a pitiful old man who has done nothing, for the nation's hoop is broken and scattered. There is no center any longer, and the sacred tree is dead.[3]

In the tradition of the great religions of the West (Judaism, Christianity, and Islam), there has been a form of social cohesion based on adherence to certain doctrinal standards, or certain ways of doing things. *Orthodoxy* (which literally can also mean "correct worship") relates to the maintenance of certain standards of belief whereas *orthopraxis* means the observance of certain standards of religious practice. As a shorthand for both terms, we shall simply speak of orthodoxy.

Most will be familiar with some type of orthodoxy. Certain Evangelicals say, for example, that the rule of faith for them is based on the

Bible as the absolute source of the will of God. Comparable claims are made by Orthodox Jews with respect to the Torah and by pious Muslims who base their belief on the Qur'an as the "speech of God."

Problems result, of course, when persons within a particular faith community advance different interpretations of orthodoxy. Here are just a few examples:

- The fierce debate among Jews over the refusal of Orthodox rabbis to recognize the legitimacy of marriages and religious conversions presided over by rabbis from the Reform wing of Judaism. In Israel, for instance, marriages witnessed by Reform rabbis are not recognized in law. The Orthodox rabbis reject the Reformed, arguing that they depart from the way of Torah.
- The past bitter struggles in the Missouri Synod of the Lutheran Church and more recently in the Southern Baptist Convention over the issue of the inerrancy of the Bible. In both cases, fundamentalists have attempted to purge the seminaries of the influence of impure doctrine.
- Conflicts between the Vatican and certain dissident theologians over the correct interpretation of Catholic belief and practice.
- Attempts on the part of certain Islamic groups (popularly called fundamentalists) to limit the influence of moderate Muslims and to establish governments that administer Islamic religious law.

To those who view such struggles from the outside, the religious argumentation involved often seems rather petty. In the nineteenth century, for example, a new American denomination (the Church of Christ) began with, among other things, an argument over the scriptural basis (or lack thereof) for playing instrumental music in worship services. More recently, the Anglican Church has split between those who wish to use a new version of the Book of Common Prayer and those who insist on the retention of the 1928 edition. Nonmembers of the Church of Christ (or non-Anglicans) might view such disputes as trivial. From the inside, however, things look different. If, as members believe, clear doctrinal standards are at stake, then such disputes are about faithfulness to God.

How does a religious community react when threatened by discord? How is its sacred canopy preserved? Of course, in some cases, the answer is that it cannot be. Especially with respect to tribal societies, it seems that disruption in the institutions of tribal life brings an end to tribal religion (though that point is controversial). In many cases, however, it is possible to classify the reactions of religious communities to discord in terms of reform (or renewal) or division.

Reform or renewal signifies a strategy to effect religious change, usually by an appeal to return to communal origins—for example, to emulate the inspiration of a founder, or to reconsider the original sources of the community's notion of the sacred. Within Christianity, for example, numerous reform movements have called for the church to emulate the selflessness, nonviolence, and/or devotion to the poor that was characteristic of Jesus. Other movements, similarly devoted to reform, have focused on a return to the "pure doctrine" contained in the Bible. Similarly, Islamic movements that usually are called fundamentalist demand a reform of Islamic societies through a return to the Qur'an and the example of Muhammad—sources that, from the Muslim point of view, provide clear guidance for those who would live rightly.

Reform movements are successful to the degree that they are perceived not to be lethal to what the majority of the older establishment sees as the irreducible core of the religious tradition. When this is not the case—that is, when the majority does identify a reform movement as "life threatening"— then reform movements often moderate their demands or channel them into some socially acceptable form of behavior. If that does not happen, then the reaction of religious communities to discord becomes characterized by division, which can take several forms.

First, the majority may declare the reform movement a *heresy*. This indicates that the reform movement is illegitimate (from the majority standpoint) and may be subject to various types of disciplinary action. In the extreme case, heretical movements may become the object of military action. Heretical leaders may be subjected to imprisonment or even death. In the case of medieval Christianity, a number of reform-minded groups were dealt with in this fashion. The Waldensians of northern Italy and the Czech Brethren provide important examples.

Division may take at least two other forms. A reform movement may become the occasion for *schism*, which here signifies its emergence as a community separate from its "parent," yet not distinct enough to constitute a new religious tradition. Schisms are often, in effect, divisions related to authority: Within a particular religious tradition, who decides which version of the tradition is orthodox? Thus the Church of England and the Church of Rome divided, in part, over the issue of papal authority, just as the Methodists, in part, broke with the Church of England over the proper designation of persons with authority.

The final form of division is one in which reform movements end up as new religious traditions. Thus, Siddhartha Gautama (the Buddha, or "enlightened One") began his religious search within the tradition of Hinduism, yet his teaching evolved into a separate religious tradition. The same, of course, could be said of Jesus of Nazareth and of Christianity. Christianity is unintelligible apart from its Jewish background, yet Christianity developed forms of thought and practice that are quite distinct from Judaism.

Both Buddhism and Christianity are religions with a specific founder. As a consequence there is a very strong impulse in those religious traditions to be faithful to the intentions of the founder. As a further consequence, the impulses that lead to schism or separation often have to do with fidelity to the teachings and example of the founder.

It should also be noted that many large religious traditions manage to accommodate a number of diverse movements, trends, or schools under a rather large umbrella. In such traditions, one does not speak of division in quite the same sense as in the cases discussed thus far. For example, in Hinduism one finds a very complex interrelationship of movements ranging from devotional practices oriented toward a specific deity to extremely austere groups whose members search for enlightenment through asceticism and meditation. The response of many scholars to this complexity is to note that "Hinduism" is in some sense an abstraction. Where there are no doctrinal or behavioral standards—in short, where there is no orthodoxy—can one speak of divisions (heresy, schism, and the like)?

Even in cases such as Protestantism or Roman Catholicism, which provide numerous classic examples of division, there is some force to this question. "Protestant" is an adjective that describes a wide spectrum, from Pentecostals to Quakers. And even in Roman Catholicism there are movements that are in tension with others in the tradition; for example, Catholic "traditionalists" look askance at Catholic "liberals," while "charismatics" have a niche in the Catholic Church unshared (and unwanted) by others who call themselves Catholics. In all of these examples we see a fair amount of diversity, tolerated within the sacred canopy of the religious community. In such cases, the key notion is *tradition*—the history and memory of the group, relative to its notions of the sacred. Thus: "We are Protestants because our memory goes back to the Reformation and we especially esteem the Bible as the rule of faith." Or, "We are Catholics because that is our tradition and we look to Rome as the center of our unity." Or, "We are Hindus because we accept the authority of the Vedas and of the sages of the Upanishads."

Tradition comes from the Latin verb *tradere*, which means to "hand over" or to "hand down." It does not take a great deal of imagination to see how important tradition is in religion. Most people who are religious in particular ways are so precisely because they have inherited certain notions from their families and religious communities. When there are religious divisions, one (or both) side(s) of the debate will inevitably appeal to tradition as a source of authority: "That is not what we have *traditionally* believed or done."

Tradition, of course, can be a blessing in its power to provide a sense of who one is and where one comes from. It can also be a means of holding back growth, progress, and achievement. The tension between the social value of tradition and its constraints merits some extended analysis.

TRADITION AND INNOVATION

At the outset of this chapter, we noted that the diverse notions of sacred reality that bind religious communities together can be a source of interreligious conflict. In the course of discussion, we also noted that religious communities are all "traditional" in the sense that they attempt to keep members in some sort of relationship to the communal past. As long as a religious community retains power, or at least a majority voice in the affairs of a given culture, this is a relatively simple task to accomplish. To put it bluntly: It is not difficult to be a Muslim if one lives in Saudi Arabia, or to be a Catholic if one lives in the Irish Republic.

What happens when a religious community, having a social bond built on its notion of the sacred, finds itself in a cultural setting that rests on somewhat different perceptions of the sacred, or even on a stance of avowed neutrality in religious affairs? This is an issue of particular urgency in a country such as the United States in which the predominant culture fosters a plurality of religious traditions that *under the law* have equal rights. Even in particular geographic regions where one or another religious community can claim a majority of the population as adherents (for example, the Mormons in Utah), there is no legal preference for that community. That community does, of course, exert considerable informal influence upon the customs or mores of the state.

The difficulty of maintaining traditional connections in such a pluralist culture becomes clear when one considers the question of marriage. Religious people often desire that their children marry within their own tradition. Indeed, many traditions place religious restrictions upon marriage "outside the faith." In Islam, for example, it is not permissible for a Muslim woman to marry a non-Muslim (though it is permissible for a Muslim man to marry a non-Muslim woman). In homogeneous societies (with a particular predominant religious community), this desire is not difficult to fulfill. In a country such as the United States, however, the issue can become acute. Some Jewish leaders, for example, worry that intermarriage between Jews and Gentiles in the United States will result in the diminishment of the Jewish community. In some parts of the United States, Jews marry outside their tradition nearly half the time. It is for that reason that many rabbis refuse to witness marriages in which one of the partners is not a Jew.

The Jewish community is not the only one attempting to maintain tradition through regulating marriage. Roman Catholics and the Orthodox Churches discourage marriage outside of their sanctuaries, and some fundamentalist churches will not sanction marriages between believers and those who are not professing Christians.

Such concern need not be seen as simply reactionary or exclusivistic. Rather, it points to another aspect of the social character of religion: Most religious communities recognize the family unit as fundamental. No matter how dominant a professional or priestly class may be in a given tradition, the family is always recognized as one of the sources, if not the main source, for passing on values and beliefs (notions of the sacred) from one generation to the next. This was true in ancient Rome with its "household gods"; it remains so for the modern Hindu family with its "home shrine," the Jewish family with its Sabbath meal, and the Christian family that prays together.

A pluralist culture engenders forces that run counter to such concerns, either by promoting attitudes that ignore the particularity of religious communities and traditions, or by espousing values that are antagonistic to religious ones. Some religious communities respond to such forces by attempting to shut them out. Among sectarian communities (see earlier discussion), this is sometimes done through separation of believers from prevailing cultural patterns—for example, among the Amish the adoption of an alternative communal lifestyle, codes of dress, and patterns of education. Other communities cope with the challenges of a pluralist culture by creating parallel structures that imitate those of the majority in every way except the path of neutrality in religious matters. Many religious groups, for example, create their own school system, which offers a curriculum parallel to that of public schools but with the addition of religious instruction, worship, and (sometimes) a religious perspective on such important aspects of the curriculum as the biological and physical sciences. The stated goal of such parochial systems is to prepare young people for a twofold vocation: life not only as a member of a pluralist culture but also as a devout member of a particular religious community.

From the vantage point of a pluralist culture, the demands of various religious groupings create challenges and sometimes frictions. To what degree, for example, can public law be stretched (or ignored) to accommodate the religious values of a particular religious community? Should state penal institutions be required to accommodate the dietary restrictions of inmates who practice Judaism or Islam? Should the Amish have the right to take their children out of school after the eighth grade? Can Jews wear a skull cap when the military regulations forbid nonofficial headgear? Can cities enforce laws that require businesses to close on Sundays (for the Christian holy day) when Muslims and Jews observe Fridays and Saturdays as holy? Can the state demand an autopsy even though Orthodox Jews regard such procedures as forbidden? Can a court order a blood transfusion for a sick child against the wishes of parents who are devout Jehovah's Witnesses or, in the case of Christian Scientists, order medical treatment?

Conflicts of this sort confront U.S. courts every day and are settled after inspection of the relation between the needs of society and those of the individual's right to freedom of religious practice. Not every case is settled to the satisfaction of all parties, of course. This underscores the main point of our discussion: the difficulties of relating particular religious traditions to pluralistic cultural settings. In many (perhaps most) cases, religious groups attempt to balance tradition and innovation in order to accommodate the realities of cultural change and the imperative of received tradition. Catholics have learned to live in pluralistic cultural settings, just as have Orthodox Jews. In both cases (and other similar ones) the long-cherished traditions of a religious community are not broken but are accommodated to or reformed with respect to the necessities of pluralism. To resist such innovation would involve either a freezing of tradition, resulting in the creation of a more sectarian model of community, or giving up the tradition altogether.

THE SOCIAL ASPECTS OF WORSHIP

The sociologist of religion, Joachim Wach, has written that religion includes, among other things, a program of ordered worship. From our standpoint, worship is an aspect of the response persons and groups make to that which they perceive as the appearance of the sacred. In the context of a discussion of sacred communities, we also can say that worship is a means by which a notion of the sacred is transmitted to members of a particular community. Thus it serves as a means for the identification and maintenance of religious groups.

The great philosopher Alfred North Whitehead once said that religion is what people do with their solitariness. Religion, after all, is the perceived relationship a person has with ultimate reality or the sacred. Every great religious tradition allows for individual experience of the sacred. Hinduism and Buddhism, for example, place a high value on the hermit ascetic who follows a solitary path in search of enlightenment. In Judaism, we note the solitary rabbi in his study; in Islam, we think of the lone person reciting the Qur'an in the late hours of the night: These are the symbols of the committed religious believer. This is similar to Christianity: According to the gospels, when Jesus, who knew privacy and solitude and silence in his life, wished to praise the person of authentic piety he singled out one who went into a room, shut the door, and prayed in secret (Matthew 6:6).

A good deal of evidence shows not only that there is room for individual piety but also that the great religions view the relationship of individual persons to the sacred as paramount. Indeed, it may be that in those solitary moments the real commitment of faith and the depth of belief is most clearly revealed.

After we make the above concession, let us further insist that worship is also fundamentally and absolutely social in character. Indeed, the very word used to describe worship in certain Christian communities is *liturgy*, which derives from the Greek term for a public work.

It is not difficult to demonstrate the social dimension of worship. As noted in an earlier chapter of this text, all religions provide for public, symbolic ceremonies to celebrate important moments in the lives, not only of persons but also of groups. It is to the group that persons turn at times of birth, marriage, and death. It is within the group that springtime is anticipated and harvest is celebrated. Furthermore, every religion that praises persons who are diligent in private prayer and meditation also provides for, and in many instances requires, participation in communal acts of worship. Protestant communities may encourage members to study the Bible in the quiet of their homes and to pray before retiring for the night, but those same communities gather as a group each "Lord's Day."

The social aspect of worship is underscored by the fact that many religious communities insist not only on correct doctrine but on correct worship. To return to an earlier term: Orthodoxy comes from two Greek words meaning "correct praise"—a right form of worship. Worship is seen as the acting out of communal beliefs; one can say that there is an intimate bond between what a religious tradition believes and how it comports itself in its religious ceremonies. Speaking from a Christian context, there is an old proverbial saying, *lex orandi, lex credendi*: The law of prayer is the law of belief. That statement has implications for religious traditions other than Christianity, too: For example, the centrality of the Sabbath meal in Judaism reflects the historic influence of the religious program of the Pharisees, those rabbis who, while vigorously criticized in the Christian gospels, are the heroes of rabbinic Judaism. According to historian Jacob Neusner, the Pharisees emphasized the home as the replacement of the Temple in Jerusalem, the table as the altar for sacrifice, and the husband/father as the family priest. Particularly following the destruction of the Temple in 70 C.E., the program of the Pharisees took hold, including the establishment of the *Sabbath* meal as a central ritual. The law of prayer (worship in the home) is the law of belief (that right sacrifice is offered in a family context).

The bond between prayer and belief is so close that in many religious communities differences in prayer or worship can provide occasions for division. It is also interesting to note that the language of worship often incorporates the perceptions of a given community about the social order of the world. Worship becomes a mirror reflecting a community's ideas of the relationship between the sacred and the profane. In traditional Chinese religion, for example, the emperor was an earthly icon of the heavenly emperor that guaranteed the order of the universe. That correlation was also present in the state religion of Japan (Shinto) and in the religion of ancient Rome as seen in emperor worship.

In a contemporary North American context, the language of worship typically incorporates biblical depictions of social order, which are often far removed from the experience of the worshipers. Thus in a suburban synagogue or church people will recite the twenty-third Psalm's reference to the Lord as a "shepherd," even though the vast majority of the congregants will never have seen a shepherd. God will be addressed as "father" (more rarely as "mother"), reflecting the connections of biblical language to the patriarchal organization of the tribal cultures of the ancient Near East—not the more complex society of contemporary North America. The current preoccupation of some Roman Catholic thinkers with liturgical forms that would reflect less hierarchy and more equality between believers and the feminist criticisms of patriarchal language in Christian worship provide clear indications of the interrelationship between worship and social consciousness.

Communal worship has two basic thrusts: the horizontal and the vertical. The horizontal thrust refers to the bonding of the community itself; the vertical thrust refers to the object of the worship, that is, the sacred. Both are exemplified in the communal prayer of Muslims gathered for Friday prayers. Row after row of Muslim men kneel and profoundly bow at the appropriate signal of the imam, or prayer leader. The horizontal character of that worship is indicated by the communal or group action of a large body of believers rather than of a single person. The prayer is a shorthand symbol of the Islamic community at worship. The profound bows indicate something of the essence of Islamic theology: Every person is called upon to make "the submission" (*al-islam*) to God. In the everyday workings of the Islamic community there may be potentates and leading politicians; but in this act of worship everyone bows as a group, not simply as an individual. Hence the horizontal and the vertical elements of worship coalesce into one act in which the theology of Islam is converted into its worship. *Lex orandi, lex credendi*: The law of prayer is the law of belief.

One last note. At times even pluralistic societies manifest a desire to join civil or political life and religious life. Hence, on some state occasion, happy or sad, a leader might ask for a common day of prayer or a moment of silence or a period of reflection so that people can sense the horizontal and vertical dimensions of their common life, however ill defined that may be. In the United States, perhaps the clearest example of such a day is Thanksgiving.

In some societies the relationship of state and religion is much closer. In Japan, for example, it was traditionally held that allegiance to the emperor was allegiance to the sacred. Similarly, in ancient Rome, the theory was that when a family worshiped the gods of Rome they expressed reverence for the state. In both cases, the world could be considered harmonious when all families expressed their allegiance through proper worship. These conceptions go a long way toward explaining why the early Christians and Jews (in the case of Rome) and Korean Christians (in the case of Japan, during its occupation of Korea from 1910 to 1945) were viewed as enemies of the state. They were politically subversive in their claim that they could worship a god transcendent to and sovereign over the power of the emperor. From the perspective of the Romans and the Japanese conquerors of Korea, the exclusivity that Christians claimed was characteristic of their god looked very much like a means of undermining the harmony of the state.

A WORD OF CONCLUSION

The relationship of religion and society is a vast and complicated subject that has held the attention of scholars for a long time. The whole area of the sociology of religion has been a rich one, with contributions not only by such classic scholars as Emile Durkheim, Ernst Troeltsch, and Max Weber, but also by contemporary writers such as Robert Bellah, Andrew Greeley, and Peter Berger. Of course, the recognition that religion has an important social dimension is the insight not only of professional social scientists but of important religious leaders. In North America, in Islamic countries, and in other parts of the world religious leaders assert that the religious community has much to say about the proper way to order human social existence. Religious figures from left to right have spoken on a whole range of issues dealing with economics, foreign policy, and social justice. Without arguing the merits of specific proposals, or even the merits of religious spokespeople making proposals for social policy, clearly very few people think that the personal, private dimension of religion exhausts its significance. Indeed, it seems that the reality is quite the opposite. Religious people argue that within their traditions there are ideas, symbols, and insights that are crucial for the well-being of human societies.

An informed observer will quickly note that the social dimension of religion has at least two sides. Religion can be a sustainer of family and state; it can also serve as a tool of revolutionary change. Religion can motivate progressive inquiry; it can also be a force for obscurantism. History affords examples of both tendencies. The one thing that is very clear is that the social reality of religious belief is a shaping *force* in human culture. To find the best evidence for the truth of this statement, read the newspaper for a week.

NOTES

1. For these and other reasons, some scholars have suggested that a third type, the "denomination," is more characteristic of American religion. See, for example, Talcott Parsons, "Christianity and Modern Industrial Society," in *Sorokin and Society,* ed. G. C. Hallen and Rajeshwar Prasad (Agre: Satis, 1972).

2. *West-struckness* is actually a translation of the title of a very interesting (and, in Iran, popular) book. Jalal e-Ahmad, *Plagued by the West (Gharbzadegi),* trans. Paul Sprachman (New York: Caravan Books, 1981).

3. John G. Neihardt, *Black Elk Speaks* (New York: Washington Square Press, 1959), p. 230. There is some question as to whether this book represents the thoughts of Black Elk or of his American translator/editor. See Clyde Holler, "Lakota Religion and Tragedy: The Theology of *Black Elk Speaks," Journal of the American Academy of Religion,* 52, no. 1 (1984), 19–45.

THOUGHT EXPERIMENTS

1. The history of the United States is littered with the memory of utopian communities and/or experiments in communal living. The only such communities that tend to survive are those with a strong religious ideology. Why should that be so?

2. It has often been observed that religion is class conscious. From your own perspective, do you think that to be true? Could you cite examples of

lower-, middle-, and upper-class religion? What factors account for such distinctive social strata in religion?

3. Can you guess the religious background of your classmates based only on your knowledge of their surnames? If you think you can make some fairly good guesses at this exercise, what does that say about the importance of ethnicity and social background for the study of religion?

4. Have you any direct or indirect acquaintance with people who have been attracted to religious cults or sects? What causes people to find such groups attractive? How do you explain the success of some groups in weaning people away from a life of crime and/or antisocial behavior?

5. From your own personal experience, can you appreciate or understand the severe tensions that sometimes arise when people disagree about the "correct" manner of expressing belief or conducting worship?

SUGGESTIONS FOR FURTHER READING

BERGER, PETER, *The Sacred Canopy: Elements of a Sociological Theory of Religion*. Garden City, N.Y.: Doubleday, 1967. A very stimulating book on religion from the perspective of the sociology of knowledge.

ECK, DIANA, *From Bozeman to Benares*. Boston: Beacon, 1993. A wonderful book on how a committed Christian views the Hindu world in an open and sympathetic fashion.

MARTY, MARTIN, et al., eds., *Fundamentalisms and the State*. Chicago: University of Chicago Press, 1993. This third volume of the "Fundamentalism Project" is especially important for the study of religious groups in relation to politics and economy. All volumes of this series are useful.

MILLER, TIMOTHY, ed., *When Prophets Die*. Albany: State University of New York Press, 1991. A collection of essays about American religious movements in the generations after the death of a founder or foundress.

MONAHAN, S., ed., *Sociology of Religion: A Reader*. Upper Saddle River, N.J.: Prentice Hall, 2001. An anthology of classic texts in religion and society.

O'DEA, THOMAS, *The Sociology of Religion*. Upper Saddle River, N.J.: Prentice Hall, 1966. A standard text in this area. Useful for definitions, concepts, and so on.

WUTHNOW, ROBERT, *The Restructuring of American Religion*. Princeton, N.J.: Princeton University Press, 1988. A highly regarded study of changing patterns in the American religious experience.

WUTHNOW, ROBERT, *Loose Connections*. Cambridge, Mass.: Harvard University Press, 2002. A sociological study of community building.

7 *The Problem of Evil*

"Vanity of vanities," says the Preacher. "Vanity of vanities! All is vanity. . . ."
I have seen all the works which have been done under the sun, and behold, all
is vanity and striving after wind. What is crooked cannot be straightened, and
what is lacking cannot be counted. (Ecclesiastes 1:2, 14–15)

Thus far we have stressed that "religion" signifies ways of thinking, feeling,
and acting that refer to a notion of sacred reality made manifest in human
experience. The discussions in various chapters of this book illustrate, in
effect, the first three components of our definition of religion (Chapter 1).

This chapter, and the two that follow, address the final component of
that definition: In various ways, notions of sacred reality address problems
of ordering and understanding human existence. To ask and think about the
nature and purpose of life, the meaning of death, and the right way to live
has always been an important aspect of the sacred quest. It is possible, of
course, to address such issues in ways that are not religious, but it is difficult
to think of a religious tradition that does not attempt to deal with such concerns. The history of humanity indicates that throughout the centuries, we
have made a persistent attempt to relate questions about existence to ideas
and experiences of sacred reality.

In this chapter, we discuss the problem of evil. This is a phrase that
actually represents not a single problem but a cluster of issues arising from
the attempt to relate a diverse set of experiences to notions of sacred reality.
Drawing on the tradition of his faith community, for example, the psalmist
asks, in effect, "Why does good fortune turn to bad?"

O God, we have heard with our ears, Our fathers told us, The work that Thou
didst in their days, In the days of old. Thou with Thine own hand didst drive
out the nations. . . . Yet Thou hast rejected us and brought us to dishonor,
And dost not go out with our armies. Thou dost cause us to turn back from
the adversary; And those who hate us have taken spoil for themselves.
(Psalm 44:1–2a, 9–10)

In a very different context, a critic of Hindu beliefs asks a different sort of question: Why do the righteous suffer, and the wicked flourish? Why is the world not a happier place?

> The world is so confused and out of joint, why does Brahma not set it straight? If he is master of the whole world, Brahma, lord of the many beings born, why in the whole world did he ordain misfortune? Why did he not make the whole world happy? . . . Why did he make the world with deception, lies, and excess, with injustice? . . .[1]

Again drawing on particular experiences, the preacher of Ecclesiastes raises questions about evil in the passage cited at the outset of this chapter. What is the meaning of life? asks the preacher. For ultimately, all people must die.

IDENTIFYING EVIL

When such questions are raised in connection with belief in God or gods, we may describe them as issues of *theodicy*, or "divine justice." Especially in traditions that stress the power and goodness of one God who rules over all creation, the occurrence of evil presents a logical dilemma. If God is good and powerful, what is the nature of evil? If God could prevent evil but does not, can God be good? On the other hand, if God is good but cannot prevent evil, can God be powerful? A satisfactory resolution is difficult to come by, as the continuing discussions within Judaism, Christianity, and Islam show.

The problem of evil occurs not only within theistic traditions, however. As Max Weber put it, even religious traditions that stress the impersonality of the sacred and its apparent indifference to human concern must deal with the imperfections of the world.[2] In general, one can say that the problem of evil arises whenever certain "brute facts" of everyday experience suggest a contradiction between the world of ordinary existence and the sense of reality suggested by a particular notion of the sacred. In the first place, religious people identify evil as an inconsistency between *what is* (the facts of experience) and *what ought to be* (the reality of the sacred).

In the modern West, no single experience raises the questions associated with the problem of evil with greater power than the *Holocaust*—the attempt by Adolf Hitler's National Socialist regime to destroy Europe's Jews and other "undesirables." By most estimates, the Nazis put to death fifteen million people between the years 1933 and 1945. Of these, six million were Jews; the rest were a combination of Gypsies, Slavs, homosexuals, and mentally or physically handicapped persons. The complex relationships between social, political, and economic factors in the development of Nazi policies are hotly debated among scholars of the period and cannot be resolved here. What is of concern, however, is the way in which the Holocaust illustrates the general point of how religious people identify evil in terms of a contradiction between the facts of experience and the reality of the sacred. The following comment by Irving Greenberg is instructive:

> The Holocaust poses the most radical counter-testimony to both Judaism and Christianity. . . . The cruelty and the killing raise the question whether even those who believe after such an event dare to talk about God who loves and cares without making a mockery of those who suffered.[3]

One might rephrase Greenberg's statement as follows: The Holocaust challenges some of the central affirmations of Jewish and Christian faith. In the most striking way possible, it poses the question: Do Jewish and Christian notions of the sacred correspond to anything real?

Why is this so? First, the Holocaust was cruel. Hitler's victims suffered greatly from cold, hunger, and deprivation. Families were broken apart in captivity. Like the title character in William Styron's novel *Sophie's Choice*, those singled out for ill treatment were deprived of their autonomy, forced to make unspeakable choices that undermined their dignity. How many mothers, upon arrival at Auschwitz, the infamous death camp where a million prisoners were executed, were faced with a choice like Sophie's? She arrives with her two children, already brutalized by a long journey in a cattle car filled with people, faint with hunger, only to be faced with the following dilemma: She must choose which of her children will survive, for one must be executed immediately. What can she do? She chooses her son, knowing she is thereby a participant in the execution of her daughter. Pain, suffering, dehumanization—all these were part of the agony of the Holocaust.

Further, the Holocaust need not have happened. Half a century after the terrible events, it seems clear that an early objection to Nazi treatment of Jews would have forestalled their destruction. That is not to mention that the artificial immigration quotas of the Allied powers, inspired partly by anti-Semitic sentiment, kept many Jews from escaping the grasp of Nazi domination.

Such factors are an important aspect of identifying the evil of the Holocaust, but they do not touch the central point made by Greenberg. Cruelty and human irresponsibility constitute the brute facts of the Holocaust, but the problem of evil arises for Jews and Christians when such facts are connected to religious affirmations. For Jews, the challenge of the Holocaust involves the relationship of the destruction of Europe's Jews to the notion that there is a God who governs history according to a plan; that God chose the Jewish people to receive and obey God's law, the Torah; and that, therefore, all the events of Jewish history have a meaning in the plan of God. For Christians, the problem is slightly different and involves the following question: In the death camps, where was Christ?

In either case, the primary question is one of meaning. What purpose did the massacre of fifteen million persons serve? In particular, what purpose was served by the systematic execution of six million persons whose only "crime" was to be Jewish? Reflecting on the death of his father, Holocaust survivor Elie Wiesel describes graphically the "brute facts" of suffering. Yet the real dilemma for Wiesel is to make sense of this death. What meaning did it—can it—have? As Wiesel puts it, his father did not yield his soul to the God of his ancestors, but to the hostile deity of the Nazis.[4]

The God of his ancestors was the "Holy One of Israel" (see Chapter 3), who long before had chosen Abraham and promised "I will make you a great nation. . . . And in you all the families of the earth will be blessed" (Genesis 12:2a, 3c). The basic, prophetic tendencies of Judaism were historically expressed in the idea of a "chosen people," the Jews, who had been set apart by God. To be chosen did not mean that the Jews would not suffer. Indeed, the book of Deuteronomy indicates that, under certain conditions, suffering becomes an important aspect of the relationship between God and God's people.

> [Moses said] See, I have set before you today life and prosperity, and death and adversity; in that I command you today to love the Lord your God, to walk in His ways and to keep His commandments and His statutes and His judgments, that you may live and multiply, and that the Lord your God may bless you in the land where you are entering to possess it. But if your heart turns away and you will not obey, but are drawn away and worship other gods and serve them, I declare to you today that you shall surely perish. . . . (30:15–18a)

The suffering spoken of in Deuteronomy is not meaningless suffering, however. Throughout their history, Jews interpreted misfortune as the will of God, the working out of the "curse" spoken of by Moses. When suffering comes (Jewish tradition indicated) the wise person will repent, ask forgiveness, and make a renewed effort to obey the Torah. The meaning of suffering lies in its power to teach. For through suffering, God disciplines God's people: "For whom the Lord loves He reproves, Even as a father, the son in whom he delights" (Proverbs 3:12).

Is such an interpretation possible with respect to the suffering of the victims of the Nazis? For many Jews, the answer is no.

> How can Jews believe in an omnipotent, beneficent God after Auschwitz? Traditional Jewish theology maintains that God is the ultimate, omnipotent actor in historical drama. It has interpreted every major catastrophe in Jewish history as God's punishment of a sinful Israel. I fail to see how this position can be maintained without regarding Hitler and the SS as instruments of God's will. . . . To see any purpose in the death camps, the traditional believer is forced to regard the most demonic, anti-human explosion of all history as a meaningful expression of God's purposes.[5]

For Christians, the Holocaust poses many similar problems. God's governance of history and choice of the Jewish people are important themes in Christian as well as Jewish theology. Yet Christian writers who contemplate the Holocaust have the additional problem of interpreting the death camps in terms of the presence of Christ. In this respect, the sacramental tendencies in Christianity (see Chapter 3) provide a context for the problem of evil that is somewhat different from that of Judaism. For Christian thought must interpret the brute facts of cruelty and human irresponsibility in terms of the New Testament affirmation that "God was in Christ reconciling the world to Himself, not counting their trespasses against them . . ." (II Corinthians 5:19). According to the New Testament, Christ defeated the powers of sin and death and inaugurated a new age in which those who trust him live to serve God. With Christ's victory in mind, those who experience cruelty or hardship may understand that their suffering will soon cease. More than that, they may affirm that God in Christ has redeemed or given meaning to their suffering:

> [W]e also exult in our tribulations, knowing that tribulation brings about perseverance; and perseverance, proven character; and proven character, hope; and hope does not disappoint, because the love of God has been poured out within our hearts through the Holy Spirit who was given to us. (Romans 5:3–5)

But where was Christ in the death camps?

In his memoir of Auschwitz, Elie Wiesel relates an incident in which he witnessed the execution of a young boy. According to Wiesel, this was a particularly troubling execution, and even the Nazi guards seemed disturbed at the prospect of hanging a young boy in front of the other prisoners. The scene grew worse, as the child did not die right away, but rather remained suspended in midair, struggling for some thirty minutes. In response, someone in the crowd asked "Where is God?" Wiesel reports his own answer, from an inner voice: God was there, hanging with the child.[6]

Wiesel's inner voice is related, as he indicates elsewhere, to the tradition of Jewish mysticism. But many Christians would affirm a similar notion, in response to the question "Where was Christ in the death camps?" The answer: With those who suffer. As one writer put it, the Holocaust might be considered "the crucifixion of the Jews."[7] In this way, the incarnation is taken as an affirmation that God in Christ has become one with humanity, especially with those who suffer. If that is the case, then Christians at least may affirm that the Holocaust is not meaningless.

Nevertheless, problems remain, because those who died did not die freely, as the New Testament indicates in the case of the Christ. The victims of Auschwitz had no inkling that their deaths might have a redemptive purpose. More than that, the killers were Christians, in some cases motivated by the idea that Jews deserved punishment for the crucifixion of Jesus. If the

Christ was present in the death camps, and present as one of the victims, what does that make of the Christian executioners?

RESPONSES TO EVIL: SOME CLASSIC PATTERNS

The identification of evil is thus not a simple matter. Certain experiences characteristic of human existence—cruelty, indifference, and the like—constitute the brute facts of evil. But the reasons why such things count as evil vary somewhat, depending on the notions of sacred reality that persons and communities bring to such experiences.

Remembering that "the problem of evil" occurs whenever people perceive a contradiction between the facts of ordinary experience and the reality suggested by their notions of the sacred, we now turn to a discussion of responses to evil in religious traditions. We identify certain characteristic patterns of response. We discuss four classic approaches to the problem of evil: karma, characteristic of the religions of India; the consolation of promise, characteristic of Judaism, Christianity, and Islam; the appeal to sovereignty, especially as it appears in the Hebrew Bible; and dualism, of which *Zoroastrianism* provides perhaps the clearest example.[8]

Evil and Karma: The Indian Context

In an earlier discussion of sacred time (Chapter 3), the notion of *karma* was tied to Buddhist and Hindu ideas of the cycle of existence (*samsara*). Karma, we noted, signifies the moral "weight" of one's actions. Good or proper action results in good karma, and in progress toward the goal of enlightenment.

In connection with the problem of evil, karma is a kind of inexorable reality that explains the destiny of human beings. People get what they deserve—at least, over the long cycle of time. Samsara signifies the way human beings work out their destiny through a long process of birth, death, and rebirth—the goal being to achieve enlightenment and be liberated from the cycle, never to be reborn again.

The inexorability of karma is the problem addressed in the Buddhist story of "The Death of Moggallana."[9] The story begins with a saying of the Buddha on the law of karma:

> Who striketh him that striketh not, And harmeth him that harmeth not, Shall quickly punishment incur, some one among a list of ten.

A number of types of retribution are listed: The wrongdoer will experience "cruel pain, or drear old age," or "failure of the vital powers"; if these do not occur, then disease or madness "him shall overtake"; the king will punish the wrongdoer or, as a last resort, "when his frame dissolves in death, In hell the fool shall be reborn."[10]

According to a standard commentary, the Buddha spoke these words on the occasion of the death of Moggallana, one of his chief disciples. Known for his miraculous powers, Moggallana had been brutally murdered by a rival religious sect. The Buddha's saying referred to the law of karma as a way of indicating that justice would ultimately be done. According to the commentary, it was so: Moggallana's murderers were arrested while fighting in a tavern. In captivity, they revealed their connections with the contrary sect, whereupon the king seized the murderers, buried them in pits "up to their navels," covered them with straw to which he set fire, "and after thus burning them, he took iron plows and plowed them into bits."[11] Evil never goes unpunished. Such is the moral of the tale.

Such a moral provides only a partial response to the problem of evil, however. And thus the story continues with the questions of Moggallana's companions. Perhaps, they say, we can perceive the workings of karma in the punishment of the killers. But how can we affirm the eternal law in the case of Moggallana? Karma means "one gets what one deserves." What then can be said of the brutal murder of the saintly Moggallana, whose association with the Buddha seemed to lead him to the very brink of enlightenment? Here it seems there is a contradiction: The "facts" of experience run counter to the reality proposed by Buddhist notions of the sacred. What is the proper response?

According to the story, the Buddha said: "The death of Moggallana was unsuited to his present existence, but suited to his karma of a previous existence." There follows a tale concerning a youth who, faced with the duty of caring for his parents, took a wife as a helpmate. His parents had insisted on this, knowing their son needed help. But soon the wife told her young husband, "It is impossible to stay in the same house with your parents." Eventually the young man's resolve broke in the face of his wife's insistence, and he conspired to take them into the forest where he killed his parents in the manner of a highwayman. Thus it is not only the death of Moggallana's killers that is appropriate, fulfilling the law of karma; Moggallana's death also exemplifies that inexorable law, for he "was" the youth in the story. That which is experienced as evil may in fact be right and proper.

From the Buddhist perspective, evil is located in the self, with its passions and desires. The brute facts of cruelty and pain are not simply the "luck of the draw," nor are they connected with the will of God. The Buddha's teaching points toward Nirvana, the state of mind that is beyond such notions. One who attains enlightenment sees through such illusions. He or she knows that the resolution of the experiences associated with evil does not depend on gods or goddesses, nor does it depend on other human beings. In the fundamental sense, the solution to the problem of evil depends on each individual person. Beginning with the awareness that life itself is painful and filled with suffering, one starts down the road that leads to enlightenment. At the end of the road lies Nirvana. In between initial awareness and Nirvana there is discipline: the way of the Buddha, summarized in the Noble Eightfold Path (Chapter 2). Ultimately, one "solves" the problem of evil by overcoming one's self.

The approach from karma, is characteristic of most types of Hinduism, as well as Buddhism, yet it takes diverse forms. In Vedantic, or philosophical, Hinduism, for example, karma explains the major events and the overall setting of a person's life. Did a person's father die early? The explanation lies in past deeds—in this life or another. Was a person born in poverty? Each life illustrates the law of karma. The destiny of beings is the consequence of past actions.

According to Buddhism, one overcomes such evils by dealing with one's self. By contrast, the way of Vedanta stresses that such evils are ultimately illusory and therefore have no real existence. Seen from the point of view of enlightenment, terms such as "evil" and "good" have no referent. Such distinctions simply do not exist. In this way, the problem of evil is "dissolved."

Further variations within the framework of karma may be found in popular Hinduism. As Wendy O'Flaherty indicates, the notion of evil as the outworking of an inexorable law may not answer all the questions raised by the facts of pain and suffering. Even those who do affirm the law of karma may ask who or what created the law in the first place. By what logic or force can one declare a world governed by karma the best or most meaningful of possible worlds? It does not suffice—at least, necessarily—to say that evil is an illusion. After all, even those who are enlightened do not seek after hunger or misfortune. Beyond this, it seems that the circumstances of some people's lives give them a better chance to attain enlightenment in the first place. Thus popular Hindu mythology points to the role of various gods and goddesses in the origin and resolution of the problem of evil, even within the framework of belief in karma.[12]

The Consolation of Promise

In the face of contradictions between the facts of experience and notions of sacred reality, it is always possible to say "evil is powerful now. But it will not always be the case. At some future time evil will be overcome, justice will be satisfied, and the point of suffering will be made clear." Such a response uses the language of *promise*, offering consolation and hope to those currently suffering. Just how or when the promise will be fulfilled is a matter on which there is a variety of opinions, both among diverse religious traditions and within them.

Both Judaism and Christianity, for example, share a belief in the Messiah: the anointed servant of God who will come to fulfill the promise of an ideal kingdom.

> And the wolf will dwell with the lamb, And the leopard will lie down with the kid, And the calf and the lion and the fatling together; And a little boy will lead them. Also the cow and the bear will graze; Their young will lie down together; And the lion will eat straw like the ox. And the nursing child will play by the hole of the cobra, And the weaned child will put his hand on the viper's den. They will not hurt or destroy in all My holy mountain, For the earth will be full of the knowledge of the Lord, As the waters cover the sea. (Isaiah 11:6–9)

In other places, the promise is stated more succinctly: The Messiah "will bring forth justice to the nations" (Isaiah 42:1b).

Judaism and Christianity differ on the how and when of fulfillment of the promise, of course. Orthodox Jews in particular wait for a Messiah who is yet to come. When the anointed one arrives, he will reestablish the nation of Israel and will rule the other nations "with a rod of iron." It is significant that a number of Orthodox groups hold that the contemporary state of Israel is not a fulfillment of this promise. Rather, they view the Jewish state as a violation of the Torah, a manifestation of the impatience and disobedience of humanity rather than the work of God.

Christianity holds, on the other hand, that the Messiah has come: Jesus of Nazareth is the Messiah, or the Christ (see Chapter 3). His life, death, and resurrection manifest the promise of God to bring about a peaceable kingdom. The work of Jesus is not yet complete, however. For he "will come again in glory to judge the living and the dead; and his reign will have no end."[13] The doctrine of the *parousia* or the "second coming" of Christ indicates that the fulfillment of the promise is yet to come. Thus Christians see the world as in between the manifestation of the promise and its fulfillment.

A similar idea appears in the Islamic tradition of the *mahdi* or "rightly guided one." Particularly among the Shi'a of Iran, the *mahdi* is identified with Muhammad, son of Hasan al-'Askari (d. 873/874 C.E.). Taken into hiding by the will of God shortly after his birth, Muhammad al-Mahdi remains in occultation to the present day. He will come or "appear" at the time God decides and will establish the rule of justice and equity on earth.

At the same time, Islam points to another version of the promise theme, shared with most forms of Judaism and Christianity: It refers to an afterlife in which good will be rewarded, evil punished, and suffering explained.

> Those who fled their homes in the cause of Allah and then were slain or died, Allah verily will provide for them a good provision. Lo! Allah, He verily is best of all who make provision. Assuredly He will cause them to enter by an entry they will love. Lo! Allah verily is Knower, Indulgent. (Qur'an 22:58–59)

Unjust suffering is a fact in this world, but God will deal with it in due time. Or again, the death of just warriors is a part of historic experience—but God will give them recompense:

> Think not of those who are slain in the way of Allah, as dead. Nay, they are living. With their Lord they have provision: Jubilant (are they) because of that which Allah hath bestowed upon them of His bounty, rejoicing for the sake of those who have not joined them but are left behind: that there shall no fear come upon them neither shall they grieve. (Qur'an 3: 169–70)

In an afterlife, through a Day of Resurrection and Judgment, God will resolve the problem of evil, ensuring that the good receive rewards and the evil, punishment.

The Appeal to Sovereignty

The problem of justice is not the whole of the problem of evil, of course. Those commenting on the occurrence of suffering, particularly in such cases as the Holocaust, often note that no future settlement could really compensate for the suffering of the victims. No punishment could ever be enough for the wrongdoers; no reward could ever "pay back" a child hanging from the gallows. Thus the theme of promise is often joined with an appeal to sovereignty. Here evil is related to notions of the sacred, which emphasize its freedom with respect to ordinary ideas of justice and its inscrutability with respect to human understanding. The sovereignty appeal finds its power in affirming that, at least from the human standpoint, there are no solutions to the problem of evil. There is only God, the Lord of the worlds. The response of suffering humanity should be the response of Job: "The Lord gave and the Lord has taken away. Blessed be the name of the Lord" (Job 1:21).

The book of Job may be taken as the archetype of the sovereignty response. As such, it has both baffled and comforted believers throughout generations of Jewish and Christian faith. The story begins with a meeting between God and Satan, the latter appearing as a sort of divinely appointed agent whose interest is to ensure that the glory of God is protected.

> Now there was a day when the sons of God came to present themselves before the Lord, Satan also came among them. And the Lord said to Satan, "From where do you come?" Then Satan answered the Lord and said, "From roaming about on the earth and walking around on it." And the Lord said to Satan, "Have you considered my servant Job? For there is no one like him on the earth, a blameless and upright man, fearing God and turning away from evil." Then Satan answered the Lord, "does Job fear God for nothing?" (1:6–9)

In a number of ways, the question of Satan is the key to subsequent events. As the story unfolds, Job is put to the test. Will he prove that his obedience to God flows from his own integrity—that is, does he do the will of God because it is right? Or will Job show that his obedience is motivated by considerations of personal gain—of rewards and punishments, of obtaining blessings and avoiding curses? Satan's position is clear. He suspects that Job is motivated by gain, and argues:

> Hast Thou [God] not made a hedge about him and his house and all that he has, on every side? Thou has blessed the work of his hands, and his possessions have increased in the land. But put forth Thy hand now and touch all that he has; he will surely curse Thee to Thy face. (1:10–11)

This God allows, first with respect to Job's possessions and family, then with respect to Job's health. Struck with boils "from the sole of his foot to the crown of his head" (2:7), Job sits in an attitude of repentance and mourning. When his wife challenges him, Job remains faithful; as the story proceeds, however, he makes it clear that he has a number of questions for God.

Chapters 3 through 32 point to Job's questions in the context of a dialogue between Job and three friends who come to sympathize with and comfort him. In so many ways, Job asks about the meaning of his suffering. His friends posit the idea (already discussed in connection with the Holocaust) that suffering is educative. Misfortune is God's discipline for those whom God loves. The proper response is repentance.

For Job, however, this explanation is unsatisfactory. The punishment given is out of proportion to any sin he has committed. Weighed on the scales of justice, Job's "vexation" at his suffering "would be heavier than the sand of the seas" (6:2–3). If repentance is God's goal, then God achieved it long ago. God should either forgive Job or kill him. In the end, the language of justice and injustice is not sufficient to settle the case. No matter what the righteousness of Job's claim, there is no one to enforce it. God always has the advantage:

> If it is a matter of power, behold, He is the strong one! And if it is a matter of justice, who can summon Him? . . . For He is not a man as I am that I may answer Him, That we may go to court together. There is no umpire between us, Who may lay his hand upon us both. (9:19, 32–33)

Job perceives his "comforters" as accusers. Their comments about justice and injustice only complicate the problem. And they, of course, see him as faithless, proud, and a rebel against God. In a way, both claims prove right. When God finally answers Job (Chapters 38 through 41), God does not claim that the testing of Job was right, at least according to ordinary canons of justice. Instead, God claims the wisdom of the creator of all things.

> Who is this that darkens counsel By words without knowledge? Now gird up your loins like a man, And I will ask you, and you instruct Me! Where were you

when I laid the foundation of the earth! Tell Me, if you have understanding. Who set up its measurements, since you know? Or who stretched the line on it? On what were its bases sunk? Or who laid its cornerstone, When the morning stars sang together, And all the sons of God shouted for joy? (38:2–7)

Similarly, Job's response is not "I was wrong," in the moral sense. It is "I am insignificant" (40:4); "I have declared that which I did not understand" (42:3); "I retract" (42:6). Job repents by accepting the finitude of human understanding and the sovereignty of the Maker of heaven and earth.

Dualism

Among the many fascinating aspects of the story of Job, the character of Satan has captured the attention of many religious minds over the centuries. When joined with other biblical passages, the story of Job has contributed to a lore about Satan that points to a last response to the problem of evil, which may be called *dualism*: The postulate that evil is the result of a conflict between good and evil powers, both of which share some of the characteristics of sacred reality discussed in Chapter 2. Both God and "the devil" are set apart, to some extent beyond the volitional control of human beings, and exercise a special prominence with respect to human welfare. Only God, however, does so by right, pointing to the importance of moral concern in dualism. From the perspective of dualism, God is good but faces a severe challenge to God's sovereignty from those powers that do evil in the world.

To a certain extent the Bible reflects the concerns of dualism. Thus, in the Gospel according to Luke, the devil tempts Jesus in the following way:

[The devil] led Him [Jesus] up and showed Him all the kingdoms of the world in a moment of time. And the devil said to Him, "I will give You all this domain and its glory; for it has been handed over to me, and I give it to whomever I wish. Therefore if You worship before me, it shall all be Yours." (4:5–7)

That the kingdoms of the world have been handed over to the devil is a sign of the power of evil. Jesus' rejection of this temptation is a sign of his choice to be on the side of God in the struggle against evil.

Luke's gospel does not, however, illustrate dualism in the fullest sense. Nor does the book of Job or the Bible as a whole. No matter how powerful "the devil" is, it is ultimately subject to the sovereign will of God. In the passage from Luke, the kingdoms of the world are said to be "handed over" to the devil. In the book of Job, Satan is an "accuser" whose primary concern is the glory of God. Martin Luther expressed quite well the biblical approach to the devil: "The Devil is always God's devil," for the devil, like human beings, is created.

A fully developed dualism requires that good and evil be on a more equal footing. Thus the best representations of the position may be Zoroastrian stories of the struggle between Spenta Mainyu ("beneficent spirit") and Angra Mainyu ("hostile spirit"), whose conflict stems from the beginning of all things and continues to the end of time. These stories, which by tradition originated with the founding teacher Zarathustra around 1000 B.C.E., exerted a strong influence on pre-Islamic Iran and on aspects of biblical and Islamic traditions. They continue as important components in the religious understanding of Zoroastrian communities in Iran, India, and Pakistan.

Spenta Mainyu and Angra Mainyu are twins, offspring of the "wise lord" Ahura Mazda, the creator of all things. Ahura Mazda's twins represent the moral choice set before all creatures. Evil comes into the world as a result of wrongful choice, and the proper response is thus to fight against it.

> The two primordial Spirits, who are twins, revealed themselves in a dream. They have two ways of thinking, of acting: the good and the bad. And, of the two, the one who acts well has made the right choice, not the one who does evil. And when these two spirits met, they established, at the beginning, life and nonlife, and the consequence, in the end, of the Worst Existence for evil, and Best Thought for good. The evil one of the two Spirits chose to do bad things, and the Most Bounteous Spirit, clothed in hardest stones, chose Truth, as is also true for all those who constantly strive to please the Wise Lord with honest actions.[14]

The hope is that human beings, choosing to participate in the work of the beneficent spirit, will eventually transform themselves and the world. That this would be right and is to be fervently desired is clear. It is less clear that it will be accomplished. The suggestion is that the transformation will take place, for the "wise lord" is ultimately on the side of good. But the principle of choice and the equality of good and evil make this answer somewhat more tentative than in some other traditions.

ARE THE ANSWERS ADEQUATE?

In so many ways, the responses outlined here attempt to address questions associated with the problem of evil. Our primary task is to understand the responses, not to evaluate them. Nevertheless, the question arises: Are the answers adequate? Do any of the classic responses really deal with the questions raised by the "facts" of evil?

The short answer must be "maybe." In their book of *Approaches to Auschwitz*, Richard L. Rubenstein and John K. Roth discuss a study of the religious beliefs of survivors of the Holocaust. Fifty-three percent of those responding to a questionnaire indicated that the Holocaust affected or at least modified their faith in God. The remaining 47 percent indicated that their experience had very little impact on their religious views. Sixty-nine percent stated that prior to the Holocaust, they believed in God, conceived either personally or impersonally; 33 percent continued to believe very strongly. But of 55 percent who, before their wartime experience, expressed belief in a personal deity involved in everyday life, a little more than one in four now rejected such belief. And of the 53 percent who said that the Holocaust had modified their faith, three out of four indicated this modification was negative—they had lost faith, or at least believed less strongly than before. Only one out of four said the modification involved a strengthening of faith. Of those continuing to believe in some way, interpretations of the Holocaust ranged from the traditional view of evil as God's discipline, to notions of an impersonal God, uninvolved in the Holocaust or any other aspect of historical experience.[15]

Of course, surveys do not constitute a measure of religious truth, but they indicate something about the questions people ask in ascertaining the justifiability of particular ideas. Specifically, they raise the following questions in assessing the adequacy of a response to the problem of evil.

Is It Logical? Is a given proposal consistent (at least) on its own terms? Much criticism of Jewish and Christian thought with respect to the Holocaust, for example, has been that it is unwilling to accept the consequences of the notion of a God who rules the world and acts in history. It has focused, as some would say, on *anthropodicy* (the justice of humanity) rather than on theodicy. The point of the criticism is that Jewish and Christian theologians are addressing only the moral aspects of the Holocaust. Yet, given the notions of sacred reality characteristic of their traditions, consistency requires an attempt to address the religious issues raised by the destruction of Europe's Jews.

Is It Coherent? Insofar as empirical claims are made, do they correspond to human experience? Part of the appeal in the Buddhist tale of Moggallana's death is to the inevitability of retribution, according to the law of karma. Some of the reasoning is not subject to empirical inquiry: for example, the story of Moggallana's past crime against his parents. But the response of karma is, at least in part, based on an appeal to observation: In life, does one reap what one sows?

Is It Psychologically Satisfying? In her previously mentioned study of Hindu mythology, Wendy O'Flaherty argues that the karmic approach, particularly in connection with the Vedantic interpretation of evil as illusory, may be rationally—that is, logically—acceptable. But is it emotionally so? Not if one takes seriously the evidence of Hindu mythology. In such myths, where the stock example of evil is the death of a young child, Vedantic or even karmic responses are not fully satisfactory. According to O'Flaherty, this reflects the experiential fact that if "one says to the parents of this child,

'You are not real, nor is your son; therefore you cannot really be suffering,' one is not likely to be of much comfort. Nor will the pain be dulled by such remarks as 'God can't help it' or 'God doesn't know about it.'"[16] One might also say that giving comfort is not a measure of religious truth. Yet O'Flaherty (and by extension Hindu mythology) reflects an important consideration: Even if a given response to the problem of evil is logically consistent, it may not be experientially satisfactory. To put the issue bluntly: Can any proposal that denies the facts of evil be satisfactory?

What Are the Moral Consequences?   One difficulty with a Jewish or Christian interpretation of the Holocaust that stresses God's action in history and thus interprets the suffering of Jews and others as divine chastisement is the question it raises about the moral responsibility of human beings. If God was punishing Jews in Auschwitz, why do we feel that those outside should have tried to stop the suffering? The logic of such an interpretation can be expressed this way: God is punishing the victims of the Nazis; we are supposed to obey God; thus God must want us to punish the victims. How could it be otherwise? As liberation theologians and others have pointed out, there is a sense in which some conceptions of sacred reality serve in practice to legitimate and preserve structures that are evil.

In the end, there may not be any perfect solution to the problem of evil. We may press for consistency and coherence; we may ask questions about the psychological and moral consequences of particular proposals. We may well narrow the scope of justifiable responses—even narrow it to one that seems most correct. Yet we may still be left with the great dilemma: How can God be all-good and all-powerful, while at the same time evil occurs?

NOTES

1. Cited in Wendy Doniger O'Flaherty, *The Origins of Evil in Hindu Mythology* (Berkeley: University of California Press, 1976), p. 5.
2. Max Weber, "Theodicy, Salvation, and Rebirth," printed in *The Sociology of Religion*, trans. Ephraim Fischoff (Boston: Beacon Press, 1963), pp. 138–150.
3. Cited in Richard L. Rubenstein and John K. Roth, *Approaches to Auschwitz* (Atlanta: John Knox Press, 1987), p. 317.
4. Elie Wiesel, "The Death of My Father," in *Jewish Reflections on Death*, ed. Jack Riemer (New York: Schocken Books, 1974), pp. 34–39.
5. Richard L. Rubenstein, *After Auschwitz: Radical Theology and Contemporary Judaism* (Indianapolis, Ind.: Bobbs-Merrill, 1966), p. 153.
6. Related in Elie Wiesel, *Night* (Toronto: Bantam Books, 1960), pp. 61–62.
7. Franklin Littell, *The Crucifixion of the Jews* (New York: Harper & Row, 1975).
8. This type of classification follows, with some revisions, that of Weber, "Theodicy, Salvation, and Rebirth," and of Peter Berger, *The Sacred Canopy: Elements of a Sociological Theory of Religion* (Garden City, N.Y.: Doubleday, 1969), pp. 53–80.

9. *Buddhism in Translations*, trans. Henry Clarke Warren (New York: Athenaeum, 1987), pp. 221–226. The reference was suggested by the article of Ronald Green, "Theodicy," in *The Encyclopedia of Religion*, ed. Mircea Eliade (New York: Macmillan, 1987), vol. 14, pp. 430–441.

10. Warren, *Buddhism in Translations*.

11. Warren, *Buddhism in Translations*.

12. O'Flaherty, *The Origins of Evil in Hindu Mythology*.

13. The Nicene Creed, as it appears in Bard Thompson, *Liturgies of the Western Church* (Cleveland: World, 1961), p. 63.

14. From *Yasna (Acts of Worship)*, 30:3ff., as cited in Gherardo Gnoli, "Zoroastrianism," trans. Ughetta Fitzgerald Lubin in *The Encyclopedia of Religion*, ed. Mircea Eliade (New York: Macmillan, 1987), vol. 15, p. 582.

15. Rubenstein and Roth, *Approaches to Auschwitz*, pp. 292–297. The study in question is by Reeve Robert Brenner, *The Faith and Doubt of Holocaust Survivors* (New York: Free Press, 1980).

16. O'Flaherty, *The Origins of Evil in Hindu Mythology*, p. 5.

THOUGHT EXPERIMENTS

1. Consider God's answer to Job (Chapters 38–42). Does this answer constitute an adequate response to the problem of evil? Why or why not?

2. Read Elie Wiesel's *Night* or watch a film about the Holocaust (*Sophie's Choice, Playing for Time*, the documentary *Shoah*, or *Schindler's List*, for example). Discuss some of the classic responses to the problem of evil as applied to this experience. How does one interpret the Holocaust, for example, within a perspective stressing the law of karma? Sovereignty? Does any one of the classic responses seem more adequate than the others?

3. Consider the following incident reported by anthropologist Gladys Reichard in a discussion of Navaho statements about the end of the world:

> The chanter . . . believed that a people different from the Navaho would succeed them. He thought the whites were the successors and for this reason was not only willing to teach them the fundamentals of Navaho belief but also deeply concerned that they should learn accurately. (Gladys Reichard, *Navaho Religion* [Tucson: University of Arizona, 1983], p. 25)

In the context of the kind of catastrophe (the defeat of Native Americans by white settlers, the restriction of tribal life to reservations, etc.), how does this statement constitute a response to the problem of evil? Is it similar to any of the classic responses discussed in this chapter, or does it suggest another pattern?

SUGGESTIONS FOR FURTHER READING

BOWKER, JOHN, *Problems of Suffering in Religions of the World*. Cambridge: Cambridge University Press, 1970. A good discussion of one aspect of the problem of evil as it appears in a variety of religious traditions.

GREEN, RONALD, "Theodicy." In *The Encyclopedia of Religion*, 15 vols., ed. Mircea Eliade. New York: Macmillan, 1987. A helpful survey of various theodicies and their place in the major religious traditions.

HICK, JOHN, *Evil and the God of Love* (rev. ed.). New York: Harper & Row, 1978. A survey of Christian responses to the problem of evil and a defense of one position.

O'FLAHERTY, WENDY DONIGER, *The Origins of Evil in Hindu Mythology*. Berkeley: University of California Press, 1976. An important study of popular Hinduism's response to the problem of evil.

8 *Religion and Morality*

The United States, it is often said, is a secular nation. Support for this judgment lies in the legal and cultural tradition summarized in the phrase "the separation of church and state." According to the First Amendment to the U.S. Constitution, Congress is to make no laws that would suggest the establishment of a state church. Nor is Congress to make laws that would inhibit the holding of a variety of opinions on religious matters or that would stifle the free exercise of religious beliefs.

Despite these facts, Americans consistently show themselves to be a religious people. According to Supreme Court Justice William O. Douglas, writing for the U.S. Supreme Court in 1952, Americans "are a religious people, whose institutions presuppose a Supreme Being."[1] What this phrase means, in legal terms, is subject to much debate. Nevertheless, it summarizes well the feeling of many Americans. It also points to the reason why many issues that are primarily legal or political are nevertheless debated in religious terms. The United States may be a secular state, but Americans are a religious people, and this makes for a peculiar state of affairs. Particularly when legal and political issues have a moral dimension, religion comes to the fore. Abortion provides the most striking contemporary example, but one can also consider civil rights and antiwar sentiment in the 1960s, or slavery in the years immediately preceding the Civil War as illustrations of this tendency.

According to opinion polls, many Americans continue to feel some empathy for the statement of former President Ronald Reagan: "The truth is, politics and morality are inseparable. And as morality's foundation is religion, religion and politics are necessarily related."[2] Clearly, Reagan's statement, as well as the beliefs of many Americans, raises important questions for American politics. It also points to significant issues in the study of religion. It is hard to think of any religious tradition or community that has not tried, in one way or another, to relate notions of the sacred to issues of morality. Yet the relationships thus established may not always be the same. At the least, there is reason to look a bit more closely at the varieties of religious expression and to ask just how it is that religion relates to moral concern.

DEFINING THE ISSUES

First, we consider what is involved in questions about the relationship of religion and *morality*. Even a brief consideration shows several issues that, while interconnected, can nevertheless be distinguished.

We might consider, for example, the claim that religion provides a foundation for morality. President Reagan's comment that "morality's foundation is religion" certainly suggests this. The issue of foundations usually involves a claim about the nature of moral knowledge. How do human beings know what is good or right or praiseworthy? They can refer to religious sources such as the teaching of a sacred scripture or the judgments of authoritative scholars within a particular religious tradition. For some religious traditions, the phrase "obey the commands of God" expresses the highest standard of the moral life. At least, this phrase appears to be the highest standard, although it often seems to mean that people should obey the commands of God as the best guide to what is good. In that case, the highest standard is really "do what is good," and "obey the commands of God" is an indicator of how fallible human beings come to know the good. Ultimately the claim that religion provides a foundation for morality raises the question asked by Socrates: "Do the gods love the good because it is good, or is it good because the gods love it?"

A second issue raised by discussions of religion and morality has to do with the definition of terms. In Chapter 1, we pointed to a variety of questions connected with the definition of religion, and we proposed a working definition in which notions of sacred reality provided the key to distinguishing religious from nonreligious ways of thinking, feeling, and acting. Certainly a great deal of inquiry about the relation of religion and morality focuses on the "definition question." If we follow the rules of definition set forth in Chapter 1, especially the rule stating the priority of ordinary use of terms, then a working definition of morality focuses on considerations of human welfare as the key. Students of ethics often point to the way that moral teaching in a variety of cultures reflects concern about a class of acts that philosopher Eric D'Arcy has termed "moral-species" acts: those acts that are so crucial for considerations of human welfare that they cannot be ignored.[3] Such acts include murder, rape, perjury, and the like. The list is not exhaustive, of course; various cultures express concern about a number of attitudes that seem to be connected with D'Arcy's moral-species acts (e.g., jealousy or hate). They also often add a number of ideal behaviors that express positive values (e.g., giving aid to others or showing love). But considerations of human welfare do supply a kind of "core" to the concept of morality. Thus if "religion" refers to ways of thinking which refer to a notion of sacred reality, "morality" may be taken to refer to ways of thinking, feeling, and acting that address considerations of human welfare. As some scholars put it, religious considerations lead one to think in "sacred-regarding" terms, moral considerations in "other-regarding" terms.

A third issue raised in discussing the relations between religion and morality is which of these two belief systems has priority. Much discussion of religion and morality presumes that the two are interconnected, and much in the history of religions supports that. There is also evidence that notions of sacred reality and considerations of human welfare may sometimes come into conflict. The Danish theologian Soren Kierkegaard (1813–1855), for example, discussed the moral problems raised by the biblical story of Abraham (told in Genesis 22). In the story, God commands Abraham to sacrifice his son, Isaac, as a way of testing Abraham's faith. Studies of ancient Near Eastern religion indicate that the practice of sacrificing the firstborn child (or ox, goat, and so forth) was commonly presented as a religious duty for men such as Abraham. In Jewish and Islamic thought, the story of Abraham poses no moral problems. Instead, it offers a legal precedent: Since, in the end, God provided a ram for the sacrifice, which Abraham substituted for Isaac, believers should understand that they may "redeem" their firstborn by offering up an animal in his or her stead.

Kierkegaard was not interested in such niceties of interpretation, however. For him, the central aspect of the story, that which made it beautiful and terrifying at the same time, was the paradox presented to Abraham by his two "loves": God and Abraham's son. Which came first, God or Isaac? Abraham was (evidently) willing to sacrifice his son at God's command, which indicates that his love of God took priority; this makes him a true "knight of faith," according to Kierkegaard. Abraham's love for God is an example of the religious point of view taking priority over the moral. As such, it is a lesson for all who claim to have faith—though, of course, the particulars of God's command to them may not be the same as the command to Abraham. For our purposes, it is not necessary to agree with Kierkegaard's analysis of the Abraham story. We might, for example, take the line of Immanuel Kant, who argued that if anyone thinks he or she hears a command like that of Abraham's, it is obligatory to ignore or renounce that directive. What is important to note is the question: In cases of conflict, which takes priority, religion or morality?[4]

RELIGION, MORALITY, AND JUSTIFICATION

Underlying all of these issues is the problem of *practical justification*, or the question of reasons for action. In this respect, the discussion of the relations between religion and morality is a part of the general study of *ethics*, or the inquiry into the nature of the good life. What does it mean to live well? Is a given course of action right or wrong? What standards should be used in evaluating particular acts or the persons who engage in them? The study of ethics focuses on such questions and involves an attempt to develop theories of the nature and foundation of human judgment—or, more specifically, of *right* human judgment.

Discussions of religion and morality play an important role in the general study of ethics. Such discussions deal in particular with the types of reasons persons give for the actions they engage in and the judgments they make. Suppose, for example, that a visitor to the United States listens to a public discussion of abortion. He or she hears arguments identified as prochoice or prolife. It will be clear to such a visitor that a great deal is at stake for those engaged in the discussion, and he or she may well wonder why there is so much passion on both sides of the issue.

If participants in the debate take the opportunity to answer this question, they will be engaging in a process of justification. They will give reasons in support of the fact that abortion is for them of crucial importance—so much so that they think it an issue on which it is difficult to compromise. The prolife side will emphasize the importance of respect for life and of rules against killing innocents. The prochoice side will refer to considerations of the mother's life and to the importance of personal liberty.

At some point, religious reasons may appear in the argument and, depending on the persons involved in the debate, may be of considerable importance. One or both of the presenters may refer to scriptural sources or to theological considerations. The prolife representative might say, for example, that the rule against killing innocents has religious significance, for it is one of the Ten Commandments (Exodus 20). He or she might go on to say that scripture presents God as interested and involved in the life of persons even before birth: "For Thou didst form my inward parts; Thou didst weave me in my mother's womb" (Psalms 139:13). Prochoice advocates might cite aspects of biblical law that imply the priority of the life of the mother over that of the fetus (Exodus 21:22–23). They might argue that the Christian emphasis on freedom and the long history of human abuses of political power establish a principle summarized as "the right to be left alone" in matters pertaining to intimate choices.

JUSTIFICATION: GENERAL CONSIDERATIONS

In any given case of action or judgment about the rightness of action, then, it is possible to ask for reasons. The attempt to provide reasons for actions and judgments involves persons and groups in the process of practical justification. The example of the arguments surrounding abortion presents one illustration of such a process. Below we present several others.

Before we move to particular cases, however, it is appropriate to identify a few general considerations connected with justification. One such consideration has already been identified: In analyzing a given case of justification, one may ask about the role of religion. Do religious reasons play a part in justifying particular judgments? If so, what part? How are appeals to religion related to other types of justification?

In addition, we may ask about at least three other factors. First, reflecting a general concern of ethics, it is possible to distinguish an appeal to duty, or a *deontological* approach to justification, from an appeal to consequences, or a *teleological* approach. The former appears, for example, whenever reasons such as "abortion is wrong because it violates the rule 'Thou shalt not kill,'" and "abortion is wrong because it violates the command of God" are given in support of a given group's antiabortion stance. The issue is one of formal adherence to a given standard of action, regardless of the good or bad consequences that follow.

Teleological appeals, on the other hand, appear whenever the process of justification involves giving reasons such as "if we say that some abortions are justified, we will open the door to many wrongful killings" and "if we permit abortion, it will make us—as individuals and as a society—less sensitive to the killing of innocents in other areas of action—abortion leads to euthanasia, which leads to doing away with 'surplus people,' which leads to the Holocaust," and so forth.[5]

Second, we may note that the distinction between appeals to duty and appeals to consequences can take on a special form in religious traditions. Particularly those traditions which indicate that present actions have consequences for one's future state—either in an afterlife or (as in Hinduism) in a future existence in this world—must deal with questions of motivation. The problem of justification includes responses to not only the question "Why do you say/do *x*?," but also to "Why should I be moral?" The ideal of many religious traditions is that one should do the right because it is right. A person recognizes his or her obligations and fulfills them, not because of selfish concern, but because of an overriding sense of duty, or because of his or her good character. Yet many religious traditions promise that there will, at some time in the future, be rewards for good conduct and punishments for wrongdoing. One might say that religious traditions often combine what the Scottish philosopher Francis Hutcheson called "justifying reasons" (arguments about the rightness or wrongness of particular actions or judgments) with "exciting reasons" (promises of rewards and threats of punishments, the purpose being to motivate persons to do what is right). In any case, it remains possible to ask what the role of appeals to rewards and punishments is in various instances of practical justification.

Third, we can further refine the distinction between deontological and teleological arguments in terms of the place of principles, rules, or other action-guides in justification. A *rule-deontological* approach, for example, not only measures acts in terms of appeals to duty but also indicates that duty can be known through guidelines that have a general form: Do not kill, do no harm, love your neighbor, and so forth. A *rule-teleological* approach makes reference to similar sorts of action-guides but understands them to be general statements concerning those types of behavior that, over the long course of personal or social experience, make for good consequences. On the other hand, *act-deontological* and *act-teleological* approaches to justification empha-size the importance of individual acts or situations in which judgments must be made. For these approaches, there are no generally valid guidelines by which human beings may know their duty or that can be said to yield good results. The most that can be said for rules, principles, or other norms is that they are "rules of thumb": They provide assistance but have little or no authority in justifying particular judgments.

PRACTICAL JUSTIFICATION: THREE CASES

For purposes of this discussion, let us consider three cases of practical justifi-cation in religious traditions. From Hinduism, we look at justifications for the caste system; in Islam, we examine the rules of war; from the Christian tradition, we consider the purpose of prayer. Following the discussion of particular examples, we consider some of the various patterns possible for the relationship between religion and morality.

As we begin, two caveats are in order. First, the issues discussed with respect to one tradition have parallels in others. For example, Christian tradition does not have a "caste system" *per se*, but it does have to deal with problems of social status and inequities. Similarly, it is not only Muslims who must deal with questions of war or Christians who struggle with ques-tions about prayer. Second, the purpose of discussing such cases is not to judge their rightness or wrongness; it is to understand the way that diverse groups have tried to give reasons for their beliefs and behavior. As we have emphasized elsewhere in this text, the primary goal of a phenomenological approach to religion is understanding, not judgment.

Hinduism: The Caste System

Our first case involves the Hindu tradition and the institution of the caste system. A major feature of traditional Indian life, the caste system has faded somewhat in the twenty-first century. Historically, however, this institution was central to the religious tradition we call Hinduism; so much so that one could say that Hinduism *is* the caste system.

What is the caste system, and how did it come into being? In its sim-plest form, *caste* is a way of institutionalizing certain forms of labor neces-sary to social life; it thus has parallels in many cultures. The four major castes—Brahmin, Kshatriya, Vaisya, and Sudra—represent the priestly, war-rior, merchant, and laboring classes. A fifth group, the "outcastes," is in effect outside the system and does the tasks that are beneath the other classes. In each case, one major aspect of the structure necessary to a traditional society is established and made secure by the fact that birth determines status, including one's assigned vocation or "duty" (dharma).[6]

Further, insofar as it is seen as a vivid illustration of certain religious ideas important to Hinduism, the system of caste explains people's varied and unequal destiny. Why is one born a Brahmin, another a Kshatriya, and still another an "outcaste"? The answer is found in the working of karma (see Chapter 7). In the process of birth-death-rebirth, justice is ultimately served, for persons reap the consequences of their actions. In this respect it is important that the various castes represent an order established at the beginning of all things. According to Hindu scriptures, the primordial sacrifice, in which Purusha, the "lord of immortality," is given as an offering, resulted in the "creation" of the various castes: From Purusha's mouth comes the Brahmin; his arms become the Kshatriya; his thighs become the Vaisya; from his feet comes the Sudra. The hierarchical implications of this order are clear: At the top of the system is the religious class; at the bottom are the laborers, and one's birth into any of the various spheres is just, as the outworking of karma.

The caste system thus represents an institution that serves to order society and that can be justified in religious terms. But it is also possible to think of the caste system in another way, one which has great interest from the standpoint of religion and morality.

Many scholars have noted that there was a great shift in Indian religious thought between 800 B.C.E. and 200 C.E. The most ancient scriptures of Hinduism, the various *Vedas*, appear in their final form by about the beginning of this period. They represent the central themes of a religious tradition that focuses on the attainment of such "this-worldly" goals as wealth, victory in war, and fame. Some of the latest texts to be included in the *Vedas*, however, seem to indicate a certain dissatisfaction with this focus. They ask about the origin of all things, and indicate a sense that the various gods and goddesses of the ancient myths may not be of much help in securing an understanding of the great questions of human existence: Who am I? What is my destiny?

> Who verily knows and who can here declare it, whence it [the world] was born and whence comes this creation? The Gods are later than this world's creation. Who knows then whence it first came into being? (Rig Veda 10:129)

These are difficult questions, and as the text continues, it seems that only a supreme God may know the answer—if an answer exists.

> He, the first origin of this creation, whether he formed it all or did not form it, Whose eye controls this world in highest heaven, he verily knows it, or perhaps he knows not. (Rig Veda 10:129)

Beginning about 700 B.C.E., the philosophical explorations collected in the Upanishads began to express the ideas that make up key aspects of classical Hinduism: the eternal core that is the true self of each individual being in creation (*atman*); the original and ultimate connection of that core with the power that gives life to all things, and fills the world (*brahman*); the union of atman and brahman as the goal of life; and the necessity of release (*moksha*) from the endless cycle of birth–death–rebirth by which karma governs worldly existence. The logical implication of this set of ideas is a kind of paradox: The goal of existence involves an escape from the laws that govern this-worldly life. The necessary condition of moksha is renunciation (*sannyasa*) of the restrictions imposed by karma in order to seek enlightenment and release from the cycle of birth–death–rebirth.

The social (and moral) implications of this conclusion are significant. The notion of renunciation implies a rejection of the social order of caste in favor of a religious ideal focused on otherworldly goals. One who renounces becomes a wandering ascetic, no longer fulfilling the vocation of his caste but rather living off the largesse of others. In a sense, the logic of the Upanishads is that of a rule-teleology, which holds out the promise of positive consequences for the enlightened sage, while denying the rule-deontological premise of duty toward society through the fulfillment of one's dharma.

Can a society survive if religious ideals are in such evident tension with the requirements of ordinary morality? To renounce the world of karma, and with it the caste system, would be to renounce the very fabric of traditional Indian life. What happens to marriage and family life, to business and the military, if people act on such an ideal?

In all probability, the teaching of the Upanishads on renunciation was an active ideal for only a narrow spectrum of Indian society. But the possibilities of the idea were evidently of concern to religious leaders, particularly Brahmins. For according to the *Laws of Manu* (collected between 200 B.C.E. and 200 C.E.), one who undertakes a life of renunciation without fulfilling the vocation of his caste commits a wrong. Members of the Brahmin, Kshatriya, and Vaisya castes may, even should, renounce the world in search of release. (Sudras are meant only to serve the other castes.) However, they must do so only when they are prepared—when their renunciation has the correct motivation. Thus renunciation should occur only after one has fulfilled certain duties. This idea is summarized by the teaching on the four "stages of life": student, householder, hermit, and ascetic. The first two correspond to the time of adolescence and adulthood, the latter to late-middle and old age. The student learns the duties of his caste; the householder marries, raises a family, and is a productive member of society; the hermit begins a gradual withdrawal from the world; and the ascetic attends to the problem of release.

The Laws of Manu and the teaching on the four stages may be seen as an attempt to reconcile the teleological concerns of renunciation and the deontological drive of the caste system. In other words, classical Hinduism developed ways to ease the tension posed by the peculiar relationship between religion and morality suggested in the Upanishads and the traditional system of caste. The Laws of Manu were not the only such attempt within classical Hinduism. The Bhagavad Gita (from about 200 C.E.) may be read as an attempt to reconcile religious and moral concern—in this case by reinterpreting the ideal of renunciation in terms of "detachment." One may, one even must, fulfill the duty set by birth into a caste—that is, one's karma—but does so with the understanding that karma is not the ultimate reality. Thus a person cultivates a spirit of detachment. "He who dedicates his action to the Spirit, without any personal attachment to them, he is no more tainted by sin than the water lily is wetted by water" (5:10).

Islam: The Justification and Limitation of War

Our second case deals with the problem of war as reflected in the Islamic tradition. As a general matter, war is one aspect of the problem of force in human relations. Although many, if not most, religious traditions view the use of force as a necessary feature of worldly existence, they do not thereby take it lightly. In particular, lethal force is a matter that requires justification. In some sense, one of the characters in Edward Bondi's play *Bingo: Scenes of Money and Death* speaks a human truth when he says: "Only a god or a devil can write in other men's blood, and not ask why they spilt it and what it cost." [7] The reasons why this is so may vary between and within diverse religious and moral traditions. Lethal force may be problematic because of a rule against killing, for example, or because it is considered an inefficient way to achieve goals. In most religious traditions, it is possible to differentiate at least some acts of killing from murder, and thus to speak of killing that is just or right. But the processes of justification always seem to be present, because there do not seem to be any religious traditions that make a virtue out of killing, in and of itself.

In the case of Islam, discussion of the religious and moral dimensions of war appear very early, in connection with the life and work of Muhammad. Following the initial revelation of the Qur'an and call of Muhammad to prophesy, Muhammad and his followers were persecuted in Mecca. According to Islamic tradition, such persecution ranged from taunts and jeers to economic boycott, eventually including physical torture and an attempt on the Prophet's life. Under such pressure, Muhammad and his community undertook the *hijra* or emigration to Medina in 622 C.E. (the year 1 in Muslim understanding). It was in connection with these developments that Muhammad received the following revelation:

> Sanction is given unto those who fight because they have been wronged; and Allah is indeed Able to give them victory; Those who have been driven from their homes only because they said: Our Lord is Allah—For had it not been for Allah's repelling some men by means of others, cloisters and churches and oratories and mosques, wherein the name of Allah is oft mentioned, would assuredly have been pulled down. Verily Allah helpeth one who helpeth Him. Lo! Allah is Strong, Almighty. . . . (Qur'an 22:39–40)

With this in mind, the Muslim community engaged in a series of raids on trading caravans traveling to and from Mecca. The raids became a war, eventually resulting in victory for the Muslim side and a situation in which Muhammad could say, prior to his death in 632 C.E., that "Arabia is solidly for Islam." War is not a thing to be undertaken lightly—it requires justification; for example, the defense of religion against those who would persecute believers. But given the presence of a just cause, war may become necessary as a means to achieve God's purposes on earth.

Following Muhammad's death, the Muslim community quickly expanded its influence into most of what is now called the Middle East. According to many scholars, the motivation for this expansion was quite mixed. But a number of (Sunni) classical Islamic jurists, drawing not only on the Qur'an but also on reports of the Prophet's words and deeds (*hadith*), legal precedents, and various forms of "independent reasoning," developed a set of rules governing the resort to war that made the expansion of Islamic territory a duty. The sole exception to this general rule involved the jurists of the (minority) Shi'i groups, who for various reasons argued that the only justified wars were defensive and ruled out wars of expansion.[8]

The justifications given for this set of rules were by and large religious. The Qur'an had taught that human beings were by nature knowledgeable about the right way to live. Nevertheless, humanity did not live up to its nature. "Lo! We offered the trust [responsibility to do the right] unto the heavens and the earth and the hills, but they shrank from bearing it and were afraid of it. And man assumed it. Lo! he hath proved a tyrant and a fool . . ." (33:72). Given the choice, most of humanity takes the road of heedlessness, and proves disobedient to God's commands. Only a few prove themselves upright, pious, practicing the submission (al-islam) to God.

The eternal choice before human beings was (and is) clear: submission or heedlessness. Classical Sunni jurists held that these choices had been institutionalized: Submission was the rule in the territories governed by Islam; in other territories, the rule was heedlessness. The territory of Islam was an abode of peace, order, and stability; the territory of heedlessness was the territory of war. This was true internally, because heedlessness leads to strife; externally, because Muslims were duty bound to try and expand the territory of Islam as a way of "pushing back" the intrusion of heedlessness into human society.

It is important to note that the classical jurists did not believe that war would make converts to Islam. The territory of Islam was not fully Muslim; far from it. Jews, Christians, and other "peoples of the book" were protected, or at least tolerated, under Islamic law, and with certain restrictions practiced their faith freely in the territory of Islam. The point of calling the territory "Islamic" was to indicate its submission to Islamic *government*. The Qur'an declared, "There is no compulsion in religion" (2:256). One cannot force another person to have faith; true belief must come from the heart. What one can do is to try to expand the influence of Islam, to remind people of the standards of good conduct that God had written on their hearts by nature, and to limit the harm done by heedlessness.

To that end, the Sunni jurists said that all Muslims must participate in a struggle to expand the influence of Islam. This struggle, called *jihad*, is broader than war, though war is its ultimate (final) resource. A prominent tradition says that Muslims must struggle to command the good and forbid the evil with the heart, tongue, and sword. The heart signifies the struggle to become a true Muslim. That is the "greater jihad." The tongue signifies missionary efforts: teaching and preaching the word of God. The sword is a last resort. If a community of people does not accept the invitation to acknowledge the supremacy of Islam, it becomes subject to war—so the Sunni jurists taught.

Such jurists also taught that the jihad of the sword must follow certain rules. Common sense and the Qur'an both taught that bloodshed is not to be taken lightly. There must be reasons given; one must make sure that wars are "holy" in the sense of "approved by God." Specifically, there must be a just cause. The war must be either to expand the territory of Islam or to defend that territory from attack, and the enemy must give provocation to the Muslims. In the case of wars of defense, the provocation is the act of aggression. But in the case of wars to expand Islamic territory, the provocation is failure to acknowledge the supremacy of Islam, indicated by the refusal of the Muslims' invitation to (1) become Muslims or (2) acknowledge Islamic rule by paying tribute. If the enemy refused this invitation, then it was the duty of the leader of the Muslims to make war against them, provided that there was a reasonable hope of success.

It is possible then to justify war to expand the influence of Islam, according to the jurists. Indeed, it is incumbent on the leader of the Muslims to lead the community in the jihad. Thus under certain conditions war could become an obligation. One might say that teleological considerations (the goal of expanding Islamic territory) provide the context for certain deontological tendencies in the jurists' teaching. Not that the "ends justify the means," at least as that is usually meant. In this regard, we must note that the Sunni jurists do not say that "anything goes" in war. A holy warrior fights in a holy fashion—he does not "cheat or commit treachery, nor [does he] mutilate or kill children, women, or old men."[9] War is an activity governed by certain rule-deontological considerations. In the end, the goal of justice and peace provides the context for an idea of war "in the path of God."

The example of classical Sunni teaching on war suggests that considerations of religion may supplement or fill out moral judgment. War can be justified, but when? By whom? How? The answers are: for the sake of religion; by the duly constituted head of the Muslim community; according to God's commands and the example of the Prophet. War, as other aspects of human existence, is governed by the commands of God.

This classical understanding is not necessarily the teaching of modern Muslims. Most modern interpreters in fact argue that the Qur'an and the example of the Prophet justify war only when it is fought for defensive purposes. Yet, since the attacks on New York and Washington, D.C., on September 11, 2001, many public figures in the United States and other Western countries question the validity of this modern claim. The *Declaration on Armed Struggle against Jews and Crusaders*, a document published in February 1998 and signed by Osama bin Laden, among others, asserts that contemporary political conditions justify the judgment that fighting against Americans and their allies is a duty for each and every Muslim able to do so, in any country where it is possible. The *Declaration* further specfies that such fighting should aim at both military and civilian targets.

In response, many Muslims offer criticisms of bin Laden, of the program of al-Qaeda with which he is associated, and of other, like-minded groups. These criticisms dispute the judgments of the *Declaration* and other pronouncements of al-Qaeda. There is much to discuss here, not least the way that bin Laden and others see their program as connected with establishing and maintaining a kind of social-political order in which religious, moral, and legal values are interdependent in ways rather different than in the United States and other Western states. It is also important to note the fact that Muslims disagree about these matters, and that all sides refer to the authority of the Qur'an and the example of the Prophet in support of their judgments.

Christianity: Why Pray?

For our final case, we focus on *prayer* and on Christian discussions of it. It is important to note that prayer is connected with the general question of worship and as such is related to some of the issues discussed in Chapter 5.

Why pray? In some ways this seems an odd question. To a religious person, especially in the context of a tradition stressing faith in a God characterized as personal, prayer may seem obvious. People pray to express the feelings of their hearts: joy, sorrow, love. They pray out of adoration or to confess their sins. They offer petitions for the things they desire. Christian reflection on prayer stresses such dimensions, as do most religious traditions in which prayer plays a part. And as in other traditions, Christianity offers to people a number of model prayers such as the Psalms, and especially the Lord's Prayer:

> Our Father, who art in heaven, hallowed be thy name. Thy kingdom come. Thy will be done, on earth as it is in heaven. Give us this day our daily bread. And forgive us our trespasses, as we forgive those who trespass against us. And lead us not into temptation: but deliver us from evil.[10]

Yet prayer does not always come naturally—for Christians or others. For this reason, prayer is said to be a duty. Even when one does not feel the need to pray, the act of praying may be important. Why? Once one thinks in these terms, the question of justification may occur. Is prayer obligatory? If so, then one may ask for reasons.

Further, if there are some prayers that are models, what makes them so? Why are some prayers better than others? Or does the form of prayer really matter? These also are questions of justification.

Finally, what does prayer accomplish? At least some prayers involve petitions—requests of God for help, guidance, or even for the coming of God's kingdom. But if God knows everything, and if God's will is in some sense inevitable, why pray? For those Christians who hold such beliefs (as many do, albeit in various forms) some prayers, at least, can raise the question: Why pray? What sorts of answers can be given?

According to some Christian writers, prayer is justified by the command of God, purely and simply. For example, Karl Barth, the Swiss thinker extolled by some as the foremost Protestant theologian of the twentieth century, wrote:

> A man prays because he is permitted to do so by God, because he may pray, and because this very permission has become a command. It is true that to pray is to ask. It is thus true that prayer is the stating of a privation and desire, the expression of the certainty of finding it satisfied in and from and through God, the uttering of a request that this may really happen. But the basis and origin of this utterance, that which makes it right asking and therefore right prayer, can consist neither in the privation and desire, the certainty, nor the asking.[11]

For Barth, one never asks for further justification: There can be none. To be sure, prayer may accomplish certain ends. It may make one a better person, in some sense. It certainly should increase one's awareness of God. Petitions may be granted; desires may be fulfilled. But these things are not the point of prayer. According to Barth, prayer is an expression of the true relationship between God and humanity, in which God is Lord and humanity is God's "covenant partner"—that is, the creature to whom God speaks and who is invited to do God's will. Prayer is thus a matter of obligation, established by the command of God. Barth's reasoning is strictly deontological and refers only to religious considerations. One could say further that Barth's reasoning illustrates a kind of act-deontology, since he stresses that the obligation to pray cannot be founded on a general rule. True prayer results from human beings hearing the command of God.

A different line of thought is expressed by John Calvin, the famed "Reformer of Geneva" during the Protestant Reformation.[12] In one sense (Calvin indicates) prayer is justified by God's command, given in the Bible. He thus provides a justification that is deontological, and refers to religious reasons. One could say further that the justification illustrates a kind of rule-deontology, because Calvin's religious reasons include the commands of

God specified in the Bible as general rules: for example in I Thessalonians 5:17: "pray without ceasing."

In another sense, however, prayer is obligatory as an act of natural justice. There is, according to Calvin, a rule known to natural reason (that is human reason as such) that indicates that one owes thanks to a benefactor. Anyone who reflects will see that God is the source of all life and good; for the Christian, this should be doubly obvious because he or she acknowledges God's gift of salvation in Christ. Prayer is one way to express thanksgiving and is therefore justified as a way to give a great benefactor (God) that which is owed.

Still, this does not settle all of our questions about prayer. Especially when one thinks of petitionary prayer, there is the problem of God's knowing what is necessary "before we ask." For Calvin, this is a particular problem in connection with prayers that ask for the gift of faith. Faith is a gift of God "so that no one may boast" (Ephesians 2:9). If prayer is a prerequisite for the reception of this gift, then it is not really a gift. Beyond this, if God governs history and decides the eternal destiny of humanity, why should God be moved by human petitions "as if he were drowsily blinking or even sleeping until he is aroused by our voice"?

Calvin's answer is that such reasoning reveals a misunderstanding of prayer. People who ask such questions "do not observe to what end the Lord instructed his people to pray, for he ordained it not so much for his own sake as for ours." In particular, God ordained prayer so that human beings might grow in awareness of God's grace and, insofar as they perceive that their prayers are answered, might be strengthened in their faith. Prayer is "familiar conversation" with God, the Father of life, and a way of cultivating certain character traits: reverence, a sincere sense of need, humility, and hope. In this respect, prayer also increases a person's disposition to love his or her neighbor and makes a contribution to moral behavior. Prayer for others (intercessory prayer) provides a good example. For Calvin, religion animates the moral life, providing reinforcement and motivation for doing one's duty toward others.

The implication of Calvin's comments is that prayer is not only justified in deontological terms; it is also an act justified by certain ends. Teleological considerations are important, too, and in this connection, prayer can become a morally relevant act, even while it remains preeminently a religious concern.

RELIGION AND MORALITY: PATTERNS

What conclusions can we draw from the examples of religion and morality discussed in this chapter? Recognizing that our cases represent only a few of the possibilities presented by the history of religions, let us consider the following patterns in the religion-morality relation.

1. In the case of Hinduism and the caste system, there is evidence of religion and morality in *tension*. Insofar as the ideal of renunciation indicates the priority of sacred-regarding over other-regarding concerns, religion and morality appear to be in competition. This is not the whole story of ethics in Hinduism, of course, nor is it unique to classical Hinduism. If we consider the example of Soren Kierkegaard, religion and morality may be in tension in some aspects of Christian thought. Indeed, the gospels themselves set forth sayings of Jesus that do not rest easily with ordinary, moral concerns: "Do not think that I came to bring peace on the earth; I did not come to bring peace, but a sword. For I came to set a man against his father, and a daughter against her mother, and a daughter-in-law against her mother-in-law" (Matthew 10:34–35). Medieval Christianity presents further examples of religion and morality in tension, as do certain types of Buddhism.

2. In the case of Islam, one finds evidence of religion *complementing* and filling out morality. Ordinary moral concern suggests that war is an act in need of justification. In particular, a theory that war is sometimes justified must specify when war can be justified, by whom, and how. From the standpoint of classical Sunni teaching, religion supplied answers to the questions, pointing to the necessity of extending or defending the borders of the territory of Islam, at the discretion of the leader of the Muslim community, according to the command of God. Again, the general thesis of religion as a complement to morality is not unique to classical Sunni Islam. With respect to questions of war, medieval Christianity taught that some wars could be considered just because of a connection with religion; that in such cases, the declaration of war lay with appropriate religious authorities; and that holy warriors should adhere to holy standards. With respect to other problems, and to general considerations of ethics, we should add that Christianity, Islam, and Judaism are traditions that by and large emphasize that religion complements the moral life by sharpening, extending, and strengthening human perceptions of the good, and human motivation to perform it.

3. Christian discussion of the question "why pray?" provides evidence of religion *animating* the moral life, that is, providing reinforcement to the will to do what is good. One does not pray primarily in order to build up moral resolve, of course. Prayer is preeminently a religious act, in Christianity as well as in other religious traditions. But it is interesting to note that John Calvin's discussion of the justification of prayer points in this direction. One could cite other examples of religion animating the moral life in the teaching of Christianity, Judaism, and Islam on martyrdom; again, in Buddhist emphasis on meditation, or in the Confucian approach to ritual.

One should only expect that such patterns would recur in numerous religious contexts. The relationship between religion and morality is not one of identity but of two distinct concerns related to the human capacity to order and understand the world. Because both command the attention of humanity, it is only natural that religious traditions should seek to comprehend the relations between the sacred quest and the quest for the good life. Sometimes in harmony, sometimes in discord, religion and morality make their diverse claims to loyalty—and contribute to the richness of human experience.

NOTES

1. In *Zorach v. Clauson*, 343 U.S., 313.

2. Ronald Reagan, in a speech to an ecumenical prayer breakfast during the 1984 Republican National Convention, *New York Times*, August 24, 1984, p. A11.

3. Eric D'Arcy, *Human Acts: An Essay in Their Moral Evaluation* (Oxford: Oxford University Press, 1963), p. 25. Note also the discussion of David Little and Sumner B. Twiss, Jr. in *Comparative Religious Ethics: A New Method* (San Francisco: Harper & Row, 1978), pp. 24–52, from which we draw much of our discussion of the definition of morality.

4. For Kierkegaard's analysis, see his *Fear and Trembling*, published with his *The Sickness unto Death*, trans. Walter Lowrie (Garden City, N.Y.: Doubleday/Anchor, 1954).

5. It is important to note that *teleological* is a wider category of argument than what is usually called "utilitarian." The former can include religious ideals, so that particular judgments are justified in terms of whether they are conducive to salvation, as well as the utilitarian's "do those things that make for the greatest good for the greatest number" of people.

6. Each caste is subdivided into units called *jati*, but for our purposes it is unnecessary to go into these.

7. Edward Bondi, *Bingo: Scenes of Money and Death* (London: Eyre Methuen, 1974), p. 42. Some of the material in this section appears in different form in John Kelsay, "Religion, Morality, and the Governance of War: The Case of Classical Islam," *Journal of Religious Ethics* (Fall 1990). Used by permission.

8. This difference relates to the Shi'i position on the true leadership of the Muslim community. In the absence of a leader designated by God to rule, there is no authority competent to lead a war to expand Islamic territory, and this situation will continue until the *mahdi* (rightly guided one) appears.

9. This prophetic tradition is cited by the jurist al-Shaybani in his *Kitab al-Siyar*, trans. Majid Khadduri as *The Islamic Law of Nations* (Baltimore, Md.: Johns Hopkins University Press, 1966), pp. 91–92.

10. Adapted from Bard Thompson, ed., *Liturgies of the Western Church* (Cleveland: World, 1961), p. 79. We note that many, if not most, Christians reciting the Lord's Prayer would add in some form the doxology found in Matthew 6:13: "For Thine is the kingdom, and the power, and the glory forever." Some of the material in this section appears in different form in John Kelsay, "Prayer and Ethics: Reflections on Calvin and Barth," *Harvard Theological Review*, 82 (1989), pp. 169–184. Copyright 1989 by the President and Fellows of Harvard College. Reprinted by permission.

11. *Church Dogmatics*, trans. A. T. Mackay et al. (Edinburgh: T. & T. Clark, 1961), III, no. 4, p. 91.

12. Calvin's most sustained discussion of prayer is found in his *Institutes of the Christian Religion*, vol. III, p. 20. All quotes in the paragraphs that follow are from the edition of John T. McNeill, trans. and ed. Ford Lewis Battles (Philadelphia: Westminster Press, 1977).

THOUGHT EXPERIMENTS

1. Consider a basic precept of Judaism and Christianity: "You shall love the Lord your God with all your heart, and with all your soul, and with all your strength, and with all your mind; and your neighbor as yourself" (Luke 10:27). Some writers understand this "double love command" to illustrate the central relation and divergence of religion and morality. Do you think this is so? Are the two commandments in tension? Complementary? Representative of some other pattern?
2. The Muslim theologian al-Ash'ari (d. 935 C.E.) argued that the only sure basis for moral knowledge was the command of God made known in revealed texts such as the Qur'an. He argued that God was the Supreme Lord of the worlds, whose commands were always to be obeyed; and he went on to say that if God commanded human beings to lie, then lying would be obligatory. Does this seem right to you? Why or why not? What view of the religion-morality relation is suggested by al-Ash'ari's comment?
3. The pacifist scholar Roland Bainton argued in his study of *Christian Attitudes Toward War and Peace* (Nashville: Abingdon Press, 1960) that holy wars—wars fought for religious reasons—tend to become crusades—wars in which the enemy is counted as demonic and worthy of total extermination. As you think of wars in the twentieth century, is this true?
4. The statement of former President Reagan quoted at the outset of this chapter continues: "We need it [religion] because we are imperfect. And our government needs the church, because only those humble enough to admit they are sinners can bring to democracy the tolerance it requires in order to survive." Consider this statement in the light of the patterns identified in this chapter: religion in tension with, complementing, and/or animating morality. Which of these are reflected in Reagan's remarks?

SUGGESTIONS FOR FURTHER READING

BROAD, C. D., *Five Types of Ethical Theory*. Paterson, N.J.: Littlefield, Adams, 1959. Comparison and contrast of the ethical theories represented by leading figures in the history of Western philosophy.

KING, WINSTON L., *In the Hope of Nibbana*. LaSalle, Ill.: Open Court, 1964. Anthropological study of ethics in the Theravada Buddhist tradition.

ROBINSON, PAUL, ed., *Just War in Comparative Perspective*. Burlington, Vt.: Ashgate, 2003. Includes an essay by John Kelsay discussing the 1998 *Declaration* signed by Osama bin Laden and others.

9 The Quest for Salvation

The quest for salvation is, according to some, the essence of the religious life. That seems fair enough for some religious traditions. One may certainly understand Christianity as a religion of salvation; at least for many Christians, the fundamental question of life is the one asked by the Philippian jailer: "What must I do to be saved?" (Acts 16:30). This question resonates through much of Christianity, especially because it is connected with the notion of life after death: Salvation implies a personal existence that continues after death, which is immeasurably enriched by the fact that one lives in the presence of God.

The notion of salvation thus has a very particular Christian "ring" about it. But it can also be applied more generally in the study of religion and indeed in the study of human culture. In fact, there is a peculiarity in the idea "salvation," which suggests that it can be applied to a variety of religious and nonreligious phenomena.

To be saved, in the fundamental sense, is to be rescued. That much is clear from the dictionary definitions and from ordinary conversation. When a ship is sinking, a person is drowning, a bear is attacking an isolated camper, or a child is trapped inside a collapsed building, they need salvation from the danger that threatens. They may be, as we say, "saved" from the danger confronting them.

The great religions ask that one expand on these ideas. Think of someone who is healthy, on firm ground (literally and/or figuratively), and not visibly threatened by any outside danger. Does this person need salvation, too?

Difficult as such a proposition seems, most of the great religions judge such persons to be in need of salvation. It is not only those having immediate and pressing needs who must ask, "What must I do to be saved?" All persons need salvation—though the precise nature of the need and the means of salvation vary considerably in connection with diverse notions of sacred reality. When Buddhists speak of enlightenment, Hindus of moksha, or Christians of eternal life, they are all speaking about salvation. But they are also indicating the diversity within that concept: For the Buddhist, the danger is ignorance and salvation lies in mystical perception; for the Hindu, the problem is the cycle of birth–death–rebirth and the solution is found in liberation; for the Christian, salvation is deliverance from death—not just as a physical end to life but as separation from God—through the power of the risen Christ. And these are only a few examples of the rich variety present in religious notions of salvation. Indeed, in the East, the term "liberation" may be the equivalent of Western notions of salvation.

In this chapter, we are interested in exploring this variety. What is it that unites religious (and to a certain extent nonreligious) humanity in the quest for salvation? What distinguishes various notions of the quest for salvation? Perhaps at the deepest level, salvation indicates the human desire not to be consigned to oblivion but to affirm that human experience counts for something. If that is so, it is understandable that the quest for salvation quickly takes on religious overtones. The central, distinguishing feature of religion is the affirmation of a notion of sacred reality that, among other things, addresses problems of ordering and understanding human life.

CONCEPTS OF SALVATION

If we consider the variety of ways human beings speak of salvation, we may be quickly overwhelmed. Here we discuss diverse concepts of salvation in terms of the answers people give to a few simple questions: *Who* is to be saved? *Where* does salvation occur? Such questions lead to a set of patterns, which may be outlined as follows:

	This World	Other World
Individual	1	2
Group	3	4

Four patterns within the general notion of salvation may thus be distinguished: *individual salvation, in this world* or *in another world,* and *group salvation,* which similarly can be either this-worldy or otherworldly.

Within each of these patterns, we may make further distinctions related to the definition of salvation: salvation from what and to what end? With respect to individual salvation in this world, for example, we can distinguish emphases on the search for meaning, the desire to be remembered, and the ideal of completion. As we move from this-worldly to otherworldly notions of salvation, ideas of an existence that transcends the boundaries of death become more significant. By contrast, this-worldly salvation has distinctly secular overtones.

INDIVIDUAL SALVATION IN THIS WORLD

As already indicated, concepts of individual, this-worldly salvation may be distinguished in terms of emphasis on (1) the search for meaning, (2) the desire to be remembered, and (3) the ideal of completion. In each case, the idea of an existence that continues after death plays only a very small role in the notion of salvation, if indeed it plays any role at all.

The Search for Meaning

In connection with the search for meaning, salvation involves a struggle with despair. Recall the discussion of the Holocaust in Chapter 7, in which we indicated that the central questions have to do with the meaning of the suffering endured by victims of the Holocaust. The real danger of the Holocaust is that there may not be an answer to this question—that is the implication of much modern thought.

In his short novel *Dawn*, Elie Wiesel tells the story of a Holocaust survivor who participates in the struggle to establish the state of Israel.[1] Required to perform actions that he considers evil yet necessary, the survivor feels that he is playing God. It is an uncomfortable role, yet one that is necessary in view of the need for a Jewish state. Here Wiesel's writing is reminiscent of the notion that the creation and maintenance of Israel is an obligatory response to the Holocaust, associated with the need to affirm that the victims did not die in vain. Wiesel's survivor feels impelled to participate in the creation of the new state as a way to give meaning to his suffering and that of others, even as he feels that the dead whom he loved might not approve his present course of action. He seeks for meaning in a world filled with contradictions, in which traditional values no longer seem valid.

Wiesel's novel presents a stark picture of the search for salvation through meaning. There are less radical examples. The popular desire to make one's life "count for something" provides any number of illustrations: The Peace Corps volunteer, the medical researcher seeking a cure for a deadly disease, the husband and wife who devote themselves to promoting strong family relationships can all be examples of the search for meaning. In a world filled with ambiguity, in which disorder and danger seem rampant, the search for meaning is an attempt to bring order to the world—at least as it affects personal life and intimate relations. As such it is one aspect of the quest for salvation.

The Desire to Be Remembered

The Renaissance of the fifteenth and early sixteenth centuries is famous as the time of Michelangelo, Raphael, Leonardo da Vinci, and others. The artistic works produced by such persons have had a great impact on Western culture. Part of the reason for such a flourishing of visual symbols was the resurgence of the ideals of classical Greece and Rome—among them, the desire for glory or, more to the point, for fame. To be remembered was a part of the motivation for the creation of such works, driving the artists and also those who provided financial support for their work.

The relations between the desire for fame and the Christian notions of salvation common at the time of the Renaissance are rather problematic. Some scholars emphasize that the Renaissance was dominated by humanist concerns rather than religious ones. And yet, the humanist desire to be remembered, to have one's work established, is not without parallels in the history of religion. In Islam, for example, the construction of mosques or, in some cases, tombs served at times as a way for exceptional personages to ensure their place in history. The famous Taj Mahal at Agra is one such memorial, signifying the devotion of Shah Jahan (who ruled in Moghul India 1627–1658 C.E.) to a woman (for whom the building was to be a tomb) and to the concept of Islamic architecture. Less grandiose but equally important to Islam is the notion of *waqf*, by which one leaves a testament to the community (money, land, etc.) to be used for religious purposes.

Perhaps most common in the history of religions is the tendency to view children as ensuring one's heritage. According to the Bible, children are a "gift of the Lord; The fruit of the womb is a reward" (Psalm 127:3). In the context of the Hebrew Bible, one who has no children suffers a terrible misfortune, second only to one whose children neglect him or her in old age. Certain traditions associated with East Asia carry this even further. In Japan, for example, certain family members (those associated with the paternal family tree) are raised to be sources of spiritual blessing upon death and for the performance of purification rites. For such persons, not to be remembered by their children is a curse, causing them to wander about the earth as a kind of ghost, bringing misfortune to the living rather than blessings.[2] Such notions point to the fact that in many cases concepts of salvation overlap—in the Japanese case, otherworldly considerations begin to impinge upon the basically this-worldly desire to be remembered.

The impulse to be remembered is all around us. Families leave monies to endow hospitals, schools, public spaces, and so on "In Memory of ———" as a way of ensuring some remembrance of a person now dead but who is granted a certain kind of "immortality" through the work named for him or her. Even the inscription of a person's name on a burial monument is meant to keep this person remembered. The ways in which we memorialize death reflect a deep desire to keep alive the meaning of a person who has died.

The Ideal of Completion

Ideals of completion vary with respect to specifics. When we think, for example, of the Taoist sage who becomes one with the power at work in all of nature, we may think of completion. Consider the statement attributed to Chuang Tzu (fourth century B.C.E.):

> The pure man of old knew neither to love life nor to hate death. He did not rejoice in birth, nor did he resist death. Without any concern he came and without any concern he went, that was all. He did not forget his beginning nor seek his end. He accepted (his body) with pleasure, and forgetting (life and death) he returned to (the natural state). He did not violate Tao with his mind, and he did not assist Nature with man. This is what is meant by a pure man.[3]

In another context, Chuang Tzu states: "The universe and I exist together, and all things and I are one. . . . Let us not proceed. Let us let things take their own course."[4]

We may also think of the ideal of completion, however, in connection with the Buddhist goal of enlightenment. To achieve Nirvana is the ultimate attainment, enabling one to see the world for what it is. The mystical goal of a certain state of mind, attained after much disciplined effort, exemplifies salvation through completion.

There are also less mystical versions of this pattern. For example, when Muhammad visited the Ka'ba in 632 C.E. (the year of his death), he proclaimed to his followers that their religion had been perfected—completed—in the sense that the Arabian peninsula was now solidly Islamic. Again, in Martin Luther King, Jr.'s famous address in Memphis, on the eve of his assassination, he invoked the example of Moses and told his coworkers in the civil rights movement: "I may not get there [the just society] with you. But I have seen the Promised Land."

Finally, we note the custom, widespread now in North America, of cremating the dead and then scattering the ashes either over the ocean, in the countryside, or on a mountainside as a way of completing the cycle of life: returning human remains to the earth from whence people first came with the (often implicit) desire that their remains may be part of the never-ending cycle of fertility and new birth in the world.

INDIVIDUAL SALVATION IN ANOTHER WORLD

If the search for meaning, the desire to be remembered, and the ideal of completion represent distinctive aspects of an individual, this-worldly notion of salvation, what are the comparable ideas within an individual, otherworldly notion? Again we discuss three patterns: (1) joining the spirit world, (2) cosmic cycling or expansion, and (3) the idea of judgment. In contrast to the secular motifs associated with individual, this-worldly salvation, otherworldly salvation requires the belief in an existence that transcends the boundaries of physical death.

Joining the Spirit World

The least complex concept of an existence that transcends physical death is an expectation that one will somehow "join the spirit world." Certain traditions, for example, assume that death is followed by a transition, a kind of rebirth into a new existence. This model is evidently very ancient. In primitive burial sites skeletal remains appear to indicate that the dead were buried in the fetal position, perhaps awaiting rebirth into the spirit world. Where might such a world be found? That is difficult to say; but anthropological data include tribal stories that attempt to locate the place of the spirits—say, on a distant island. In other contexts, spirits are likened to air, and traditions speak of the spirits dwelling in the sky.

In ancient Greece and Rome, and also in the Hebrew Bible, we find indications of a spirit world located somewhere "below." The Hebrew *Sheol* refers to burial places, especially cave-tombs that apparently were connected with particular clans. The story of Jacob or Israel (Genesis 25–50) ends with a reference to such a place. In Genesis 49:29–30, Jacob charged his sons:

> I am about to be gathered to my people; bury me with my fathers in the cave that is in the field of Ephron the Hittite, in the cave that is in the field of Machpelah, which is before Mamre, in the land of Canaan, which Abraham bought along with the field from Ephron the Hittite for a burial.

Jacob goes on to say that his ancestors and his own wife are buried there, and he wishes to join them.

A tradition of burial sites does not in itself imply an afterlife. There is in fact much scholarly controversy as to the precise nature of conceptions of afterlife in the Hebrew Bible. With respect to Sheol, the references are rather obscure. Scholars are not sure what the word itself means. Again, the spirits in Sheol are described as "shades," which perhaps implies the shadow of one's former self or the kind of entity some would call ghosts.

In Greek and Roman tales the place of the dead is called by various names, among them *Hades* or *Dis*. Located underground, it is inhabited by spirits who, while recognizable, are mere shadows of living beings. Virgil's *Aeneid*, for example, describes the various levels of Dis in great detail. But when the reader encounters Achilles, the great warrior, he or she is told that life in this world is far superior to even the highest level of existence in Dis. Virgil, of course, draws on the much more ancient traditions found in Homer's *Iliad*, which expresses the very same ideas.

Cosmic Cycling or Expansion

A second type of individual, otherworldly salvation posits the existence of an eternal soul, spirit, or mind that experiences a cosmic cycling or expansion. The former implies rebirth and is central to Hinduism and some forms of Buddhism. Some versions of such cycling depict the eternal spirit as leaving this world and journeying into a world of spirits, where it experiences a time of rest and renewal prior to reentering the world of human existence. Stories that reflect this notion may also indicate that the eternal spirit can choose when and where it will be reborn. Most often, however, the force called karma is said to determine these facts, so that the timing and even more the status of the spirit's rebirth depend on actions undertaken in its previous existence. *Reincarnation* exemplifies one type of cosmic cycling, in which spirits are reborn in new, usually human existences; *transmigration* refers to another type of cycling, in which the eternal soul may be reborn into human or nonhuman forms of existence.

Closely related to cosmic cycling is the idea of cosmic expansion. Earthly existence, it is said, is limited and confining. Salvation is achieved when the eternal spirit joins with a larger consciousness. Thus in Hinduism the process of cycling ends when the spirit achieves *moksha* or liberation, thus joining the infinite, Brahman. In Mahayana Buddhism, expansion and cycling are similarly related.

In Western culture, similar ideas are often associated with Plato and his intellectual offspring. The idea of the *logos* or absolute reason provides a basis for this association, particularly when Plato's writings are taken to mean that individual persons are in a way participants in the logos, whose goal is to shed attachments to the physical world (the body, it is said, is the "tomb of the soul") and thus achieve union with absolute reason. In the platonic view, the physical world is but a shadow of the ultimate—just the reverse of those notions associated with "joining the spirit world."

The influence of platonic conceptions of the logos and the soul was, historically speaking, enormous, particularly with respect to the development of Christian thought. Such important teachers as Clement and Origen of Alexandria (second and third centuries C.E.) were influenced heavily by platonic ideas and identified Christian notions of eternal life with the union of the eternal soul and the logos, here described as God. Although certain aspects of the platonic position—in particular, the idea of the body as the prison of the soul—could not be sustained by Christians reflecting on the creation stories of Genesis 1 and 2, wherein God calls the created world good, the idea of an eternal soul did remain a central theme in the Christian tradition.

The Idea of Judgment

The idea of judgment or, more to the point, a Day of Judgment is central to notions of salvation in Orthodox Judaism, Christianity, Islam, and other religious traditions. The Qur'an provides some of the most outstanding illustrations of the theme, for example in "The Cleaving":

> When the heaven is cleft asunder
> When the planets are dispersed,
> When the seas are poured forth,
> And the sepulchres are overturned,
> A soul will know what it hath sent before (it)
> and what left behind . . .
> Lo! the righteous verily will be in delight.
> And lo! the wicked verily will be in hell;
> They will burn therein on the Day of Judgment,
> And will not be absent thence.
> Ah, what will convey unto thee what the Day of
> Judgment is!
> Again, what will convey unto thee what the Day of
> Judgment is!
> A day on which no soul hath power at all for any
> (other) soul. The (absolute) command on the day is
> Allah's. (82:1–5; 13–19)

In Islam, as in Christianity and Judaism, the Day of Judgment is a day of reckoning, when good is rewarded and evil punished. That the idea has important connotations for the problem of evil (Chapter 7) as well as for salvation seems clear.

Reflections on the idea of judgment in the three great Western traditions suggest an important tension between this theme and the idea of an eternal soul. Many of the biblical and Qur'anic accounts of the Day of Judgment suggest, not that the soul enters into the presence of God (or alternatively into Hell) upon the death of the body, but rather that Judgment is performed at the end of time, following a *resurrection* of the dead. There is a significant difference between the two ideas, not least because the idea of an eternal soul implies that death affects only one aspect of the person—and that the least important one. The soul "sheds" the tomb of the body and goes on to inherit its eternal reward. Resurrection, on the other hand, implies the death of the entire person, and eternal life—whether for rewards or punishments—is accomplished by the power of God.

In the three great Western religions, the idea of judgment implies great fear. Every person will face God and will provide an account of his or her deeds. Yet judgment also inspires great hope, for, according to biblical and Qur'anic traditions, God is merciful, and forgiveness is a reality. In many ways the idea is aimed at the reformation of behavior in this life. Rewards and punishments then serve as a type of "exciting" inducement intended to encourage moral conduct (see Chapter 8).

GROUP SALVATION IN THIS WORLD

Modern conceptions of salvation often presuppose that the object of salvation is the individual person. But the history of religions provides numerous examples of group salvation, some of them quite significant. Under the rubric of group salvation in this world, we may consider salvation (1) through the people, (2) through the tradition, and (3) in the Kingdom of God.

Salvation Through the People

The concept of "the people," and particularly the continuation of the people, is common in the history of religions. In Chapter 6, we discussed the importance of the group for personal identity, and provided examples of the way in which a group catastrophe can imply the end of meaningful, personal existence as well. In such a case, personal identity depends upon association with the group. Outside the social unit, a man or woman may have the form of a human but lacks the connections that give substance (or meaning) to life.

When participation in the continuing life of a people is at the heart of the quest for salvation, the obligation to bear and nurture children becomes important, a concern expressed in certain parts of the Torah. In Deuteronomy 25:5–10, it is said that the brother of a man who dies without leaving a son should "go in to her [the widow] and take her to himself as wife and perform the duty of a husband's brother to her." The firstborn son of this union must bear the dead man's name, "that his name may not be blotted out from Israel." Again, when Abraham was dying (Genesis 24), his primary concern was to find a wife for his son Isaac from among his own people.

In modern times, the notion of salvation through the people may be seen in connection with various types of patriotism. Sometimes religious, sometimes not, the kinds of behavior associated with patriotism reflect a sense that the nation is more important than any single person. The actions of *kamikaze* pilots in the service of the Japanese emperor during World War II provide one outstanding example; the martyrdom of young Shi'i Muslims during the Iran-Iraq War provides another; and the frequency of self-immolating martyrs both in Iraq and in Israel is still another. To be a martyr is both to gain paradise and to honor Islam.

Salvation Through the Tradition

Related to salvation through the people, yet with certain distinct themes, the idea of salvation through maintaining a connection with tradition presents an important theme in the history of religions. Perhaps the most outstanding contemporary example is found in Judaism, where Emile Fackenheim's discussion of the "614th commandment" expresses a sense of urgency about maintaining Jewish tradition after the Holocaust. In the light of that event, says Fackenheim, Jews

> are first commanded to survive as Jews, lest the Jewish people perish. Second, we are commanded to remember in our very guts and bones the martyrs of the Holocaust, lest their memory perish. Third, we are forbidden to deny or despair of God, however much we may have to contend with Him or with belief in Him, lest Judaism perish. Finally, we are forbidden to despair of the world as the place which is to become the kingdom of God lest we help make it a meaningless place in which God is dead or irrelevant and everything is permitted. To abandon any of these imperatives, in response to Hitler's victory at Auschwitz, would be to hand him yet other posthumous victories.[5]

The social and traditional character of Fackenheim's claim is striking in contrast to the struggles of the Holocaust survivor in Elie Wiesel's novel *Dawn*, discussed earlier in this chapter. While considerations of the people and the tradition are undeniably present in the story of the latter, the focus is on the effort of the individual to find or create meaning in a world filled with contradictions. For Fackenheim, on the other hand, the focus is on the duty to maintain the people and its tradition. "Do not give Hitler any posthumous victories" seems to mean: "Close the ranks. Maintain the tradition. The Jewish people and their Torah must not perish, else we [Jews] will perish with it."

Salvation in the Kingdom of God in This World

The kingdom of God is on the border between this-worldly and otherworldly concepts of salvation. As it pertains to this world, the idea points to the advent of a reign of justice and equity. God in person, God with angels, or God in Christ are variously depicted as ruling and reordering the world so that justice and peace prevail. The coming of the Kingdom is the fulfillment of a promise (see Chapter 7) to eradicate evil—a promise made by God through God's prophets. Therefore, judgment is usually implied, as well as the rule of justice and peace.

When will the Kingdom come? Most Christian and Jewish thought points to the end of time, or to a "time beyond time," for the establishment of the Kingdom. Some, however, interpret the biblical promise as a goal for this world. Christian thinkers, in particular, sometimes interpret the New

Testament proclamation that "God was in Christ" (II Corinthians 5:19) as an indication that the Kingdom of God has already arrived in the life, death, and resurrection of the Christ. Protestant theologians such as the American Walter Rauschenbusch (1861–1918), the leading spokesperson for the Social Gospel movement in early twentieth-century America, proclaimed the Kingdom of God as an ideal for which people can and should strive: a real possibility within human history.

In recent times, the most striking examples of such thinking appear in the various *liberation theology* movements within Christianity. Liberation theologians argue that the Bible tells a story about the action of God in history to achieve justice for the poor and oppressed. The words of the prophets and the message of Jesus are understood as a warning: If a person or community is not on the side of the poor, he, she, or they are not on the side of God. This commitment frequently is called the "preferential option for the poor." This message is common to religious thinkers who work in otherwise quite diverse contexts: Latin America, African American liberation movements, and the struggle for women's rights. For such thinkers, the power of the Kingdom of God lies in its role as a symbol of hope and a directive for action to achieve group salvation in this world.

GROUP SALVATION IN ANOTHER WORLD

In a sense, our discussion of individual, otherworldly salvation already anticipates much of what might be said about group salvation in another world. Although the focus of joining the spirit world or the idea of judgment seems to be on individual or personal existence, certainly elements of group concern appear in either emphasis. The most striking example of otherworldly group salvation is related to the Kingdom of God, for that symbol never stands for individuals saved in isolation, even when it is applied in an otherworldly way. Those who are saved become a part of the community of the just—in Christian terms, the communion of saints. They live eternally in the presence of God, not only as individuals but as a part of the community of the blessed. In Judaism, Christianity, and Islam, the Kingdom of God (as an otherworldly symbol) points to the establishment of an ideal society "beyond time." It comes at the end of history, usually through an *apocalypse* or cataclysmic end to the world. War, famine, disease, fire, flood all will play a part in the coming of the end.

Following the apocalypse, the Kingdom of God begins. The logic of the Western traditions is that this Kingdom is eternal, though sometimes there is a stipulation that it lasts for a specified period, perhaps a thousand years (see Revelation 20). The Kingdom of God implies a rule that is perfectly just, but its perfection is not only in terms of justice. There will be no evil in any form: Sin, death, and disease will all pass away. The just will live in perfect harmony, reunited with all those who have loved and served God.

In this way, the Kingdom of God becomes a symbol for otherworldly, group salvation. It is, in essence, the community of the blessed—those who by well-doing have lived a life that bears fruit in the fulfillment of the quest for salvation.

Now That Distinctions Have Been Made

It should be said that the distinctions between individual and group, this-worldly and otherworldly notions of salvation, while helpful, are not absolute. They are often, in fact, mixed. For example, an individual may strive mightily for a meaningful life that will be remembered, and leave behind a family so that his or her group will be preserved, all the while hoping for personal salvation as a part of the Kingdom of God. The various concepts of salvation, and their diverse relations, point to two things: the unity and diversity inherent in religious phenomena; and the difficulty of talking about what is, after all, presented by most religious traditions as a deep and abiding mystery—the mystery of salvation.

Paths to Salvation

Thus far we have focused on concepts of salvation, with questions of who shall be saved and where. We have also dealt with definitions of salvation: what salvation consists in. Now we must turn to the how of salvation. And, as one might guess, the answer to this question depends in part on the answers to our earlier questions. How, that is, is strongly related to who, where, and what.

For purposes of this discussion, let us consider five paths toward salvation, each of which is distinctive, though in any particular context they may be combined in various ways: (1) knowledge, (2) action, (3) aesthetics, (4) submission, and (5) grace. In discussing each we focus on its distinctive characteristics. We should always keep in mind, however, the high degree of interrelation among the five paths.

The Path of Knowledge

The path of knowledge is often associated with the great traditions of the East: Hinduism, Buddhism, Taoism, and Confucianism. Indeed, the theme of enlightenment, especially in Buddhism, involves a very deep awareness of oneself and the world. This is also the goal of the practice known as *jnana yoga* (knowledge discipline) in Hinduism. The principal goal is to understand the true nature of things. A person who "sees" is one who understands or knows the truth and thus is liberated. Liberation, then, is the Eastern equivalent to "salvation" in the West.

Yet knowledge is also valued in the great traditions of the West. Judaism and Islam have long esteemed study, so much so that it is a religious obligation. And Christianity, while not making study a formal obligation, certainly exhibits a concern with knowledge in its efforts to provide precise translations of the Bible in various languages, and in the interest in theology. Western traditions, then, emphasize knowledge as important in the sacred quest, just as the traditions of the East do. Yet there are important differences, tied in some sense to differing notions of sacred reality. In the West, knowledge signifies learning, an understanding of the sacred books. In the East, knowledge signifies the exploration and understanding of the true self. The two are not mutually exclusive, but there is an important difference in emphasis, even as there is a shared quest for salvation.

The Path of Action

Those who seek knowledge may withdraw from the world, at least for a time. That is a part of the ideal of the one who "renounces" to achieve *moksha* (see Chapter 8) in Hinduism. It has also been a part of the Christian ideal of the monk, who withdraws in order to contemplate the workings of God. By contrast, the path of action runs squarely through the things of this world. Individuals or groups, in connection with this-worldly or otherworldly concepts of salvation, emphasize action, especially right action, as an answer to the question "What must I do to be saved?"

In Hinduism, the path of action is called *karma yoga* (duty discipline). Recalling the discussion in Chapter 8, we may say that this notion refers to an acceptance of the social lot given to persons by the working of karma. One who is born into a specific caste must fulfill his or her duties in that caste: Such is the point of the caste system, supported by the Laws of Manu. However, karma yoga takes the compromise of the Laws of Manu and the four stages of life one step further. Following the suggestion of the Bhagavad Gita, we understand karma yoga to imply that one who performs his duty in a spirit of detachment is doing right, that is, practicing a form of discipline that leads to salvation. Right action yields good consequences, in this case, for an individual, or at least for his or her eternal soul. The Gita, in fact, advises that a person best does one's duty by referring all things to God in a form of devotion called *bhakti* or love.

Similarly, Confucianism and Buddhism stress right action, though in diverse ways. Confucianism, for example, stresses the performance of duty, defined according to the role one is playing at the time: husband, father, son, official. The person who does his or her duty properly plays a part in the development of a prosperous nation or in the fulfillment of a group-oriented, this-worldly notion of salvation. The great religions of the West also stress the importance of action: in Judaism, adherence to the Torah; in Islam, following the *Shari'a* or religious-moral law; in Christianity, the performance of deeds of thanksgiving. These are all significant aspects of the quest for salvation in terms of the path of action.

The Path of Aesthetics

The path of aesthetics is closely linked to action but deserves some special consideration. It involves a special type of action: the action of those whose special talents incline them in the direction of bringing beauty into the world. In various contexts, artists, musicians, dancers, architects, and athletes have all been models of this path to salvation. Think, for example, of the Renaissance painters or of the architects of Islam, as discussed earlier. Again, in the Islamic tradition Sufi mystics have understood poetry and dance to be a part of the experience of sacred reality, which lies at the heart of their quest for salvation. And in Japan, beauty is nearly a religious form, particularly the beauty of nature. Thus, aesthetics may serve as a path to salvation.

The Path of Submission

The path of submission arises from a sense of the utter dependence of human beings on sacred reality. As such, most religious traditions exhibit some interest in this path to salvation. Human beings are to make their wants and needs "fit" with a notion of sacred reality, manifest either in the structure of the universe, the structure of society, or a revelation from God. This last points to the tradition most characterized by an emphasis on submission. In Islam the pious always indicate that their plans are subject to sacred reality with the conditional clause *insha'allah* (if God wills).

Islam is not alone in stressing submission to the will of God. The Hebrew scriptures tell a long story of the struggle of the people of Israel to submit to and trust the will of the one true God. Many of the restrictions of the Torah serve primarily as reminders that God is in charge, so that prescribed actions, clothing, foods, and times of prayer serve as an exercise in submitting to God.

Christianity also places the will of God above the will of any person. In some cases, the tendency in Christian circles (as in Judaism and Islam) has been to see everything as conforming in fact to the will of God. Jonathan Edwards, famous as an outstanding preacher and theologian in New England during the eighteenth century, for example, once thanked God for God's providence in moving boards in such a way so that no one was seriously injured when a church balcony collapsed. Such an absolute conception of God's providence or governance of events is certainly implied in other aspects of Christian tradition, most notably Jesus' prayer before his arrest: "not as I will, but as Thou wilt" (Matthew 26:39). Those whose primary focus is on the path of submission take comfort when evil occurs by saying, "It is God's will." They also trust that somehow the event must have meaning within God's great plan.

Such persons do not, however, want evil things to occur. Even Jesus prayed, just before the line quoted above, "My Father, if it is possible, let this cup pass from Me." The other side of submission, then, is supplication. Recognizing the human condition of utter dependence upon the sacred, those who submit ask for the things they need. Prayer is thus an important aspect of this path, by which salvation is linked with submission to sacred reality.

The Path of Grace

In some traditions, the sense of dependence on the sacred is so great that the quest for salvation, and even more the notion of paths to salvation, seem a contradiction in terms. Thinking that human beings can do anything to "earn salvation" seems, in such traditions, a type of arrogance. For historical Christianity, for example, salvation can only be a freely given gift; human beings are saved by *grace*. In fact, the Protestant Reformation occurred in part because Martin Luther (1483–1546) and his followers thought that the Catholicism of their day placed too much emphasis on the path of works as opposed to the path of grace even though it is the offical teaching of Catholicism and Orthodoxy that we are saved by divine grace.

The radical emphasis on salvation by grace remains a central theme in Protestant Christianity. It was not only Luther, founder of the Lutheran branch of Protestantism, who emphasized this idea. John Calvin (1509–1564), founder of the various Reformed churches, developed the idea further through the doctrine of *election*. The point was (and is) to say that, because humanity is sinful and estranged from God, human beings can do nothing to bring about their own salvation. Those who are saved are reconciled to God through a free gift, the gift of faith, which God creates in them through God's grace.

The implications of this doctrine, which is sometimes called *predestination*, were debated by Christian thinkers long before Calvin and continue to be debated to this day. That there are questions of justice, and thus of theodicy, involved in such a position is clear. How can God be just if God elects people to salvation (and correspondingly to damnation) without reference to what they do? Can the path of grace really be separated from the path of action? Such questions follow from the Protestant emphasis on grace, and yet Protestant believers may well say that such questions miss the point. At its heart, an emphasis on grace, even as developed in the doctrine of election, does not focus on "Who is to be saved?" and "Who is to be damned?" but rather on the radical need of humanity and, correspondingly, on the immeasurable love of God. Salvation by grace is not emphasized so that the saved may boast, but so that all people will know of the utter dependence of humanity on God.

A CLOSING REMINDER

It should be clear that the differences among paths to salvation are, like those among concepts of salvation, not so clear-cut as our distinctions imply. Such distinctions point, by and large, to matters of emphasis. Most of the great traditions find ways over time to incorporate not only the five paths discussed here but others as well. The ability to do so is a measure of the scope of the notions of sacred reality in such traditions; it is also a measure of the differing psychological, social, and intellectual interests of human beings. The quest for salvation is a quest to understand and order the world. In religious contexts, this means to understand and order the world in connection with a notion of sacred reality. We hardly need to say that it is the ultimate goal of all religious life, for the discussions in this and other chapters all incline toward the question of the Philippian jailer related in the book of Acts: "What must I do to be saved?" What must human beings do to understand and bring order to life?

NOTES

1. Elie Wiesel, *Dawn*, published together with *Night* and *The Accident*, trans. Stella Rodway (New York: Hill and Wang, 1972).
2. On the Japanese practice, see H. Byron Earhart, *Religions of Japan* (San Francisco: Harper & Row, 1984), pp. 59–63.
3. From the translation in Ch'ang Wing-tsit, *A Sourcebook in Chinese Philosophy* (Princeton, N.J.: Princeton University Press, 1963), p. 192.
4. Ch'ang Wing-Tsit, *A Sourcebook in Chinese Philosophy*, p. 186.
5. Emile Fackenheim, *God's Presence in History* (New York: Harper & Row, 1972), p. 84. Jewish tradition historically held that there were 613 commandments in the written and oral forms of the Torah. Thus Fackenheim's claim is that the Holocaust creates a new commandment.

THOUGHT EXPERIMENTS

1. Outline your personal concept of salvation. Where do your ideas come from? Your family? Religious training? What path(s) to salvation do you see yourself following, if any?
2. When the Buddha was asked what happens after death, he often said that the question was irrelevant. He meant that one's focus should be on the here

and now and on the search for enlightenment. In your opinion, is the question of what happens after death irrelevant to life in this world? How does a notion of continuing existence after death actually affect life in this world?

3. Talk to one or more religious leaders (of varying persuasions) to ascertain their ideas about the nature of salvation. Be careful to ask questions about who is saved, where, from and for what, and how. Explore with such leaders some of the ideas you have read about in this chapter. How do the things you hear from religious leaders compare and contrast with your expectations, based on the material in this chapter?

4. What do you make of the current popularity of novels that describe the end of the world and who is saved and who is not?

SUGGESTIONS FOR FURTHER READING

BARNES, M., *Theology and the Dialogue of Religion*. Cambridge: Cambridge University Press, 2002. The world religions, the issue of salvation, and dialogue from a scholarly Christian perspective.

HICK, JOHN H., *Death and Eternal Life*. San Francisco: Harper & Row, 1976. A broad, comparative approach by a Christian theologian interested in a "global theology of death."

KUNG, HANS, *Eternal Life? Life After Death as a Medical, Philosophical, and Theological Problem*, trans. Edward Quinn. New York: Doubleday, 1984. A systematic approach by a Christian theologian interested in the relation of theological and other perspectives on death.

LEWIS, C. S., *A Grief Observed*. New York: Seabury Press, 1961. The introspective observations of a popular Christian writer on his reactions to his wife's death. Painfully and powerfully honest.

Glossary

ablutions ritual washings, in various traditions.

adoration acknowledgment of the sovereignty of the sacred over the individual.

allegory a story, usually fictional, that makes an instructive point. Every character and incident in the story stands for or represents a reality outside the story itself.

Amaterasu Omikami sun goddess; clan ancestor to the Japanese imperial family; see **Shinto**.

aniconic "no images"; referring to traditions that do not encourage visual imagery in religion.

anthropodicy questions concerning the justice of human beings; compare **theodicy**.

apocalypse the cataclysmic end of the present world in Judaism, Christianity, and Islam.

avatar the incarnation of a deity (Hinduism).

baptism in Christianity, the sacrament employing water for the forgiveness of sins.

bar/bas mitzvah the ceremony by which a young person becomes a "son" (bar) or "daughter" (bat) of the commandments; see **Judaism**.

Bhagavad Gita the "song of the Lord"; one of the scriptures of **Hinduism**.

Bible literally "book"; sacred scripture in Judaism and Christianity.

bodhisattva in Mahayana Buddhism, one who achieves enlightenment but postpones Nirvana in the interest of bringing truth to the world.

Buddha the "enlightened one"; Siddhartha Gautama, founder of **Buddhism**.

Buddhism the religious tradition founded on the teaching and example of the Buddha.

canon originally, "measuring reed"; the list of authoritative scriptures in a particular tradition.

caste   the system of division of labor in **Hinduism**; the four castes are *Brahmins* or priests, *Kshtriya* or warriors, *Vaisya* or merchants, and *Sudra* or laborers. "Outcastes" are those who do not belong to one of the above.

Christ   the anointed servant of God (see also **Messiah**).

Christianity   the religious tradition founded on the teaching, example, and person of Jesus of Nazareth (the Christ).

church   a socially recognized religious organization that makes its appeal to all members of a society, that has a stake in the well-being of the larger society, and that claims to be the custodian of religious truth.

Confucianism   the great religious-political tradition of China founded by Confucius (551–479 B.C.E.).

cosmology   ways of thinking that attempt to relate the various aspects of the universe.

cosmos   world or universe.

cult   a religious group founded by a charismatic leader that claims it has a new revelation or insight that perfects, changes, or invigorates an older tradition; and that is viewed with extreme suspicion by the older, more established religious traditions.

cyclical   views of time; emphasizes the eternal repetition of time, as in **samsara** or, in some traditions, in the repetition of the change of seasons.

deontological   from the Greek, "that which is binding"; refers to an approach to ethics based on duties.

dharma   "law," "duty," or "teaching"; in **Hinduism**, especially associated with duties of one's **caste**; in **Buddhism**, the teaching of the **Buddha**.

disciples   students, followers of a religious teacher.

dualism   a way of thought, especially with respect to **theodicy**, that stresses the opposition of good and evil powers in the universe. See **Zoroastrianism**.

Easter   Christian holiday, in spring, celebrating the resurrection of Jesus.

election   God's choice of certain persons for salvation (**Christianity**).

eschatology   discussion of the "last thing," that is, questions of the end of the world and the eternal destiny of human beings.

ethics   the study of practical justification or of various answers to questions of the "good" life.

Eucharist   originally "giving thanks" (Greek); Holy Communion or the Lord's Supper in Christianity.

exegesis   the process of drawing out or interpreting the meaning of texts.

Exodus   the liberation of the Hebrews from slavery in Egypt (see **Passover**). Also, the second book of the **Bible**.

fasting   deliberate refraining from food or water for purposes of **purification** or discipline with respect to the sacred.

functional   referring to definitions of religion that stress the role of religion in human responses to suffering, death, despair, and the like.

grace   in certain forms of **Christianity**, signifies especially that God gives salvation freely, apart from anything persons do to earn or deserve God's favor.

Hades   classical Greek name for the place of the dead.

haggadah   "narrative"; sacred stories in the Jewish tradition.

heresy   a word used by members of a religious community to indicate an illegitimate idea or movement.

hierophany   the appearance of the sacred in human experience.

Hinduism   the predominant religious tradition in India.

Holocaust   the term used to signify the Nazi destruction of European Jews under the leadership of Adolf Hitler; also called the *Shoah*.

icon   "image"; in particular, visual images that mediate notions of the sacred to believers.

imam   leader of prayer in **Islam**; for **Shi'i Islam**, also a divinely designated leader of the religious community.

immanence   describes those notions of the sacred that stress its inherence in the world. (Compare **transcendence**.)

incarnation   the "becoming flesh" of the sacred, especially in **Christianity**.

Islam   the religious tradition that begins with the life and work of Mohammad; the "submission" to the will of God.

Jainism   a small but important religious tradition in India.

Jesus   Jesus of Nazareth, founder of **Christianity**; according to Christians, the **Christ**.

jnana yoga   in **Hinduism**, refers to the discipline of knowledge of the true nature of God and the self.

Judaism   religion of the Jewish people; see **Exodus, Messiah, Moses, Passover**.

Ka'ba   the ancient, cubical structure outside Mecca; holy to Muslims as the place of worship constructed by Abraham and his son Ishmael.

kami   sacred beings and powers in **Shinto**.

karma   in Hinduism and Buddhism, the inexorable law of cause and effect.

karma yoga   the discipline focusing on doing one's **caste** duty in a spirit of detachment.

linear   views of time; depiction of time as having a beginning, middle, and end.

liturgy   derived from a Greek work meaning "a public work"; in religion, refers to the form of **public** worship of a particular group.

logos   Greek, "word"; signifying absolute reason or mind; according to **Christian** doctrine, the **Christ** is the **incarnation** of the logos.

mahdi   the "rightly guided one"; the equivalent for **Muslims** of the **Messiah**.

Messiah   God's anointed or chosen servant; see **Judaism**; also **Christ**.

moksha   release or liberation from the world, especially in **Hinduism**.

morality   ways of thinking, feeling, and acting that focus on concern for human welfare.

Mormons   followers of the **prophetic** mission of Joseph Smith; religious movement begun in the United States during the nineteenth century.

Moses   the great **prophet** of **Judaism**.

Muhammad   the great **prophet** and founder of **Islam**.

Muharram (Shi'i Islam)   the month of memorial for the martyrdom of Husayn, grandson of the prophet **Muhammad**.

Muslim   one who practices **Islam**; thus, one who "submits" to the will of God.

mysterium tremendum et fascinans   the mystery that both terrifies and attracts; Rudolf Otto's term for the experience of the sacred.

mystical   aspects of religious traditions that focus on the appearance of the sacred to persons achieving a certain "enlightened" state of mind.

myth   a narrative that focuses on sacred reality and its relationship to humanity.

Nirvana   the sacred reality in **Buddhism**; signifies the extinguishing of all desire and release from the cycle of time (see **samsara**).

orthodoxy   indicates the standard for "right belief" set by a particular community.

orthopraxis   similar to **orthodoxy**, but refers to "right practice."

parable   a story, usually fictional, in which the thrust of the story is to make a particular point but in which (by comparison with **allegory**) the characters do *not* "stand" for realities outside the story itself.

Passover   Spring holiday and their rituals in Jewish tradition; celebrates the **Exodus**.

penance   making restitution for ethical impurities in order to be fit to approach the Sacred.

petition   to ask or beg favors of the sacred.

phenomenology   an approach to the study of religion that focuses on description of the concrete beliefs and practices of religious people and/or groups.

pilgrimage a sacred journey, usually to view a relic or to worship in a sacred place.

practical justification the process of giving reasons for the judgments one makes (see **ethics**).

prayer a deliberate attempt on the part of a person to communicate with the sacred; can take different forms (see **adoration, petition**).

predestination the notion that the ultimate destiny of persons has been eternally established by God; associated with **election**.

priest religious specialist associated with **sacramental** elements of religious traditions.

profane "outside the temple"; that which is ordinary, not sacred.

prophet religious specialist associated with **prophetic** traditions.

prophetic aspects of religious traditions which focus on the appearance of the sacred through words; see **revelation**.

purification ritual preparation for an approach to the sacred; may involve **fasting** or **ablutions**.

Qur'an the holy book or sacred scripture in **Islam**.

reincarnation the concept that a spirit or soul "takes on" or moves from one body, one life, to another (see especially **Hinduism; Buddhism**).

relics physical items (bones, teeth, clothing) associated with a holy person and preserved by believers for their connection with the sacred.

revelation the disclosure of sacred truth.

ritual a ceremonial act or repeated stylized gesture used for specific occasions.

Sabbath from the Hebrew *shabbat*; the day set apart for rest and remembrance of the sacred in **Judaism**.

sacramental elements of religious traditions which focus on the appearance of the sacred through the medium of material reality.

sacrifice from Latin *sacrum facere*, that is, "to make holy"; for example, by dedicating something to the sacred.

sage religious specialist associated with **mystical** traditions.

samsara the cycle of time (**Hinduism, Buddhism**) governed by **karma**.

schism a split within a religious body.

scriptures "writings," especially those writings which are considered authoritative or sacred by a particular religious community.

sect a religious group which demands conformity to certain standards in the behavior of its members, is exclusive in its membership, distinguishes its well-being from that of the larger society, and claims to be the bearer of religious truth.

seder ritual meal, part of the **Passover** celebration.

shaman   a person thought to have special, sacred powers, for example, as a medium for spirits or a healer.

Shari'a   Islamic religious law.

Sheol   Hebrew word for the place of the dead.

Shi'i Islam   minority tradition in **Islam**; prominent in Iran.

Shinto   indigenous religion of Japan.

Siddhartha Gautama   the **Buddha**.

srauta sacrifice   in **Hinduism**, great public sacrifice in ancient India.

stupa   burial mound for a holy person; a sacred site in **Buddhism**.

substantive   in definitions of religion, the attempt to identify an essence or core idea which distinguishes religion from other (for example, moral ways of thinking, feeling, and acting).

Sunni Islam   majority tradition in **Islam**.

systematics   the techniques of using **exegesis**, history, and other tools to set out a comprehensive account of the beliefs of a particular community.

Tao   the "way" or "power" of harmony and balance among all things.

Taoism   a system or practice for following the **Tao**.

teleological   from Greek *telos*, indicating the goal or end result; in **ethics**, signifies approaches which focus on the consequences of actions.

theodicy   discussions of divine justice; the attempt to answer questions about the sacred arising from the experience of evil.

theology   believing reflection on the faith of a particular community, with the goal of clarification of the logic and grounds of a notion of the sacred.

Torah   the "instruction" of God in **Judaism**; the first five books of the **Bible**.

torii   gate marking the entry for a sacred place in **Shinto**.

tradition   from Latin *tradere*, to "hand down"; the collection of symbols, **rituals**, **scriptures**, and customs associated with a particular group.

transcendent   that which "goes beyond" or "stands over," as in religious traditions which present a notion of the sacred as transcending ordinary experience.

transmigration   see **reincarnation**; the movement of a soul or spirit from one existence to another.

transubstantiation   the Roman Catholic doctrine that the elements of bread and wine are transformed, in the context of the **Eucharist**, into the body and blood of the **Christ**.

tripitaka   the "three baskets"; sacred scriptures in **Buddhism**.

Upanishads   writings of Hindu sages, approximately 700–200 B.C.E.

Vedas   ancient scriptures in **Hinduism**.

via negativa   "the way of the negative"; especially signifies those types of religious language which describe the sacred in terms of what it is not.

worship   to show reverence or devotion for the sacred.

Yoga   literally "yoke" or discipline, especially in **Hinduism**. See **jnana yoga, karma yoga**.

Zen   form of **Buddhism**, especially important in Japan.
Zoroastrianism   religious tradition originating in the seventh century B.C.E. in Persia; see **dualism**.

Index